The Search
for Existential Identity
Patient-Therapist Dialogues
in Humanistic Psychotherapy

James F. T. Bugental

THE SEARCH FOR
FOR
EXISTENTIAL
IDENTITY

Jossey-Bass Publishers
San Francisco • London • 1989

THE SEARCH FOR EXISTENTIAL IDENTITY
Patient-Therapist Dialogues in Humanistic Psychotherapy
by James F. T. Bugental

Library of Congress Catalogue Card Number LC 75-44882

International Standard Book Number ISBN 0-87589-273-6

Manufactured in the United States of America

JACKET DESIGN BY WILLI BAUM

FIRST EDITION
First printing: February 1976
Second printing: January 1979
Third printing: December 1981
Fourth printing: March 1984
Fifth printing: February 1986
Sixth printing: February 1988
Seventh printing: May 1989

Code 7601

The Jossey-Bass
Behavioral Science Series

For Elizabeth Keber Bugental

PREFACE

One of the rewards (and hazards) of writing a book about human experience, I have found, is the response it evokes. When *The Search for Authenticity* was published in 1965, I didn't anticipate getting moving, personal messages from men and women who heard what I was saying. But now this has become one of the important satisfactions I find in writing, and I look forward to such letters.

Several years ago a young man who lived a continent-width away wrote to tell me about the impact of my book on him and about his hopes for his own change and growth. We exchanged several letters, and then he said he was coming to Los Angeles and wanted to meet with me. So we set a time for him to come to the office.

When he arrived, almost the first thing he said was that he was thinking of giving up his job and moving so that he could come into therapy with me. This was a heady tribute indeed, but then fifteen minutes later he was weeping. And he was weeping because he was so disappointed in me. I mean, he was disappointed in me *as a person*.

From the heights of enjoying his appreciation I dropped to deep dismay. He told me how he found me so much less authentic,

so much less the embodiment of what he had expected from reading what I had written. And, of course, he was right. To tell the
truth, I have wept about that same sad discrepancy myself, and
more than once.

That dismayingly perceptive young man wept in disappointment with himself too, knowingly or not. It is a pale comfort, however, for I know I still fall far short of what I envision. Yet, I love that
vision and want others to share it. Just as the young man needed
to recognize how much he was seeking an ideal image with which
to identify, so I need to respect my own efforts toward fuller living
while recognizing how much more is always possible.[1]

I am a psychotherapist. When you read that sentence you
probably make an instant judgment about me. You may decide I
am an almost-magical healer, a charlatan, a latter-day priest or
shaman, a tinkerer with crackpots, an archaic from another period,
an adviser who knows all about human beings, a tool of reactionary
forces trying to preserve the establishment, or a dangerous radical
seeking to overthrow all that is good and worthy. The strange
thing is, you may think any of these things even if you, yourself, are
a psychotherapist. Moreover, I'm confident I could find psychotherapists (or at least people who claim to be) who would fit all of
these characterizations.

I really wish I could find a new name for what I do. I'd like
to discard words like *psychotherapy, doctor, patient,* and *treatment*
and replace them with a whole fresh glossary that would more
truly describe what I do, the attitudes I and those with whom I
work have about our mutual enterprise, and (most of all) our roles
or parts in that undertaking. To date, however, I haven't found
any replacement words that satisfy me, so I still use those I grew up
with. But although the words are the same, their meanings continually grow and evolve and my experience of what I still call
psychotherapy confronts me over and over again with new vistas,
new challenges, and new opportunities.

When I say that I "do psychotherapy" what do I mean? I
mean that I help people who are distressed about their lives try to
make those lives more satisfying. I mean I work with people who
want to be more the kinds of persons they feel they can be but

haven't yet been able to be. I work with people who sense there is more waiting inside of them than they are able to awaken to full life. I work with people who want to be genuinely close with other people and get past the barriers that would keep us in our invisible cells.

What does it mean to say, "I work with"? Well, that's elusive too. I listen a lot. I tell people when I get the feeling they're not leveling with themselves and with me. I open myself to experience within myself what these people tell me they're experiencing within themselves. When I sense that my inner experiencing is in some accord with what my patients are describing (although not necessarily the same as their experiences), I may tell them some of the associations I find set up within me. These may include my own inner reactions and may link what they are telling me now with what they have related at other times. I listen more than I talk, but sometimes I talk a great deal. Mostly I let the people who come to me set the course, but sometimes I challenge the route they're choosing. Usually we're pretty warm and like each other as we work together, but sometimes we're angry and shout at each other or at life or at things we can't name very well. Sometimes we cry together. We're also—one or both of us—often scared during the hours we talk with each other.

What I'm trying to convey is some feeling for an activity that is quite different from most of the activities with which we are familiar in our culture, an endeavor that has many contradictions within it, that involves two people acting and reacting together emotionally and intimately, and that can have powerful impacts on some lives, prove almost completely futile in others, and—to be completely straight about it—can do some real hurt in still others.

But in addition to whatever psychotherapy does to affect the lives of the therapist and his patients (and both certainly do have their lives affected), it does something else that makes it pretty much unique in our culture: It provides a time and a place for sustained observation and thought about what it means to be a human being. *Observation and thought* don't quite satisfy me as the right terms for the process. You may get the idea of what I mean if I remind you of how completely you give your attention to whatever activity most involves you. It may be listening to music or fishing or studying the financial page or planning a new project in your work or playing golf or something else. Whatever it is, when you're really "lost" in doing it, you're also really most yourself, paradoxical as that sounds. As you'll probably also recognize when you stop to think about it, those times are ones when you're finely tuned, your sensitivity is high, your ability to think of a number of aspects of what you're doing at once is greater than usual, and you find yourself more creative and flexible and generally "really there." This is the kind of *observation and thought* I'm trying to characterize.

Being a psychotherapist gives me a special seat at the human drama. It lets me see behind the scenes to some extent, and it demandingly involves me so that I cannot be a passive spectator but repeatedly find myself part of the action. I am again and again powerfully caught up emotionally in the life revealed to me and also in the meanings I sense in it. And repeatedly I also find I want to step back a pace and reflect on what I am experiencing and share my reflections with others. That's what the following chapters are about. This book contains my reflections on the lessons about being alive that my patients and I are teaching ourselves.

But when I come to try to express what I feel I am learning from my work with my patients, I find that it is seldom in abstract terms. Again and again, what I discover within me takes the form of memory clusters of how, at various times, several different people and I have grappled with some issue of living. Rather than emerging as crisp, declarative sentences, these impressions are entangled with the kinds of emotions we had for each other, with other events that were going on in our lives, with other people who were in one way or another caught up in the flux of our experiences. They are phases of human stories, episodes of human experience.

I want to make clear that each insight opened to me about our human condition has never been unique to a given person. Quite the contrary. Each lesson I have learned, I have learned because first one and then another of my patients taught it to me, bringing out various aspects, helping me to sense beyond the incidental and toward the abiding.

So it is that when I come to set down my learnings to share them with others, I find that I must talk in terms of people, if I am to communicate with any validity and vitality. This book tells about people—Larry, Jennifer, Frank, Louise, Hal, Kate and myself—in order to talk about human experiences and the meanings that are an intrinsic part of human experience.

These are not objective case studies in the traditional detached form of such reports. Objectivity can be the illusion of the timid and the justification of the vindictive. To talk about human lives and human strivings for greater realization of latent potentials objectively would be a distortion or even a perversion. Writing and reading these pages often brings tears or smiles or poignant feelings to me as I experience again a moment of discovery or of companionship or of anguish. I hope my readers may experience some of the aliveness of these people, for in that way readers will have pierced beyond the communicative fiction to the experiencing persons. When that occurs, the reader will have found his way to his own human core as well.

In writing this book I have in mind a group of readers for which there is no one appropriate designation. I hope to speak to both professional psychotherapists and lay people (at least as far as the field of psychotherapy goes). These are readers distinguished more by an outlook on human life than by a single vocational title —an outlook of respect or valuing or trust. It is a way of thinking and feeling about one's own life and about the lives of those with whom one shares time and space. It sees beauty and wonder in the common birthright of all human beings: the will to actualize what is latent. It laments and struggles against the very real forces that seek to deny or limit that life force. It is my hope that this book celebrates the growth toward emergence, and thereby lends encouragement and comfort to those who share a dedication to such growth—whether in their work or in their personal questing.

When I try to be more specific as to who the likely audience of these pages may be, I find that it divides into five groupings. First, I want to address my fellow professionals in the practice of psychotherapy. I know that many of them are already moving toward or engaged in the kinds of work I describe here, and I know too, how candid sharing of our experiences may encourage each of us to be more courageous and more creative. As one who has so often profited from the writings of others, I want to put my own contribution into this health-nourishing pool of experience.

Professionals will find it useful to compare certain aspects of the work represented in these cases. I have tried to portray faithfully—in the spirit more than the letter—certain pivotal aspects of the course of intensive psychotherapy of an existential-humanistic orientation. These considerations are: (1) initiation of the therapeutic relation, development of a therapeutic alliance, and evolution of the transference; (2) principal resistance patterns presented, their elucidation, necessary confrontations, and the working-through process; (3) kinds of management problems encountered, some of the issues in planning for contingencies, and difficulties in resolutions; (4) my subjective participation in the therapeutic process, counter-transference concerns, involvement and nonattachment; and (5) the principal existential meanings that I find in my work. All of these considerations are set in what I hope will be manifest throughout: my deep sense of commitment to the people I am writing about, and who so greatly trust me, and the value for my own life of their courage and dread in meeting their lives.

Next, I want to write for the student in the professions that practice psychotherapy or personal counseling—psychology, psychiatry, social work, nursing, teaching, and so on—and to discuss other ways of being with patients or clients than those that emphasize technique or manipulation. I know that many students who are drawn toward working with others in pursuit of life-enhancement get turned off by approaches that do not involve deep relating or humanistic confrontation. I have tried to write a different kind of account of our work, one that will provide real support to humans concerned about human beings and not just impersonal abstractions. I hope this book will be a reassurance to students and will help them get an organismic sense of the processes and deeper personal meanings in intensive psychotherapy.

Similarly, I hope that these pages will speak to the growing numbers of paraprofessional counselors—people who are volunteering for training and practice in helping others find greater fulfillment in life. I believe these paraprofessionals are an expression of a new sense of human community that is a response to the massive alienation of our machine-and-computer society. The paraprofessionals are demonstrating that we need not turn over meaningful person-to-person relationships to the specialized disciplines. Working together, professionals and paraprofessionals can extend the human nurturance of caring and skilled relationships to many more people than could possibly be reached otherwise. The following accounts will, I hope, describe to these paraprofessionals the deeper potentials of the work they are engaged in and will suggest the importance of continuing training, growth, and dedication to self-knowledge and authenticity in relating.

Fourth, I want to write to the person who is considering undertaking this adventure for himself, who is thinking about going into intensive psychotherapy. It is and should be a deeply weighed decision, but very often such a person has not been able to find out much about what he would be choosing. I hope this book will provide one answer, and I also hope it will offer a sense of the excitement and potential opportunities that accompany such an expedition into one's inner being.[2]

Finally, I want to talk to the intelligent reader who is not professionally concerned with psychotherapy, but who is seeking to increase his own experience of vitality in being. For him or her, I have tried especially to highlight the kinds of confusions we all engage in and that rob us of deep meaningfulness in our living. Also, I have sought to illustrate for this reader the ways in which our own beings may be differently experienced as we gain in authenticity in our own lives.

To speak to all of these people is an ambitious goal, I am aware; but it is mine. In trying to realize this goal, I will speak quite dogmatically, without all the proper disclaimers of "I think . . . ," "It seems that . . . ," and other reminders that I don't have the final answers yet. When I—or anyone—presume to talk about the nature of life and death (the real focus of this book), it ought to be exceedingly evident that we're giving our own biased and very personal views. There are, in all reality, no others. Most readers of this book will know this very well already. If some do not, this may not be their kind of volume. I will say it as best I can as I see it and expect you to test what I say against your own experience. In the "Notes and References" section (placed at the end of the book to avoid intrusion on the narrative flow), I include some quotations and citations to relevant parallels in the literature of psychology.

I have written this book with what I believe to be greater openness than is usual for audiences such as I have described. I have tried to set forth some of the formative experiences of my life, to describe some of my major life struggles, and to disclose my inner experiences as a psychotherapist. I do so because I believe that psychotherapy is more an art than a science and that the reader must therefore know who I am as a person if he is to understand the processes that express my encounters with my patients.

Acknowledgements

How does one remember all the many people who have given generously to such a project as this? Any list of names is not more than one third complete, for sometimes it is only a few words spoken at a critical time that means a renewal of hope, and other times it is hours upon hours of devoted, detailed work. These friends particularly contributed: Tony Athos, Patria Basayne, Mary Conrow, John Levy, Helene Schaeffer, Sylvia Tufenkjian, Susie Wells, and Kay Williams. Bill Bridges and Brian Heald painstakingly and skillfully gave professional guidance and personal support. Lynda Abbott, my secretary, was unflaggingly patient with my hard to read copy and my continual need for work done instantly. She deserves and gets my sincere thanks.

Forestville, California   James F. T. Bugental
December 1975

A Note to My Patients

I am rereading the pages that follow for the last time before this manuscript goes to the publisher to be committed to type. Right now it feels like such a cold process to put down on paper and send to strangers these accounts of what we have known together. It's like turning love letters over to public view.

Yet I want to pass on what you have taught me. You and I know that I am not a scholar and that the pages that follow are not a distillation of the wisdom of great and prominent thinkers. You and I know that I am not a scientist (at least not in the familiar model of scientists), disinterestedly recording the actions of other creatures. In these pages I'm mostly just talking about you and me as human beings trying to awaken more of the lives we feel sleeping deeply within us.

In these accounts I have tried to create something other than an instant replay; I've tried to convey what we experienced together. I find that is a very subtle essence to breathe into words and paper. I have worked with verbatim typescripts of therapeutic interviews and know they distort even as they transmit objective exactitude. I feel, in contrast, most faithful to our times together when —as I write or read about those times—I choke up with tears or laugh with pleasure or grow tense with apprehension.

Thus I have drawn incidents and exchanges from several of you to combine in each composite—and thus fictionalized—patient. Yet I have tried to remain faithful to the experience back of such incidents—to your experience and to my experience. I hope you will feel my caring and respect for you in each chapter while knowing that none of the portraits is a complete portrayal of how in fact I see any one of you.

Probably the most fictionalized event in the book is the group session involving Jennifer and Louise. Yet I know several of you will recognize incidents in our groups' lives which are close to that occasion.

I would not want to embarrass any of you by disclosing your personal journeys with me in such a way that those who know you might feel they were having inappropriate glimpses of your private experience. To some of you who have read drafts of these chapters and reassured me of your comfort with my presentations, my special thanks are gladly given.

You, each of you, have been my teachers and my com-

panions. I cherish our time together and hope you do so also. Let this book bespeak my caring and my salute to you.

Jim

Dedication

I dedicate this book to the person who truly made it possible, Elizabeth Keber Bugental. Only with her love and support could I have found my way to trust in my own being sufficiently to speak as candidly as I have in the pages which follow. What is portrayed in those pages but incompletely expresses what I experience in my life as continually new and exciting possibility.

CONTENTS

The Search
for Existential Identity
Patient-Therapist Dialogues
in Humanistic Psychotherapy

THE LOST
SENSE OF BEING

I have listened for well over thirty years, through more than 50,000 hours, to men and women talking about what they want out of their lives. Engineers, policemen, prostitutes, lawyers, teachers, executives, housewives, secretaries, college students, nurses, doctors, nuns, cab drivers, ministers and priests, career soldiers, laborers, professors, clerks, actors, and others have invited me to be with them as they searched deeply within themselves to discover what they sought most dearly, as they struggled through the agony and soared on the joy of their seeking, as they encountered the dread and mustered the courage for their personal odysseys. From all of their rich teaching, I come increasingly to the conviction that the rock bottom concern of each human being is the simple fact of his or her own being alive.

Each of us knows he is alive, and each of us seeks to be more alive, for each knows that far too often he is not as alive as he could be, as he really wants to be. Yet that is the way it is with us. Some days we are so alive, and some days we feel ourselves slipping under the death tide that is inexorably gathering within us. It is the great tragedy of the human experience that time and again we are blind and deaf to the opportunities for fuller living.

There are so many unchangeable, external obstacles to our

full aliveness; chance, illness, death, and the intrusions of social, political, and economic forces. We all face such losses and fight against them however we can. But the losses we bring on ourselves because we did not know in time what was possible or what we most dearly wanted for ourselves—these are the most anguish-filled, the most bitter to contemplate.

Trying to have more of life and less of death is what it's all about. The continually shifting balance between life and death within us is the main barometer of how our lives are going. Too often, we have been blind and deaf to our own needing, our own wanting, our own sensing of the opportunities available to our lives. We have had too shrunken and paltry a view of our own natures, and we have not known how to claim the life that is our birthright. Many of us do not have effective access to our true centers. In my work with people who are trying to claim more of their lives, the primary focus is to help each person hear within himself more fully and accurately so he can direct his own life more satisfyingly.

I have been talking about being "blind and deaf" to our own needing and about learning to "hear" ourselves more fully in order to have more of life. These metaphors point to an awareness that has been missing or only partially present for so many of us. But they are more than metaphors. I am convinced that there is a sense dimension, part of our natural endowment, which many of us have lost the ability to use fully.

The most important point I will make in this book—and the one most easily overlooked or too little appreciated—is this: Each of us is invisibly crippled. I believe quite literally that each of us is a handicapped person, diminished in vitality, and intuiting, either acutely or vaguely, that our nature holds unrealized potentials.

This book is about our lost sense. It is the sense that is the key to our being fully, vitally alive. We have been maimed by a variety of influences; we are handicapped in the same way that a blind or deaf person is limited. We have not fully used our potentials. More fundamental than sight or hearing or touch or smell or taste is our lost sense, the sense of our own being. This lost sense is the inward vision that makes it possible for us to be continually aware of how well our outer experience matches our inner nature. This is the existential sense.[1]

What does it mean to say that I "listen" to my own experience? There is no ready set of words to describe this sense dimension. If a person has been blind or largely so from birth, the only way we can tell him about the sense of sight will be by unsatisfactory analogies with hearing and touching or the other senses. Figuratively speaking, most of us have been blind (or blindfolded) from our earliest years. We have learned very little about the sensing of our inner being, and often we have been taught to ignore it or devalue it. ("You don't really feel that way," "That isn't what you really want, now is it?" "Don't be so emotional," "It doesn't matter what you want; you've got to deal with the real world.") Thus, when I talk about this sense modality which we have not fully known we had, my words are awkward hand-me-downs from other experiences.

Inner awareness is actually an expression of my whole being, just as is my feeling love, anger, hunger, or emotional involvement in a project. As such, inward vision informs me moment by moment of how well what I am experiencing accords with my own unique nature.[2] Since it is the basis of my knowing where and how I am in my subjective being, it serves me in somewhat the same way as does my outward vision. It gives me orientation and helps me know the directions I want to take *within* myself.

The sense organ of my inner awareness is not an eye that allows me to look inward, nor is it an ear by which I listen to my own experiences. Rather, it is my whole being, the pattern or gestalt of who I am. For our discussion here, however, it is useful to speak of the inner awareness of my total being as though it were a distinguishable sense organ. In this way, I hope to be able to bring forcibly home the great loss we have all suffered.

This existential sense, as we may think of it, provides me with direct perceptions—as do all my other senses. This is a point often misunderstood. My eyes tell me there is a page in front of me, not a white rectangle with black marks on it, from which I have to deduce that this is a page with words, sentences, and meanings. Similarly, when it is functioning naturally, my inward sense gives direct awareness: It tells me, "I'm not enjoying this conversation with Clete," rather than only providing data from which I must draw deductions, such as, "I notice I'm restless physically . . . so maybe I'm bored by this conversation." But many of us can only observe ourselves in this latter and distant way, and so we must then speculate about the causes of our restlessness.

The inward sense is open to an immense range of stimuli—to sensory input, to memory, to anticipation of the future, to fantasy, to intentions, and to all the other forms of inner life. We use it well when we attend openly to all this flow as our very being in the moment. Unlike the outer sense of sight which we squint when we want to improve its functioning, the inner sense works best when we adopt an unstressed openness to what comes naturally. Functionally, inner awareness is similar to the process of hearing. For this reason, I sometimes think of my inner sense as a listening eye—it encompasses both inner vision and inner hearing. The phrase is appropriate, for it suggests a larger entity than any one sense organ. What I am saying is that the listening eye is the *listening I*. It is *I* who is listening, *I* who is the very process of the listening itself, and in an implicit way it is *I* who is listened to as well.

In thinking about these ideas, the trick is to get back within ourselves. We need to consider these thoughts in terms of immediate inner experience (rather than trying to analyze each idea in terms of usual, external conceptions). In other words, this idea of a listening I, or inner sense, that provides awareness of how things are within us may seem odd when our perspective is outward, thinking about people categorically. Similarly, when we try to reason about ourselves in the same outward way, looking at "me" and "myself" as objects, then we have difficulty recognizing this inward sense. When, instead, we reexperience within ourselves the *feel* of our inner awareness when we are vitally caught up in some activity, then the notion of this inward sense is familiar.

What is plain is that *I* am the center of my own life. *I* is the word we use to refer to what is for each of us a unique experience, unique in that *I* does not point to an object to be seen but to the very process of seeing objects. Just as the eye in my head cannot see itself, so the "I" of my being cannot see itself, cannot make an object of itself. It is the very seeing, the actual process of becoming aware.

If I am fully to experience my life, I must experience it at its center—that is, I need to feel my "I-ness." That's what inner awareness is about. It's the experiencing of I-ness.

I experience my I-ness when I know that I want something clearly and that I want it because *I* want it, not because somebody or something told me I should want it or that most people want it or that four out of five medical authorities recommend it. My consciousness of wanting it is immediate, beyond question, and unreasoned. (Of course, I can go back and find reasons or raise questions and so on, but that is a different matter from the direct experience of my wanting it.)

I want to stress that in no sense am I devaluing the role of my reasoning, my critical powers, my awareness of the needs of other people, or my concern for the future—or any other aspects of total being—as they contribute to the eventual course of *action* which I may take. For example, I do not view my reason and my feelings as opponents vying for domination of my life, a view apparently popular in some quarters today. I cherish an ideal of wholeness, which I am convinced is a direction always to travel and never to attain. My inner sense is—when most fully understood—an aspect of that potential wholeness which is my true nature.

Sometimes I have to take the time to attend to my inner sense. It may be that I have a vague sense of being hungry. If I don't run to see what's in the refrigerator or look at a menu or think up things to suggest to myself, then I can do a different thing: I can just open myself up and let my stomach, my mouth, and my whole awareness tell me what I—just I—really do want to eat or drink. It's significant that if I do this regularly, and follow what I discover reasonably, I probably won't have much problem with weight or diet or getting the right balance of such things as protein, carbohydrates, and fats, as the Pearsons have so well described.[3]

I can experience my I-ness in other ways than the wantings I hear within me. I can gain a sense of vital involvement when I let myself know and experience the emotions that are genuinely my own . . . when I let ideas flow out of me without trying to pre-shrink them in terms of whether they are logical, proper, sensible, or meet any other criterion than just being mine . . . when I move my body in free and joyful and spontaneous ways . . . when I am really open to and with another person who is with me in the same way . . . or when I explore deeply within my own thoughts, feelings, memories, and impulses in the process we call depth psychotherapy.

I am most alive when I am open to all the many facets of my inner living—desires, emotions, the flow of ideas, body sensations, relationships, reasoning, forethought, concern for others, my sense of values, and all else within me. I am most alive when I can let myself experience and genuinely realize (make real) all of these facets even as I am truly feeling and expressing my wholeness. So said, this sounds like an impossibly demanding prescription. Actually, it is only so when spelled out in this fashion. Human beings are capable of assimilating enormous amounts of material from diverse sources and subtly and unself-consciously unifying them in ways still far beyond the powers of the most sophisticated and complex computers.[4] The failure of our species to recognize and value that unity is one important root of many tragedies which we have brought on ourselves. Too often, we have chosen sides—spiritual versus sensual, behavior versus experience, intellectual versus emotional, considered versus spontaneous—rather than claiming the wholeness that is our potential.

Since being inwardly aware is so clearly an expression of our basic nature, why do we not use our inner sense continually in all of our living? As I have already suggested, much of our early training taught us to ignore—either partially or totally—the guidance of the inward sense. Parents and teachers, with the best of intentions, often feel they must "socialize" (tame?) the child so that his own wantings, feelings, and inclinations will not bring him into conflict with the expected patterns of his world.

A strong, subtle influence making us less sensitive to our inner life is western society's long love affair with the objective.[5] We have come to think that *subjective* is an adjective with flavor rather closely akin to *overly sentimental, undependable,* or *inconsiderate.* As a result, we try to rid ourselves of the taint of being who we are—inwardly experiencing persons—and set about treating ourselves as products of some Detroit assembly line, largely interchangeable and having little of value in whatever uniqueness slipped through the inspection. The virtue of objectivity is to hold in abeyance some parts of our experiencing at times in order to discern more of the environment's nature. But an authentic value has been subverted by those who do not trust the wholeness of human beings, and objectivity has been allowed to claim all of existence as its domain. The behaviorists, at their most extreme, have not been content with the special lens that the objective stance has provided; instead, they have insisted that all other views were but phantoms. Now the reaction is setting in, as might well have been anticipated, and antiintellectualism is elevating subjectivity and dethroning reason.

The inward sense about which I am concerned can be as effectively blinded by the denial of the objective as by its domination. I may decide to read a certain book because it is widely praised and force myself to finish it even when I find it is not rewarding to peruse. When my only motivation is a desire to be in on the popular thing or a self-deception that my tastes are the same as those who are supposedly "in the know," it should not surprise me if I have trouble finishing the book—but all too often it does. Too often, I may hesitate to tune into my inner awareness because I anticipate that it may not accord with what is socially expected of me. So I sit uncomfortably in a meeting, denying my inner prompting to move, so that others will not think me "restless" or inattentive; yet, in fact, I am unable to keep my thoughts on the proceedings. Sometimes it is a fear of confronting what is most truly in my core that makes me suppress my inward sense. When I busy myself with my work, with social occasions, and with continual activity to avoid confronting the realization growing within me that I am mortal and that I am aging toward my death, then it is inevitable that work, friends, social events, and most everything else will fail to bring me genuine satisfaction.

In summary, among the important consequences of being attuned with the inward sense are the following: greater integration of the many aspects of our being, increase in the feeling of vitality, better mobilization for action, more committed choices, and more authenticity in relationships. Of course, I still make mistakes and have problems, bad moods, and conflicts, but when any of those

things happen—as when positive things happen—I'm really involved with them. I have a great deal more of me to meet any
situation than when I'm out of touch with my inner sense.

In the hospital in *Catch 22*,[6] there is a man-thing completely
covered in bandages, fed through a tube from an overhanging
bottle, having its wastes removed through a tube to a bottle under
the bed. Is this a living person? Does it have any inner awareness?

At one time I was a consultant at a hospital in which there
was a patient who had been a boxer. For fourteen months, from the
night of his last fight until the day he died, the patient was in a
coma. He never regained consciousness during that time. Was he
truly alive? Did he have any inner "I-ness" before his heart finally
shut down?

At a state mental hospital, I occasionally saw another patient,
a middle-aged catatonic woman who lay in a bed, was fed intra-
venously, and soiled herself as an infant does. She responded neither
to her own body nor to any visitor. Was she alive as a human being?
Had she even a dim sense of her own inner vision?

In the same hospital there was a paranoid man who was
convinced—and sought to convince everyone else—that he was
the "Holy Ghost." In terms of that mystical identity, he was very
responsive, but he could not be reached in terms of "David Morton,"
the name on his hospital records. Somehow he felt more alive than
the catatonic woman; surely he knew something of his own I-ness.
Still, I'm curious if he, some place inside of him, had ever wondered
about the life he started out to have.

George Bannerman is thirty-four years old when his parents,
with whom he has always lived, bring him to see me. He has never
dated, and he has no real friends his own age. He works occasionally
as a handyman for sympathetic neighbors. He is not feebleminded
or psychotic, but he is socially undeveloped and has no evident
motivation to change. Is he genuinely alive in an existence better
suited to a fourteen year old? Does he have any real grasp of his
subjective life or of his own being in an "I" sense?

Donald Florenz is married and has two children. He works
as a records clerk in a large firm. Each day is much the same for
him. He gets up at 6:40 A.M., has breakfast, takes the bus to work,
goes through a day of routine, takes the bus home, arriving at

5:37 P.M., has dinner and watches TV until he goes to bed at 11:15 P.M., right after the first part of the news. How much is he truly alive? His ability to listen to his inner experience must be minimal.

And then I look in the mirror: Is he really alive? And how much? And how much more might he be? Can I hear and really know my own inner sense?[7]

I am asking the ancient question: What does it really mean to be alive? I listen to my friends-teachers-patients as they wrestle with the death that is in them and try to claim more of the life that is also within them. And, of course, I don't come up with The Answer. Yet slowly I come to realize how all of us—if we will but really look and listen—can sense the life pulsing within. We can tell when it is beating more strongly and when it grows faint—even though none of us can really define in proper academic fashion just what that deep intuition is. What we can do, though, is to recognize, by our own inner awareness, how we can experience our own beings in changed ways.

Getting dependable awareness through the inner sense and using it fully are the central avenues for the most exciting and rewarding psychotherapy experiences my patients and I have together. When someone with whom I'm working really catches the spirit of this effort, he becomes so turned on to the enterprise that we both are eager for our sessions together, for the adventure and discovery that has become possible, and for the resulting realization of personal growth. We talk of "rebirth" and of having new and deeper hope for our lives. And I feel nourished and deeply instructed by our work together.

I am describing a very different kind of psychotherapy than that practiced by orthodox psychoanalysts or by the behavior modification people. Indeed, the word *psychotherapy* itself takes on new meanings when applied to this sort of enterprise. It is no longer based on a repair model; rather, I think of this engagement as an evocation, a calling forth—of the life that is stifled within us, of the inner sensitivity we have learned to suppress, of the possibilities for being which we far too seldom bring into actuality. Whenever a person comes to me, I try to determine the extent of his or her inner awareness, whether he or she has some degree of appreciation for the experience of listening within. I try to disclose the influences that may be blocking or limiting his hearing his own subjectivity and to encourage him to put forth every effort to regain or enlarge the role of the inner sense in his living. This is the starting point in the most successful journeys my patients and I take together. When we can really concentrate on inner awareness, all else is incidental, and we both know it. Sadly, I am unable to help every person who comes to me to find his lost sense, to get in touch with the center of his being, but I'm continually trying to do so.

In seeking the inner sense, I am not, of course, asking questions that have not been asked before. Probably since man first had an inkling of that troubling, unique, and paradoxical gift of his awareness of his own being, he has stared at his own image in the forest pool and asked the awe-full question, "Who am I?" Certainly throughout recorded centuries, philosophers and prophets, kings and commoners, scientists and mystics, and all of the rest of us have tried to recognize that inescapable face in the mirror.

In these pages I write not from scholarship in philosophy or religion, or even in psychology. What I portray about the nature of our being comes chiefly from the hues of the many people who have trusted me with so much of their lives. Of course, it is likely that those colors are mixed with the pigments of my own experiences. I cannot tell how generally faithful are my portraits of our human countenance. I am warmed that more than a few people have expressed their recognition of kinship with the faces I have drawn from my palette.

I will not attempt to trace historically the many speculations about human identity. Suffice it to say that the question of "Who am I?"[8] is still very much an open one and that those who presume to have answers for it underestimate both themselves and the issue. Within the brief span of modern psychology, it has been fashionable to dodge the question or to handle it by quasireligious dogma (as is particularly the practice of the positivists). However, the humanistic force in psychology has begun to *re*-recognize man's subjectivity.

Abraham Maslow, one of the pioneers of the modern resurgence of humanistic psychology, called attention repeatedly to the importance of the person's inner awareness of his own unique being. At times he termed this "listening to the impulse voices."[9] Maslow has also written:[10]

Thinking in this way [of neurosis as a failure of personal growth] has had for me at least the one special advantage of directing my attention sharply to what I called at first "the impulse voices" but which had better be called more generally something like the "inner signals" (or cues or stimuli). I had not realized sufficiently that in most neuroses, and in many other disturbances as well, the inner signals become weak or even disappear entirely (as in the severely obsessional person) and/or are not "heard" or cannot be heard. At the extreme we have the experientially empty person, the zombie, the one with empty insides. Recovering the self must, as a sine qua non, *include the recovery of the ability to have and to cognize these inner signals, to know what and whom one likes and dislikes, what is enjoyable and what is not, when to eat and when not to, when to sleep, when to urinate, when to rest.*

The experientially empty person, lacking these directives from within, these voices of the real self, must turn to outer cues for guidance, for instance eating when the clock tells him to, rather than obeying his appetite (he has none). He guides himself by clocks, rules, calendars, schedules, agenda, and by hints and cues from other people.

Colin Wilson[11] speaks of "a kind of mental eye," and again of his "real 'I' " which he distinguishes from his self. Others have similarly recognized this lost sense: Theodore Reik's "Third Ear"[12] is a clear example. Alan Watts[13] seems to be pointing toward a similar inward knowing in many of his writings.

Erich Fromm[14] traces the path by which we lose the acuity of our inner sense:

To start with, most children have a certain measure of hostility and rebelliousness as a result of their conflicts with a surrounding world that tends to block their expansiveness and to which, as the weaker opponent, they usually have to yield. It is one of the essential aims of the educational process to eliminate this antago-

nistic reaction. The methods are different; they vary from threats and punishments, which frighten the child, to the subtler methods of bribery or "explanations," which confuse the child and make him give up his hostility. The child starts with giving up the expression of his feeling and eventually gives up the very feeling itself. Together with that, he is taught to suppress the awareness of hostility and insincerity in others; sometimes this is not entirely easy, since children have a capacity for noticing such negative qualities in others without being so easily deceived by words as adults usually are. They still dislike somebody "for no good reason"—except the very good one that they feel the hostility, or insincerity, radiating from that person. This reaction is soon discouraged; it does not take long for the child to reach the "maturity" of the average adult and to lose the sense of discrimination between a decent person and a scoundrel, as long as the latter has not committed some flagrant act.

On the other hand, early in his education, the child is taught to have feelings that are not at all "his"; particularly is he taught to like people, to be uncritically friendly to them, and to smile. What education may not have accomplished is usually done by social pressure in later life. If you do not smile you are judged lacking in a "pleasing personality"—and you need to have a pleasing personality if you want to sell your services, whether as a waitress, a salesman, or a physician. Only those at the bottom of the social pyramid, who sell nothing but their physical labor, and those at the very top do not need to be particularly "pleasant." Friendliness, cheerfulness, and everything that a smile is supposed to express, become automatic responses which one turns on and off like an electric switch.

Rollo May speaks of the "*I-am* experience" in characterizing what it means for the person to be aware of his own being. Although May is chiefly concerned with the intentionality aspects of the "*I-am* experience," and therefore with the potentiality to become, he is certainly identifying the same process within the person which I am terming the inner or existential sense. Of the "I-am experience" May[15] writes: "First, the '*I-am*' experience is not in itself the solution to a person's problems; it is rather the *precondition* for their solution." Later, he says: "The therapist's being able to help the patient recognize and experience his own existence [is] the central process of therapy."[16]

This book tells of seven people who reclaimed portions of their lives through gaining awareness of their inner beings. Each of these people taught me much, and I will attempt to relay those learnings. I hope the reader will really immerse himself in these people's stories rather than learn about them detachedly. If the reader lets these accounts resonate with his own experiences, then he may be helped to enrich his own life. For each of us—I who am writing and you who are reading—achieves our sense of well being to the extent to which we truly are on that inner beam of our lives. In that way, as in so many ways, the people whose stories I now relate are the same as we are.[17]

2

LAURENCE
Nothingness and Identity

Who or what am I? At rock bottom? Under the titles and roles and degrees and all those labels stuck on me? Under the jobs and relationships, under even name and personal history? Who am I? What am I?

The most fundamental lesson I have learned about life is this: *The essence of my being is that I am subjective awareness continually in process.* Ultimately I cannot identify myself with any substance (for example, my body), anything I produce (my words in these pages), any supposed attribute (my interest in others), my past, my prospects for the future, my thoughts of the moment, or any *thing* else. In short, I am *no thing*, nothing. I am solely the process of my being—as an example, I am the process of *writing* these words, but I am not the content of the words or the ideas they express. I am the *being aware* of writing, the *choosing* of ways of expressing thoughts, the *hoping* for communication, the *enjoying* of the emergence in thoughts and images of what I have experienced.

This recognition is hard to come by, for nearly every teacher has taught other ways to identify ourselves. We are told to find identity in education, in relating to others, in vocations, in records of achievements, in objective things. By so doing, we may hope to be *somebody,* to *amount to something.* But it is a powerful turn-on, a psychedelic experience,[1] when at last we cut loose from all that

14

objectivity and discover the freedom which is our deepest nature. Then we sense what truly being alive can be like; then we sample the various possibilities awaiting us and toward which we have ventured only timidly thus far. Then the pulse of life is firm and strong.

Laurence is a man struggling toward the discovery of his being, toward getting more genuinely and meaningfully in touch with his subjectivity. Unusually gifted, he has a long string of accomplishments that he has put together to make a sense of identity. Until fate stepped in, Laurence felt he had it made; then he crashed against the insubstantiality of substance, the transitoriness of the objective.[2]

I learned a great deal from Laurence because I had, as he had, put such trust in accomplishments. My adolescence was preoccupied with getting recognitions that would be merit badges sewn on my Boy Scout sash or entries under my name in high school and college annuals. In adult years my efforts went to building a long list of achievements for my personal résumé. It seems that only recently have I taken time to ask myself what I, just I within myself, really want to do. My listening-I has so often been deafened by the tyrannical *should's*.

October 28

When he calls to make his first appointment with me, Laurence is off-hand to the point of breeziness. "I've got a small matter on which I'd like to have your opinion. My time's pretty flexible, and I know you're very busy; so just tell me when will be convenient for you, and, hmmm, I'll look forward to meeting you." Those are his words on the phone, and the clear impression is that we need simply to talk over some trivial details. It will be some time before I learn how full his own schedule is and how much he is prepared to rearrange all manner of obligations to seize the first appointment I can offer him.

November 12

He arrives promptly, even a minute or two early, for our interview. As he comes into my office, he is impressive indeed. He wears a simple but obviously expensive suit, and he carries a hat, which is unusual in California. In all, he holds himself with a kind of stiff dignity without actually seeming rigid.

Laurence accepts the chair I indicate, carefully takes an excellent cigar out of a tube, offers it to me, and when I refuse, courteously asks if I mind his smoking. All the time he is chatting urbanely about the weather, the traffic, and the Egyptian souvenirs I have in my office. Although he is very smooth about it, I notice that Laurence is keeping such careful control of the conversation that, under usual social circumstances, I would have no opportunity to do other than listen and agree with him. As it is, I content myself with waiting for him to approach his concerns in his own way.

Abruptly, he straightens his already composed posture and speaks directly at me. "I suppose you're wondering why I am here?" It seems more an instruction than a question, but I admit its accuracy and at once get a brief, intense look followed quickly by a "good-fellow" smile. "Well, to tell you the truth, I wonder that myself, but, on the other hand, I always get the best men I can for every job, and I've been told that you are the best. So of course, I come to you. . . ."

And on Laurence goes, liberally praising me, then gradually sliding over to let me know his own qualities. He describes his education in Ivy League tradition, his foreign travel and study, his important assignments for the government, his success in several different lines of business. Then there comes another pause.

"You still haven't said why you're here."

"And, of course, you are absolutely right." His face again shows that instantaneous intensity quickly followed by the good-fellow smile. That brief intense look says something vastly important, but I can't read its message. Now Laurence tells me rapidly, and in a way which conveys how trivial he deems these matters, of several recent business reverses, of an auto accident a year ago, and of an apparently minor dispute with his wife over the children's bedtimes.

And he pauses again, that brief intense look flashes, and suddenly I know I am looking at a man drowning in abject terror. I take a calculated risk: "You're scared shitless!"

His expression freezes in the good-fellow smile, but frozen, it now looks as though he is about to shriek. He is silent a very long minute. Then he exhales noisily and slumps in his chair as if he has been held erect only by the breath he has just released. "Yes. I am." A flat voice contrasting dramatically with the modulated tones he's been using.

And so Laurence begins his psychotherapy.

We sit silently looking at each other, realizing we've made a naked contact for which neither of us was fully prepared. I feel breathless, cautious, and so I wait. Slowly he rallies. I detect his impulse to put back the urbane, competent mask. Instead, he seems to feel too weary to lift its weight.

"I am scared. Just as you say, I'm scared shitless. It's a relief finally to say it to someone. I've. . . . I've had no one to. . . . I've been very alone with. . . . I find it very hard to tell you about this. It's not that I don't want you to know. It's just that I don't seem to have the words. I mean, what I am experiencing seems outside of words or something like that. Do you know at all what I mean?"

"Not concretely, of course. But I surely do know that words just can't keep up with our deepest feelings." How quickly he regains control!

"Yes, yes, that's so. But this is something more or something different too. It's like trying to describe a color that isn't a part of our spectrum. It is related to our usual experience and yet somehow beyond it at the same time." Pausing, reflecting. "Yes. Hmmm. That's the best I can say it right now. What I'm experiencing and what has me so terrorized is similar to other things I've experienced and still it's something more than any other experience. And that 'more' is something for which I can find no words." He makes an odd little humming sound, without being aware of it, when he considers his inner feelings.

"As you talk to me, you seem to be recovering from the emotional depth you were in a few minutes ago."

He is surprisingly formal, pedantic. "Yes, that's so, isn't it? Well, I'm glad of that. Hmmm. Frankly, it's an experience I don't want to have again. In fact, that's why I'm here."

"How do you mean?"

"The feeling I had a few moments ago when you recognized how frightened I was is a small sample of the kind of panic that comes over me in waves at times. I really *have* to do something about those panics. I am utterly disabled by them. Hmmm, I mean when one of them hits I can't think clearly. I certainly can't talk lucidly—although, come to think of it now, they almost always come when I'm alone, and so I don't have to talk. . . . I'd really hate to be with others when one hits; I'd be pretty much an emotional basket case, I'm afraid. I mean, hmmm, I just cannot function in any reasonable way when these panics settle in on me."

"It seems strange to me that the important thing to you is that you can't function, as though you were a machine, rather than that you experience such terror in your self."

"Yes, well, of course, the terror is the whole thing. I really am quite undone by it." Pause. "Hmmm. It really is a relief to be telling someone about it. I feel much better already." The good-fellow smile is back. "Really, Dr. Bugental—do I pronounce that correctly? With a soft 'g'? eh? Well, perhaps if we have some interviews to discuss this whole thing, I'll be able to get back to work as I need to."

He hasn't really heard me at all. He doesn't distinguish his inner emotional experience from his outer efficiency of action. He's back in control, and the terror is already being thrust into his underground—from which it will, sooner or later, erupt again. I doubt he can really deal with these feelings now, but let's see.

"You feel better, and now I see Laurence Bellows back in what is obviously his more familiar way of being. The terror is. . . . "

"Yes, yes, you're right. It feels good to be discussing this with you and setting about correcting the situation."

Wow! He's not even going to let me get close to reminding him of the terror. Okay, okay, this is the first interview. Learn more about him before pushing.

And so for some minutes Laurence, very much back in charge of himself and the situation, tells me his story. His work, his success in developing his business, his recognition by others in the field, his hopes of building his company to a point that will allow him to work less intensely—these are the main concerns through which he lives. These are the attributes he wants me to consider when I think of him, and clearly, to value him for.

As the hour draws toward a close, Laurence glances at his watch and without any prompting from me prepares to take charge of the next matter on his agenda. "I travel a lot, you know, and it will be hard to set a dependable schedule, but of course, I'll do what I can to give you notice whenever I have to be away. Now, this is a Tuesday morning. Would you like to see me every Tuesday that I'm in town and at ten, as this morning?"

"Mr. Bellows, if we decide to work together, I will want to see you at least three times a week and preferably four, and you will need to arrange your affairs so that you rarely miss a session."

Let's get this thing straight right now. He wants to dismiss his terror as a minor matter. I'm damn sure it is not. Wish I knew more about him before dealing with the frequency of interviews; must have been challenged by the smooth way he took over, and so I'm having to reassert myself! I'm amused at myself, but it's probably just as well anyway. He needs help to take his pain and his life seriously.

"Four times a week!" Consternation, a bit overdone. "I really don't see how I can manage it with my commitments, but. . . . " His pause is well calculated to get me to offer some adjustment. He *is* skillful in interpersonal dealings, no doubt about it. Best to just keep quiet and wait.

"Well, if you think it's really necessary. . . . Hmmm. I could try to work out three interviews a week for a month or so, I imagine. I mean, you know your business, I suppose, and. . . . "

He's nettled—a little dig in that "I suppose." Yet he's beginning to let himself think more seriously about the prospect of therapy. Don't want to play elusive games with him; he's really in great pain and terror, and I don't know much about him or why he suffers so. "I'd be willing to try three times a week, as long as we really made those times regularly. But, Mr. Bellows, let's level with each other. This is not a matter of a month or so, if I can make any judgment knowing as little as I do about you."

"How long a period do you estimate, doctor?" Level, careful.

"That's really almost impossible for me to say at this time.

I hardly know anything about you yet. And, frankly, even when I know more, it will be doubtful how well I can estimate the total time you'll want to work with me. I put it that way because it will always be fundamentally your choice whether you continue or leave. What I can tell you is that most people with whom I work continue their therapy between two and three years; although some, of course, stop sooner and some keep going longer."

"Two to three years. Hmmm. This really is quite a different matter than I had anticipated, and I'm not sure. . . . " Pausing, contemplating, not quite so smooth now.

"Yes, it is a major undertaking, Mr. Bellows. It needs to be thought of as one of the major events of one's life, for what we attempt to do here is to reexamine the whole course and meaning of the way you're alive."

"Well, yes, mm-hmmm. But that seems much more comprehensive than I think I require at this time. I'm sure it would be quite worthwhile, if one had the time and resources. Hmmm. Yes, quite worthwhile." Considering, hesitating.

"But you wonder if it is what you want to undertake right now."

"Yes, you see, I'm very busy right now. That accident last year, you know, I was out of operation for six months almost completely. Whiplash to the neck and thus little or no physical activity, plus some kind of strange tracings on my EKG so that they wanted me to take it very, very easy physically and emotionally as well. The result is all sorts of work backed up for me. Can't really see taking off three or four mornings a week—even if only for a few hours—right now. Hmmm. Yes." Considering. "Do you really think that such a comprehensive program is required simply to alleviate these episodes of panic which I described?"

"Mr. Bellows, I frankly have very little idea of what may be required for that purpose. I have barely met you. I will be glad to talk with you six or eight times, if you like, and then together we'll reassess what may be indicated." He brightens, starts to speak, but I push on. "But I don't want to mislead you. My educated guess is that at the end of that time I will make the same recommendation I have just made—for two reasons: First, I very much doubt that these panics are some peripheral or isolated problem separate from the rest of your way of being. Thus, to get into what brings about the panics, we will almost certainly open up other parts of your inner experience." His eyes are tightening slightly; no other evident reaction. "Second, I believe significant, lasting changes only come from this kind of thoroughgoing inquiry into a person's life. Now in regard to this second point, you should know that there are a number of other competent people in this area who do not work as intensively as I do, who do not believe it is required, and whose names I'd be happy to give you."

"Yes, well. Hmmm. I appreciate that and your candor, Dr. Bugental." Stalling, thinking rapidly. "I suppose what I'd better do is take some of those names and then consider all that you've told me over the next few days. I can then call you toward the end of the week or the first of next week."

"That seems like a good plan. As I said, if you do go ahead with me, this undertaking needs to be one of the major events and commitments of your life. Certainly you don't want to plunge into such a program without careful thought."

So we wind up the hour, I give him three names, and we politely shake hands and bid each other good-bye.

After Laurence leaves, I walk to the window and look out at the gray day, thinking of this competent machine which is so un- aware it is a man. He doesn't value, hardly even knows there is a life going on within himself. He just wants to get fixed so he can operate more efficiently and dependably, wants to be repaired without too much "down time." Yet his background is one rich in other possibilities, studies in philosophy and literature, travel in this country and abroad. What happened to it all? Those panics. . . . Wait! Those panics just might be the only real touch he has right now with his inner aliveness. The panics are the frantic signals of his lost subjective center. Aha! The inner sense can scream, as well as listen and look inwardly.

December 28

As it turns out, it is nearly six weeks before Laurence calls again. When he does, he is quickly apologetic for not communicating with me sooner. Then he asks for as early an appointment as possible. Since I have a cancellation for the next day, I can see him then.

The way he comes into my office is similar to his entrance on our first interview, except now there is a sense of urgency and impatience in all of his movements and in his tone of voice.

"Thank you for seeing me so quickly. I really should have been back to you much sooner. Sorry, just so many demands on my time and thoughts."

"I understand."

"I went to see your colleague, Dr. Kennedy . . . or Kenny. Afraid I don't have his name right."

"Kenny."

"Of course. Hmmm. Saw him, and he seemed like a good man. Liked his way of talking. But I just never got around to following up on my visit to him. You know, your proposition—I suppose that's not the right term; your recommendation—gets to me in a way. I used to be much more reflective. Business takes that out of you or makes you push it aside, I suppose. Hmmm, anyway, I found myself returning several times to the idea of really looking at things and getting your ideas on my way of life. But. . . . "

"Mmmm?"

"But I didn't think I was ready to take that big a plunge, especially with the pressure from the office right now, but. . . . "

"You're having trouble trying to say something right now, I think."

"I read a story the other day on the plane from New York. A story about the Amazon. . . . Travel magazine the hostess handed me. . . . There was a story in there. . . . On the whole it didn't amount to much, but there was this kind of aside about the natives. They, uh. . . . "

Abruptly I realize that he's fighting a terrible battle within himself. I don't know what it is, or much about it, but I can feel the intensity like a wave of energy pushing against me.

"You're in the midst of some kind of struggle right now. Why don't you let the story go for the minute and see if you can tell me about that fight that's going on inside of you?"

Composure draining away. His face is tight, so deliberately masked that it hurts to see it. "Yes, well, I want to tell you about

this thing I read. . . . I mean I got the first insight I've had into.
. . . I find it very hard to talk about this, because I'm afraid it will
provoke the same thing that happened on the plane. Ughh! It's
amazing how physically painful this is."

"What happened on the plane?" A simple, factual question
may help him get traction.

"I had one of those panics." He sits very still, waiting,
listening within himself. The panic is forcing him to listen within, to
try to get in touch with his inner sense. "I read this item in the
travel magazine, and then I suddenly found the feelings building up
in me. I didn't know whether I could hold on. Felt like the plane
would just open up and drop me from forty thousand feet or something like that. Almost wished it would! Managed to down a couple
of stiff Martinis and finally it eased. Had another drink to keep the
thing down, wine with dinner, and brandy after. By that time,
I was able to relax and watch the last half of some stupid movie I'd
had in front of my eyes all along and had hardly been able to focus
on. Damn well could become an alcoholic doing that. Hmmm.
Those panics are the worst experiences I've ever had." More composed now, telling the event has helped.

"Can you tell me about the item in the magazine now?"

"Hmmm. Yes; yes, I believe I can. Sorry to have such a
time of it. Well, it was about the. . . . Oh! It does start up again
inside of me so quickly when I think about the story. Hmmm. Well,
let's say it. These Amazon natives get ahold of one of their enemies,
and then they smear his body with honey, and they stake him out
right in the path of the army ants. And the ants . . . thousands of
the bastards . . . the ants just eat the man alive. Uhhh! Hmmm.
My God! They eat him alive! Just imagine how he feels, what he
thinks, as they take all those little bites! Awghh!"

"Awful."

"My God! Just imagine it. It's impossible. A man would go
insane. I would. I hope I would. I hope I would just lose consciousness—not be aware of what was happening. I know I'm probably a physical coward. . . . No, I can think of some times when
I wasn't—but that's not the point. Whether I'm a coward or not,
there's something about that story that is worse than just the
physical suffering." He is gripping the arms of his chair and strug-

gling almost without awareness of me. "Hmmm. It's those little ant bites. It's seeing one's own flesh disappearing, one's own body just dissolving away into the ants. . . . Awghh! Oh, God damn it, I don't want to go into another of those panics. I don't think I can take it."

We sit silently for a minute or two. It's too early to urge him to let go to the panic. I haven't established a good enough relationship with him yet. He'll need that to know he has a lifeline to help him find his way back. Later on though, he'll almost certainly have to make that trip into his personal hell. Just now he's exerting fantastic amounts of energy to regain what he regards as necessary control. Maybe I can help a bit.

"Laurence, you are mobilizing tremendous forces in yourself to put down this panic."

"Yes." Practically through clenched teeth. "Yes, I just don't want to have another of those times."

"Something in you seems determined to break out and overwhelm you with terror."

"I keep seeing those ants. It's as though I can feel them on my own body! I've got to break out of that picture."

"Have you used drinking before as a way of stopping the panic?" Factual questions should help him shift away from the image.

"No. Yes. I guess I have. I'm having trouble thinking clearly right now. It seems like I have. Hmmm, oh, of course, now I remember. In Chicago in the spring, I had to meet a contractor after dinner, and during dinner—I was eating alone—I felt the panic starting. I stopped eating and had a couple of fast doubles."

"How'd it work?"

"It did the trick. I was a little bit unsteady during my talk with Kemper, the contractor, but it went off all right. Hmmm. I don't think he noticed anything." More comfortable now. Interesting that his measure of whether the encounter went "all right" depends on whether the other man noticed anything. I note also that his "hmmm's" seem to be a way of "doing something" when he otherwise would be silent.

The rest of the interview is taken up with Laurence's account of his present work, with his life situation, and with setting a schedule for him to come in three times every week. He doesn't say why he's here rather than with Dr. Kenny. My guess is that it's because he recognizes, at least partially, the pervasiveness of his anxiety and because he values the idea of a thorough life review—especially after having six months of enforced idleness.

As we work together in the months after that interview, Laurence's story comes out. He is, indeed, an unusual man, highly successful in his work—at least in terms of money earned and of respect won from others in his field. He is apparently indifferent to his seemingly conventional home life. He is on the governing boards of several civic and philanthropic organizations. In short, by the standards which most of us were taught, Laurence is a man who has made it. As I come to know him, that phrase *he's made it* has just the right flavor for Laurence. He has made it vocationally and financially, in his community, church, social settings, and—at least from an outside view—in his home life. Yet Laurence is truly a man in terror. Why? Because Laurence finds himself increasingly gripped by a horror-filled recognition. Like a doomed mountaineer discovering that the slope beneath his feet is beginning to slide and agonizingly realizing he is caught hopelessly in an avalanche which is carrying him over a precipice, so Laurence feels his rational footing giving way to a realization which is carrying him over the edge into endless space. The realization is that he, Laurence, does not exist!

I mean that quite literally. Laurence finds himself struggling frantically and futilely against the unrelenting and sanity-devouring conviction that he, himself, is nothing . . . nonexistent.

July 1

We come to a full appreciation of Laurence's conviction that he does not exist during a phase that occurs nearly seven months after we began our work together. These were months of building a foundation and testing our relation with each other, of Laurence's learning to explore within his own awareness, of his discovering the importance of his subjective life and thus beginning to get in touch with his "I-ness," and of the thousand other crucial but unexciting, details that are part of a truly thoroughgoing psychotherapeutic course. When he comes in today, his ability to "go to work" therapeutically without preamble testifies to the gains he has made already.

"When I left here last Friday I found I kept thinking about that whiplash I had last year. It was as though we had stirred something up, but I couldn't quite get ahold of it. Hmmm. I want to try to feel into it now." He is settling himself on the couch, as usual arranging the pillow under his neck very carefully.

"Why don't you just tell me about the accident and what followed as though I'd never heard any of it, Laurence."

"Very well. Hmmm. I was on Sunset, out where it curves around so much, you know, toward the beach. I came around the bend, and there was this pedestrian halfway across the street, so I slammed on my brakes and stopped, but this man in the Olds behind me didn't see what was happening in time, so he just ploughed into my rear end. Snapped me forward, and my head went back so sharply that right at the time, I really thought, 'My God, my neck's broken!' and I'm lucky it wasn't. The car was a total wreck. I wasn't hurt much otherwise, but I was in shock and so dazed I don't remember much of what happened then. I heard later the driver of the Olds went through his windshield and probably was dead by the time he hit the back of my car. I'm just glad neither car had any other passengers in it. Hmmm. They took me to Santa Monica Hospital, put my neck in traction, patched up a couple of ribs that got cracked against the steering wheel. You know, the usual routine. After a week of hospital observation I came home, and then the agony set in.

"Bennington, my own doctor, had insisted on a complete work-up, and in addition to the neck and ribs and some bruises, they found my heart was doing strange things on the electrocardiograph. Couple of cardiologists looked at the tracings, but nobody was quite sure how to interpret them. So they gave me those incredible, stupid instructions only a doctor can hand out with a straight face: 'Just relax and don't worry about it. Oh, no, don't try to do anything. Just take a rest. Stay in bed; don't get worked up about anything; don't move around too much . . . ' and so on and so on. 'Just relax and forget that your head nearly got knocked off your neck and that said neck may or may not have permanent after-effects and always have to be in a collar. Just relax and don't think about how your heart seems to have picked up a strange rhythm that may mean it's about to quit altogether but, on the other hand, may not mean anything at all. You know, just relax.' So I relaxed. The hell I did. I tried to be a 'good patient' for a month, but it was really very depressing."

"Depressing?"

"Maddening. I don't know. At first it seemed depressing. I was moody, irritable, snapped at the kids and Helen a lot. Then I began sulking, I guess. Hmmm. Didn't want to talk to anybody. Tried to get interested in TV. My God! 'Wasteland' is right. Tried to read. Used to love to read. Hmmm. For a while it was better. Went through a book or two a day. But pretty soon, I don't know, after a month of so, I could feel I was running away to the books. I was scared to come out of them. Hmmm. Didn't know why, but I could feel that I was frightened not to be caught up in a book, anxious when I finished one, couldn't wait to get into the next. So I tried to stop. Hmmm. By then I could move around a little, talk to people from the office. I got them to let me work a couple of hours a day—after all my heart was still going, even though still acting funny. But it was too frustrating. I'm not the world's best delegator. Hmmm. I wanted to get in and do things myself. I couldn't. Had one sharp flare-up when I disobeyed orders. Taught me they weren't kidding. I really do have a heart that isn't quite what it should be. Got to take it seriously. Hmmm." Pauses, seems to reflect.

"Hard to do? Hard to take it seriously that your heart isn't as good as you'd like?"

"Yes. Hmmm. Yes, it is. I don't like to think about that."

"Tell me."

"I'm not sure I can. Feeling of being less than I should be. Hmmm. Like I'm guilty or something. Like I'm not all there. I don't know. It doesn't make much sense. It didn't even then. But it troubled me. I guess it still does. Hmmm. The last two months or so were really miserable. I'd do a couple of hours work with people who'd come out to the house to see me or on the phone, and then I'd have to stop, and that was frustrating. But I couldn't get my thoughts to stop, even though I tried. They just kept eating away at me. And then. . . . "

"Then. . . . "

"Then I got to trying to find some other resources within myself, something besides work, or watching TV, or reading. It seems like I used to have more of my own, inside me, you know. But I couldn't seem to do it. Hmmm. Couldn't seem to find something in me that wasn't hooked up to doing something outside of me. Bugged me. Kept finding my thoughts working at it, chewing it over. Still bothers me. . . . "

"Laurence, I'm struck by the words you've been using, 'eating away at me,' 'bugged me,' 'chewing it over,' and so on. You couldn't get your thoughts to stop chewing on you. . . . "

"Yeah. Yes. Hmmm. Like so many little creatures biting me and not giving me any peace. Wait! The Amazon story, the ants eating the man? Yes! Yes, of course! Those thoughts seemed to be eating me up too."

"Past tense?"

"No, sometimes they still do. When I get the panics. That's very interesting! But why the panic? I'm not really disappearing into some alien things. . . . Or am I?"

"Are you?"

"Hmmm. I can't say why, but. . . . 'Disappearing into some alien things. . . . ' Hmmm. Yes, in some way." Pause. "It's so elusive. . . . "

"Those little thoughts keep eating away at you, chewing on you." He's close. He's trying; yet he's resisting. He would like to work it out abstractly, intellectually. He doesn't really want to go into the hell of his panics in order to recover his being.

"Eating away at me, but. . . . I don't know. Hmmm. I can't seem to think of anything further."

"You'd like to solve it, but you don't want the feelings to get too strong in you right now."

"Well. . . . Hmmm. I can't think clearly when the panic sets in. I mean I find it just scatters my thoughts."

We are silent for several minutes as Laurence ponders within himself, and I reflect on his predicament right now. He is restlessly fidgeting with the bolster on the back of the couch on which he lies, clearly wanting to get on with the task of understanding his feelings and equally clearly wanting to avoid being swept away by his emotions.

Like so many of us, Laurence still believes that "orderly thinking," such as that which our fourth grade teachers rewarded, is the right way to work on any matter—arithmetic problem or emotional disruption. Actually, that sort of thinking is a puny tool of little use once we move beyond long division and essays on the theme of "What I Did on My Summer Vacation." Laurence knows this at least implicitly in other areas of his life, but he can't risk opening his thinking when he's so near his panics.

The sort of orderly thinking that Laurence has need of now is a much more widely ranging, subtle, and emotionally informed process than that which he consciously seeks at this moment of apprehension and possibility. He is like a man who needs to know what is in a dark cave he fears to enter, and so he stands on the outside, futilely peering into the opening. What Laurence must do if he is to make any headway in understanding or changing his panic experiences is to enter into his experiencing center. He needs to be at one with his I-ness. Only in this way can he really know what it is that panics him and what he needs to free himself. Yet Laurence senses, quite accurately, that knowing his panics means that he must be *in* them—and being in them, he fears, will literally overwhelm him.

I will try to help him move into the cave a bit.

"Laurence, I know that the main thing you rely on is your thinking, but it is important to get to your *feelings,* even if that means you do not think as clearly as you like."

"Well, hmmm, yes, I suppose so, but. . . . "

"But you still don't want to feel the panic, and right now you'd rather argue about whether you should feel it than risk getting into it."

"No, no. If you say I should get to the feelings, of course, I'll. . . . "

"I feel that we're getting very far away from them right now; don't you?"

"No; well, perhaps so. Hmmm. I'll see if I can get back to them."

"What are the thoughts that eat at you? Say them just as concisely as you can. No other words—just the thoughts that chew at you."

"Well, 'what can I do except work or other things outside of me?' Or 'is there anything of my own inside of me which does not depend on the outside?' Or 'who am I?' Or, maybe, 'what am I except what I do?' Yes, that's closer. 'What am I, if I don't count what I do on the outside?' 'Is there any me apart from outside things I do?' Yes, that's it. I can feel it now. I mean I'm excited because I can feel how it all ties together, but I'm scared too because I think I'm on the edge of going into a panic. I don't want to go into it. I really don't."

"Laurence, see whether you can risk it. Sooner or later you will have to go into those feelings, into that place inside of yourself, in order to find out who or what you are."

"Well, yes. Hmmm. Quite possibly at some point. . . . But I just don't think I want to attempt that now. I think you're telling me just to let go to that panic and see what happens, but I can't do that. I've never been brave about my emotions. I never have, and I can't be now."

"It is frightening to think even of doing so, I know, Laurence. But give it as much of a try as you can. It really is important."

"It just feels too big, too overwhelming. I've got work I have to do—mind you, *have* to do—at the office today. I can't afford to be knocked out. . . . "

"Your functioning as a business machine seems so much more important than your feelings, than the fact you're living in constant fear that the panic will overwhelm you."

"No, of course not. Really, that's a stupid thing to say." Angry, anxious to get onto almost any other topic, including a disagreement with me.

"You're angry with me for holding up a mirror to your fear."

"Yes. Yes. You are a damned aggravating person sometimes."

"That's what you pay me for. But now you're getting further and further away from confronting the panic, just as you meant to, at least unconsciously."

"Oh, very well. I'll give it a try. Hmmm. Well, we were

thinking about who or what I am—apart from what I do. Hmmm. That seems a very philosophical question. Hmmm. I'm not sure I know how to proceed."

"That's probably true, Laurence. The thread you needed to follow was the anxious feeling you were experiencing a minute ago. When we got off on our debate about whether you were brave or not, or whether you could afford to listen to your feelings when you had work to do at the office, the essential lead to the panic got lost."

"Yes, well, hmmm. Let me see if I can recover it."

But he doesn't get any further. The rest of the session is largely intellectualized discussion of the nature of identity. Still we both feel this session has brought together some important strands.

Laurence has been forced by his own relentless mind to look into a terrifying mirror. He seeks an image of himself which will reassure him of his own substantiality, but he finds none. The image in the mirror grows transparent, wavers, and threatens to vanish entirely. "Who am I?" he asks, for he is no longer comfortable with answers to the question, "What am I?"[3] His past attainments are just that—past. They no longer sustain him. They are as dated as photographs in a family album. Now he is in flight from the nothingness which continually threatens to creep up on him. His momentary refuge is only in how others see him. He can find no sense of his subjective center.

July 3

At our next session, Laurence is eager and impatient when I greet him in the waiting room. He quickly enters the consultation room, tosses his coat on a chair and begins talking even as he lies on the couch, barely even fussing with the pillow at his neck.

"As soon as I left it was all clear. I mean I almost turned around and came back, but I knew you would be busy. Hmmm. I suppose you saw it all along, but suddenly I just heard my own words, and I was saying it all, wasn't I?"

"Tell me."

"Well, you know, it's so clear now that I feel I've always known it but somehow couldn't let myself face it. I just don't know who I am. I mean if you set aside what I do, my functioning so to speak; well, then . . . I mean, the question is, is there any *me,* do I exist in any way in my own right?"

"Mm-hum."

"And usually when I get to asking that question, I really get frightened. I seem to remember thinking about it in one way or another all my life. When I was about 17, I went through a period of panics . . . terrible sweaty, frightened times. Hmmm. Then, it was around the idea of dying, of just not existing any more, while the world went on without me. These panics today are similar to the death fears; yet there's a difference. Hmmm. Then I felt sure that I existed. At least right at the moment I knew I was alive. I didn't know whether I would be alive in some later moment— usually many, many years ahead. But no matter how far ahead I put my death—and I was sure I would keep healthy and medical science would make tremendous advances to help me stay alive— no matter how long I put it off, the idea that sooner or later I would die pressed in on me, and I would lose my breath and get a cold sweat all over and feel as though I couldn't stand the thought."

"But now. . . . "

"Now, it's like that and yet different. Now, I know I'll die some day, and that still is frightening, but it's off in the future some place. But the thing that is terrifying to me now is that I don't think I. . . . No, I'd guess it's closer to. . . . Hmmm. It's strange. One minute it's all so clear, and then the next I can hardly remember what we are talking about."

"You really don't want to think or remember what makes you feel the panics right now."

"That's true. I really don't."

"You'd like to just forget the whole thing."

"If I really could, yes, I would like that. When I was laid up for that six months or so, I tried to froget it in every way I could. I've told you about the reading, the TV, the two hours of business. I haven't begun to tell you all the things I tried. Did you know there are whole books of things for bedridden people to do? Knitting, solitaire, puzzles, addressing envelopes for worthwhile organizations. . . . I tried them all, and. . . . "

Interrupting, "And you're trying something similar right

now. Trying to keep us from really getting a direct recognition of what panics you."

"No, I just thought that. . . . Hmmm. Well, maybe. . . . Anyway, the thing of it is that I just get this awful feeling that really I don't exist, that in a sense I'm only something that I imagine. Hmmm. I don't know what that means. It reminds me of Berkeley's, 'To be is to be perceived.' And if no one perceives me, then I don't exist. If I don't do anything, I don't exist. And suddenly, I'm fading away, just disappearing."

"You don't sound very frightened about it now." In fact he sounds very scholarly and distant from his frightened self. Quoting Berkeley, indeed!

"I have it walled off. I can feel how carefully I'm keeping it abstract, like something in a course in philosophy."

And he keeps it walled off for the rest of this session and for some time after. Occasionally during the hour, Laurence does genuinely try to let himself get in touch with his panic, but he is either too fearful to let go to it fully or too detached an observer of himself to break through.

September 1

Sometimes the panic returns—although Laurence thinks it is less frequent now. He is diligently seeking some way to forestall those episodes and repeatedly tries to find some sense of his personal identity. About two months after the above interview, Laurence sketches the current stage of his seeking for reassurance of his own being.

"I can't believe in God, you know. At least not the God I learned about in Sunday School when I was a kid. And besides, that isn't really an answer to my question. Hmmm. Oh, I'm talking rationally and calmly about it now, but sometimes at night when the house is still and I start thinking about it, the panic sets in. I can't breathe; I can't lie still, can't even stay in bed. I get up, put on a robe, go prowling around like I'm looking for something, but I don't know what I'm looking for. Hmmm. Or I guess I do. Myself. I'm looking for myself, but I'm not sure I'd recognize it if I saw it. . . . "

"It sounds like you're looking for some tangible, physical thing, like you might go walking into the kitchen and suddenly discover your self lying there on the table where you had put it down but forgot it."

"Yes, I know. Hmmm. But I really know it's not like that. Though I don't know what it is I am looking for. I just know that I can't really rest until I find it. Even now that I'm back working full-time, I still find the questions popping up when I least expect them. And then the sweaty feeling begins and my throat hurts and. . . . "

After Laurence leaves the office, I reflect that what he was looking for so despairingly was right in the office with us and that he could not see it. His being was expressed in the fact of our conversation itself, in his commitment to our work together, in his unsaid but evident conviction that he would ultimately discover his identity. His identity was not in the *content* but in the *processes* of his talking, his continual recommitment, and his belief in our work.

January 26

At times, Laurence pushes all concern with his fears into the background and immerses himself in work, a familiar refuge for him. In work he can often quiet his own misgivings by getting others to react to him in ways that affirm his existence.

I focus repeatedly on his dependence on being busy and on his need to make an impression on others in order to experience his own presence by seeing it bounce off of them. Again and again I try to help him recognize that valuing his work and his effectiveness with others—while these things can be pleasant—cannot lastingly give him the sense of his own being for which he frantically seeks. He is an addict who needs these "fixes" to keep going; he can't believe he can get along without them.

But slowly as we pursue him into these retreats on which he has so long relied, slowly he begins to mobilize his courage, begins to face his dread more directly, and now a different Laurence is emerging. This new Laurence is less pedantic, less flowery in speech; he is more blunt, more frequently really happy, really sad, or really angry. He is more in touch with his life's pulse, and he is beginning to know his inner experiencing more genuinely.

He has been lying silently on the couch for several minutes, busy with many thoughts, his face mobile. In some way I sense that he is thinking about himself in a kind of detached, subject-looking-at-object manner. Rather than being open to the flow of his inner living, he's looking at and pondering about his self. How I know what he is thinking, I can't really say, but I'm confident that my guess is correct. I am considering saying what I sense, feeding my perceptions back to him, but before I can do so, Laurence begins speaking in what I have come to term his "busy executive" voice.

"In my business it's always essential to give the impression that you've got everything going your way, and you don't need any-body or anything. Hmmm. Just yesterday, there was a meeting that. . . . " He pauses abruptly.

Laurence's detachment is now apparent in his language, so I decide to focus on it. "I notice you're talking in the second person." Almost always, the inner sense, the I-ness, expresses itself in the first person singular.

His answer surprises me with its sudden anger. "Hell, first or second person, it doesn't matter. The thing is, people aren't going to invest tens or hundreds of thousands of dollars if you—or if I, if you like that better—seem to them. . . . Well, you know what I mean."

"What do you mean?" Blandly.

"Oh, for Christ's sake, Jim! You do play dumb about the most obvious things." Now the anger is more evident.

"Laurence, I think you'd rather get in a fight with me than face how much you depend on your image to others."

"Will you just tell me why you are making such a big deal about whether I say 'I' or 'you' when I talk?" Pause. I wait but keep silent. "Oh, very well, so I'll say it in the first person just to please you." Again he pauses, and again I wait. Now his voice changes and becomes less forceful and more uncertain. "Well, uh . . . as I was telling you, uh. . . . " A long pause. His voice changes. "Jim, you'll never believe this, but I can't remember what we were talking about."

"I believe you; in fact I'm pretty sure that you got so

worked up for the same reason you've now forgotten what you wanted to say: You're alive only in how people see you. At some level, you know that. And it scares the hell out of you to depend on your image that way."

"Oh, yes, of course, I remember," ignoring my comment. "I was trying to tell you that in my line people go a lot on how confident they think I am. If I look like I'm hungry for money, they run away. If I look like I couldn't care less whether they come in on the deal, they beat the door down."

"And so you have to put on a good show for them, eh?"

"Yeah, that's business." He settles himself more comfortably on the couch.

"You're relaxing now after being all steamed up."

"Well, I forget sometimes that you people don't know the kind of dog-eat-dog world most of us have to live in."

"You want me to think that this is just one of the realities of the world and not directly important to why you've been so upset by this feeling of not really existing."

"Hmmm. Well, that's just the way it is, and I . . . we ought not to waste our time on what can't be helped." The angry edge is coming back into his voice.

My voice is also sharp. "You really don't want to look at how hooked you are on keeping that confident image up. In fact, you're trying to pull it on me right now."

"Oh, damn it! Why don't you drop it, Jim?" Pause. "Oh, well, if it will make you happy, I'll look at it, but it's just the way business is. You just talk to anybody who's been out in the jungle, and they'll tell you the same thing. Hmmm. You sit here in your fancy office and have people come to you so I can't expect you to understand. . . . "

"Okay." Interrupting. "I get it. You're going to give me a lecture about how naive I am. Then by the time you're through, we can argue about that and forget all about how you have to look good or be scared to death. You clearly need to fight with me more than. . . . "

Now he cuts me off. "Look, I'm ready to look at anything that needs looking at, but I don't see any point in wasting my time and yours just because you don't know your . . . elbow from a hole in the ground about business, and. . . . "

"Why did you change what you were about to say?"

"What do you mean?"

"You started to say that I don't know my 'ass' from a hole in the ground and then you changed 'ass' to 'elbow.' How come?"

"Oh, well, I guess I was getting kind of worked up. There's no use being nasty about it."

"There's no use showing how you really feel, you mean."

"Well, I don't want to be angry."

"Hell." Harshly. "You *are* angry. That isn't the question. You just feel that way. So do all of us at times. What you don't want is *to be seen* as angry."

"Well, yes, that's so." Now his tone is thoughtful. "Yes, I was angry, but for some reason I didn't want to let that show."

"And that 'some reason' isn't to swing a business deal." Persistently.

"No, hmmm." Now definitely reflective. "No, I'm not trying to sell you anything."

"Yes, you are. You're trying to sell me the same thing you're always pushing: the image of Laurence-the-good-fellow, Laurence-the-always-confident, Laurence-who-never-needs-anyone, and Laurence-who-is-always-calm-and-reasonable. And it scares and angers you when I don't buy it."

"You're a direct bastard." There's affection and recognition in his voice.

"Laurence, the warmth you're giving me right now feels good, but it's just one more layer to hold off the fright."

"Hmmm. I don't know what you mean." His voice is not as firm. He's no longer the busy executive.

"Getting confused is the easy way out right now, Laurence. It's your way to avoid facing that constant dependence on how you look to others." It is important to help him stay with himself now, and yet I can sense his impulse to escape.

"Yes. Hmmm. I know what you mean, I guess." His voice is sunken in his chest, and he sounds unsure. We both are silent for some time. His breathing seems short and shallow. His eyes are open but unfocused.

"It feels good when I'm in the midst of negotiations, getting things organized, putting over an idea. . . . That's the way I felt a minute ago talking to you . . . but then there are the other times . . . like last night . . . I finished a long distance call about six-thirty, and the offices were empty. Down the hall I could hear the janitors talking. Out of the window it was getting dark and rainy. . . . Then I heard the janitors leave our suite, and the door whooshed shut. . . . Suddenly I had the feeling there was no one out there, no one out in the hall, no one out in the streets, no one out in the world." He pauses, gathering himself for what he needs to say next. "Then I knew it wasn't that there was nobody out there." Again he pauses. Clearly he is fighting to control his voice and speech.

"It seems so important to you right now to talk in an even voice and without letting your feelings through."

"What good does it do to whimper?"

"It's hard to let yourself just be who you are."

"Who am I? What am I?" His voice is a wail, startling, frightening. "That's what I asked myself in the office last night. First I thought there was nobody out there, but then I knew that wasn't it. . . . There was nobody in here, in my office, in my chair. That's the truth of it. There is nobody right here in this room now. Nobody on this couch. Don't you understand?" His voice is a harsh whisper, desperate. "Nobody. What am I? If I didn't go to those meetings, somebody else would. If I weren't here now, somebody else would be. How could you tell? You wouldn't even know if somebody else had called you and come to see you and taken these times that I have. You wouldn't even know that *I* might have been here. Oh, what's the use. The words don't say it." He falls silent again, but his face is grimacing, miserable, conflicted.

As he is quiet, I begin asking unwelcome questions within myself. What does it mean that I'm the one with Laurence now? It could be Al or Gerry or someone else. One day it *will* be someone else with another Laurence. I won't be here. I won't be anywhere, as far as I know. My consciousness teeters. I know where that thinking pathway goes, and I don't want to go there. My stomach tenses. I look at Laurence. He is busy with his own inner turmoil. I want Laurence to go into that place. I am convinced that only in that way can he emerge with a truer sense of his own identity. But I don't want to go into that place myself. I try to excuse myself by saying I have to keep my attention on Laurence. I know it is a shallow evasion. Facing it squarely, if I go into my own fearful place, it's most likely that I will really be with him.

I try to think about life as process, about it being without substance, the wind known only by its passing among the trees and grass. The words are dry sticks stuck in a bleak plain, meaningless. Suddenly Dali's twisted, molten watches make sense. I find an eager grasping at that insight; it will rescue me from anxious awareness. Reluctantly, I put it aside to allow myself to feel the emptiness. "I am the one thinking now," I tell myself in a silent whisper. It is no comfort. I am trying to make myself into a graspable being by thinking about myself this way. It won't work. What happens when I don't think? Am I then nothing?

"What makes it so frightening?" His voice is a whisper, but it startles me. For a moment I am unsure which of us asked the question. But he is asking himself more than me. I keep silent, my own inner feelings asking the questions with him. "It's not just death. I'm frightened of death, but that's different." His voice is stronger. "It's some way I feel afraid to let go, to give up something. I want to see my tracks behind me, to make a mark where I have passed, to put my name on something. And I know I can't. Not really." He pauses. His voice is growing husky again, but it doesn't sound weak. "Not really. It's like trying to write my name on the river. It's like writing my initials with sparklers on the Fourth of July, like we used to do when I was a kid. The first letter is gone before I finish the second. But it was there. It was. I am here. I am. Oh, God, I wish I could really believe that." Suddenly, briefly, he is sobbing.

He lies silently again. Seconds pass, and time stretches out. His face twists with his fear and despair. He is fighting a lonely fight, and I feel close and yet hopelessly far from him. My own throat hurts with strain. Finally, Laurence shuts his eyes so tightly that his mature, businessman's face dissolves into the grimace of a frightened little boy fighting off terrors in the darkened bedroom. He lets out a long sigh and seems scarcely to take any air back in.

Now my eyes burn and begin to swim, and abruptly I realize I am holding my own breath.

Over the next several months we descend into our personal underworlds perhaps a half dozen times. Gradually, the terror diminishes. Laurence finds he is developing a new sense of his identity. It is elusive and hard to render into words, but we both can sense that it is slowly emerging. It is a product of his determination, persistence, and courage. Only by confronting his dread of being nothing[4] is he able to *experience*—directly rather than in words—*the continuity of his being, the never-seen but always-present one who fears and persists and emerges*. This is a subtle learning, and one not easily arrived at. No effort to "teach" it would be sufficient. It is only through the despairing recognition of the death of thing-like-being that one can climb into the free air of process living.

During this period Laurence enters a therapy group. He experiences a great struggle within himself as he feels compelled to create an impressive image for the other group members rather than risk relating to them just as another person. Although in our individual sessions he is more frequently able to set aside his "busy executive" role and voice and talk to me simply and directly, in the group he is still driven to be seen as preoccupied with important matters or as paternalistic.

April 10

It is a fine spring day with a trace of rain in the air and the first of summer's promise when Laurence takes another step in his journey. As he enters the office he seems completely out of phase with the day. He slowly takes off his coat, sits down on the couch, adjusts the pillow, lies down.

"Well, I muffed it. I mean. . . . Hmmm. I did it, and I did it myself. You remember the San Antonio proposal I told you about? Well, it doesn't matter now whether you remember it or not. I just fumbled it right out the window. I didn't think fast enough or carefully enough or. . . . Hmmm. I don't know, Jim. It really makes things rocky financially. I think we'll make it okay, in the long run that is, but . . . I don't know how I could have missed so badly. . . . And I was so sure last month. . . . "

"You sound pretty down."

"You know it. Hmmm. One thing I thought I really knew how to do was to figure out these kinds of propositions, weigh in all the costs, adjust for the personalities, estimate the market trends, sniff the political winds, whatever. I really thought I was pretty good at it. After all, we built the whole business in eleven or twelve years. You know our gross last year? Well, that's not the point, but. . . . "

"You seem to say that if I knew your gross, I'd know how good you are."

"Yes. Hmmm. Something like that. Nonsense, of course. But I am good, or. . . . But, boy, this San Antonio fiasco! Hmmm. I don't know if I'm getting soft-headed or. . . . "

"Maybe you're not what you thought you were."

"Maybe so. . . . Hey! Hmmm. Say, what are you suggesting?"

"What are you thinking?"

"I don't know. Well, yes, I do. Hmmm. Maybe I'm not some natural-born genius of this business. Maybe I'm not a sure success. That's getting close to it, isn't it?"

"Is it?" I say it interestedly yet leave the play entirely to him.

"Yes, yes. Hmmm. Maybe that's not who or what I am. Then who am I? I don't know. Wait! Wait! I'm the guy who just bungled the whole San Antonio deal. I'm the guy whose company is in hot water! How do you like them apples?" Excitedly. "Hey! How about that? I'm finding my identity. I'm a klutz who fumbled away an eight-million-dollar contract. I may be the genius who has just ruined a perfectly good company. I mean this is a funny business I'm in. If the word gets around that we're slipping we might never get a really good job again. I've seen it happen. . . . " His animation fades.

"Then who'd you be?"

"I'd be mud, that's who. No. Hmmm. No, I'd still be me." Excitement returning. "I'd be the character who ruined his very promising and successful company. I'd still be. . . . I'd still be. . . . What the hell, I'd still be around, but I wouldn't be the guy I and a lot of other people think I am. And yet I can't really feel too scared by that. Hmmm. I'd still be around. I'd do something. Ha! I'd still be around."

I am excited with Laurence. Indeed he would still be around, for he has crossed over the great continental divide of personal identity. On one side he was chained to thingness, to attributes and achievements. He was at the mercy of contingency and could never rest from his vain attempts to build a secure structure from the sand of his actions and their products. Seemingly solid because it rests on what is visible, tangible, and reportable, identity founded on objectification is actually the most vulnerable; yet it was that kind of identity pattern in which Laurence was trained from his earliest years—as were most of us. On the other side of this great watershed, Laurence is discovering the possibility of true freedom, freedom to express his being in each moment without dragging along the heavy, inert shell of the past. In this way of knowing who we are, we do not seek to see ourselves for we know we are the very *seeing*; we do not repose our trust in what we have done for we know we *were* the *doing* but *are* no longer. This is an identity that is vital in the deepest sense. And, as Laurence is also discovering, it reduces our vulnerability to the vicissitudes of success and failure, of approval and disapproval.

When we seek to find our identities solely with our external senses—through what we can see and hear, for example, as in titles or money or achievements—then we are chained to the objective and we are time-vulnerable. When we open our inward vision, when we are in tune with our own experiencing and recognizing its central place in our being, then we are truly freed. I-ness is much more than a source of inner information; it is the solid fiber of our aware being. When we are thus in our centers, external input is not devalued, but it is no longer dominant.

August 27

Now comes a time in which Laurence experiences many swings of mood. Sometimes he is elated over having a new sense of identity not tied to what he does or how well he does it. At other times that recognition is meaningless, so many empty words. Sometimes he comes close to experiencing the old panic of nonbeing, but again there are other times when he is confident, assured, unselfconsciously expressing his being in action. A new element, glimpses of which we've had before, emerges gradually—a long buried rage. He becomes more irritable, less the carefully composed, urbane man of affairs.

"Sorry I'm late," he says, coming into the office briskly, tossing his coat on a chair, loosening his tie, sitting on the edge of the couch. "Some son-of-a-bitch was just dreaming his way along at twenty all down Santa Monica Boulevard where they've got it torn up. God! I'd have loved to smash into him. I honked a couple of times, but I think he only went slower. I suppose I left the office late too, but that damn kook slowing me up was just the last straw." He pauses, seems to be getting past the first flurry.

"You're angry a lot these days, it sounds like."

"Yes. Hmmm." His voice is different now, directed less to me than to his inner consideration. He lies down. "Yes, I am. Really, Jim, I feel a bit frightened at the degree to which I'd have liked to have torn into that poor, slow driver. Thinking about it now, I know I'm just using him—do the same thing with my family, my secretary—to justify letting some of the anger out. I'm going around pissed off at everything and everybody. I just want somebody to do something so that I can eat them out; yet. . . . "

"Yet?"

"Yet, it's not really just the feeling that I'm mad. Hmmm. It's more like something in me is trying to get out, something that's been caged up so long that I don't know what it is or what it would do if it ever got out."

Laurence's words are reasonable enough, but I'm aware of a tension starting between my shoulder blades. In some way I'm picking up a desperate urgency from him.

"I mean, I guess, that I'm really kind of concerned about this feeling." He seems to be unsure what he wants to say.

"You don't know how seriously to take this wild animal feeling you have inside of you, La . . . Laurence." Huh? I almost said, "Larry."

"I think I better take it seriously. I mean, I really would have loved to plow my car right into that guy today, and I know I'm going to have to watch the way I talk to my wife and kids. Lately I've been growling or shouting at them all the time."

"You sound pretty detached about it right now."

"I suppose so, but. . . . " He pauses, and when he speaks again, his voice no longer sounds calm. There is a tension and apprehension in his tone that reawakens that tightness in my back. "It's the old image thing, Jim. I was telling you about the rage in me but hiding how really strong it is and how much I'm beginning to be afraid I'll do something I'll regret." Again he pauses. His tautness is now even more evident. "But the thing is, I'm not sure I want to keep that wildness in me caged up any more. I have to keep reminding myself what might happen. . . . "

"What might happen, Lar . . . Laurence?" Softly. Again almost said, "Larry." My tension is rising, and I imagine him urgently trying to hold a door shut while it is slowly being pushed open by an uncontrollable and powerful force. I know those feelings. I repressed my own rage for many years.

"Oh, I don't know, I might really hit somebody or smash up something."

"You're pulling away from your feelings now. They must be getting too threatening to look at right now."

"Maybe so. Hmmm. I know I don't want to feel them build up in me without finding something to do about them." He is silent for several seconds. "That's funny. I don't know how I got here, but suddenly I'm thinking of the summer I was seventeen." His voice seems less tense, and I'm relieved, although I know that the brewing storm has not really been resolved. Laurence seems reflective as he goes on, "I had gotten a job as a counselor at a boys' camp. It was going to be a great summer. I really was looking forward to it, and then I didn't get to go for some reason, and it was a big letdown," suddenly weary and dispirited.

"What happened, La . . . Laurence?" Again I start to call him "Larry," a familiar name that once would have been out of place with this man.

"I don't remember now. Hmmm. It seems that there was always some reason that things I wanted didn't work out." He is restless on the couch. "I think I'll sit up, okay?" swinging his legs to the floor and suiting his action to his words.

"Why didn't you get to go to camp, Larry?" There, the name has come out; surprisingly he doesn't seem to notice. I'm playing a hunch; his physical restlessness suggests a wanting to get away from something.

"Oh, that. I don't know, Jim. It's not important. There were many times like that. I'm sure that my folks thought they had some very good reason. They were always so reasonable."

"You're being pretty reasonable yourself now, but you don't seem to be focusing on anything." I decide to let the summer camp issue go and pay attention to his sudden decrease in involvement.

"Well, yeah, I suppose so. Wait a minute, let me just listen inside, huh?" He is silent a minute, screws his face up, seems intent. His manner reminds me of all the months when he tried to find inner awareness but could only come up with vague generalities about himself. Larry has come a long way, and I feel good about our work together.

"Nothing," he reports. "I just seem to be blank. Don't feel especially good or bad or anything else. Thinking about the fact there's only about twelve or thirteen minutes left, about going by the shoe repair shop, about your calling me 'Larry.' [He noticed; I might have known.] It felt nice, haven't been called that in years."

"Larry—and you do feel more like 'Larry' these days—I don't understand what's happening, but I think at some level you've pulled out on your feelings. There's just too big a contrast between the intensity you felt only a few minutes ago and now this shallow calm."

"Maybe so, but. . . . " Pause. "I don't know. I just feel kind of confused and uninvolved." His hand is adjusting the couch cushion in an unaware, tidying up way. "I can't even remember very well what we were talking about."

"You're still being very reasonable, but you are so detached from what's going on in you that I can't believe you are really open to being more emotionally involved."

"Yeah, I suppose so. Well, let's see. . . . " Again a silence. I can sense a very slight shift in him in the direction of being more open inwardly.

"Main thing I'm aware of is a distant tension, like a storm just over the horizon. I'm afraid of it the way I was afraid of those panics for so long. Well! I didn't know that. Yes, it's the same sort of ominous anticipation." Pause. "I really learned to fear what goes on inside of me, didn't I? I feel like something is going to emerge one day that will destroy me. First the panics about not existing, now the rage that wants to just smash anything and everybody. Hmmm. Jim, I really can feel that building up in me now, and I'm not at all sure I want to risk letting it out."

"It's so powerful that you don't know whether you'd still be able to be in charge of yourself, is that it?" I am sensing, like a very faint change in the air, a shift in Larry's inner experiencing. I am picking up a subtle tightening of his muscles so that he sits more rigidly on the couch and a change in his breathing, which is becoming shorter and slightly faster. Probably I am getting other clues too. He is back to tidying up the tissue which I put over the pillow, hands carefully smoothing it, aligning its corners with the pillow's corners in exact precision.

"I'm confused." Voice sunk in his throat.

"You need to be confused evidently." Persistently.

"Maybe so. I can't seem to think very clearly right now."

"It would be too frightening to let yourself really know what's going on in you."

"Yeah, I know I'm close to being scared, plenty scared."

"You are confused so that you won't feel the scaredness."

"I feel like I have to hold it off, *have* to."

"It's very important to hold off that feeling some way."

"Yeah, I guess so." His voice changes. He is starting to pull away from feeling the intensity he verged close to. His hands are busy again with the pillow.

"Now you're pulling back and tidying everything up. Just like you're taking care of the pillow and making sure that the furniture is all neat." I have no idea why I say "furniture" just at that point;[5] it must have come from Larry's unconscious in some way. However it got into my words, it is the spark in a powder keg.

"Fuck the furniture!" Larry shouts and suddenly throws the pillow across the room with such force that it knocks a picture from the opposite wall. He is on his feet, his face twisting, tears starting from his eyes, and inarticulate sounds coming from his mouth. "Always the damn furniture! Fuck it to hell! And the car! And the lawn! Fuck them all!" His hands are clutching air angrily. He drops down on the couch and hits it savagely with his fist, but clearly it is too yielding, too insubstantial.

I was startled when he burst out and felt a moment's fright as the pillow flew and the picture fell. Now, however, I feel exhilarated. And yet, there is an animal alertness in me, a poised readiness to spring. The futility of hitting the couch or a pillow angers me, for it threatens to abort what Larry is working out. On impulse I shove a chair with a padded seat toward him. "Hit it!" I say. He swings his fist in an arc directly into the seat of the chair. It makes a satisfying, solid thump, but I can tell it hurts him too. And that seems to please him. Quickly he hits it a half dozen more times, both fists now pummeling.

"Always it was 'Take care of the furniture, Larry boy. Be careful of the woodwork.' Always! Always! Always!" A little breathless, he pauses and looks at me with a hint of delight in his eye. "Are you especially fond of this chair, Jim?"

"Not especially, Larry. You don't have to take care of it."

"Oh, I'm going to take care of it all right." He stands, picks up the chair by its back, raises it to head level and brings it crashing down on its back legs at an angle nicely calculated to snap them. The chair creaks and cracks, and there is the rewarding sound of something breaking, but the legs hold on. Larry lifts the chair again and brings it down with even greater force. The snap this time is definitive and one leg dangles as he raises the chair for the third time. It takes an amazing three more hits to break off the other leg. Then the front legs are amputated in another series. By this time, he is settled into his task with workmanlike intensity and concentration.

I find myself fascinated by the channeled rage and energy and by the way in which Larry has found a vent for his fury. Once again I realize, as I have numberless times before, that when I begin to trust a person's feelingful awareness, I must be really open to him. When I am, he will—in his own way—find appropriate and effective routes. Larry's rage has to come out. When I demonstrate my understanding of how furious he is and my trust in his being the

one in charge of his emotion, he finds a way—albeit a violent one—
to let his passion work itself out. The loss of the chair is trivial compared to the loss of life that Larry has been subject to for years.

Now he is systematically using great stamping thrusts of his
feet to break the chair's back, shatter the seat, and reduce to rather
small kindling the once sturdy chair. He has a grim intensity that
still conveys a great inner satisfaction. He looks up as he tears the
plastic covering from the shattered back with a rich ripping sound.
"You know why I didn't get to go to that damn camp?" He is
grinning, with a ferocious quality to the grin.

"Why, Larry?"

"Because I'd broken the living room couch roughhousing
with a friend, so I had to stay home and work all summer to earn
the money to help replace it! That damn couch!" He breaks a back
support by ramming his heel onto it where it is propped up on
another piece. "That goddammed couch!" He kicks and tears
broken pieces into smaller bits. "And then, after I'd worked all summer, they didn't take the money but told me to put it in my savings
account for college! They were going to replace the couch anyway!
Damn them!" He is near tears now.

I wait. Larry has found his own route to working out an old
hurt; he can be trusted to continue to do so. I find myself briefly
wondering what the people in the offices downstairs think about the
crashings and stampings that have been going on. I hope they aren't
too disturbed, but I find that my wish is more perfunctory than a
deep concern. Perhaps my not-so-hidden self-righteousness is involved here as I judge my work more important than theirs.

Meantime Larry is energetically tearing the plastic chair
covering into uneven strips. "Hey! You know what?" He is suddenly delighted. "You know, that was the summer I first had sex
with a woman, a girl really! Ha! They kept me from the good
moral influence of a camp, so I committed the awful sin of sex!
Somehow that pleases me. You know, I don't know which was the
greater sin though; being careless with the furniture—with prop-
erty—or getting sexual with a girl. I'll bet they couldn't have decided." He gives a laugh and snaps the only remaining chair leg.
Suddenly we both know the orgy of destruction is over. Larry sorts

out one of the largest pieces of wood remaining and hands it to me with mock ceremony, "There, doctor, is the trophy of this hunt!" Then he turns and sweeps together the bulk of the wreckage, drops it in the wastebasket, grins at me while giving me a thumb and index finger "okay" sign, and leaves. I sit back exhausted and twenty minutes late for my next appointment.

The destruction of a chair[6] is, in itself, meaningless. The act was an ancient ritual, a primordial rebirth drama, a revolt against things and thing-centered being and against being a thing. The act of destroying the chair is Larry's proclamation that he is no longer a thing but is a living being with power in his life. It is appropriate that he has accepted a new name to celebrate that rebirth.

December 11

It is slightly over two years from the day Laurence of the dapper exterior first came into my office. Today Larry of the slightly casual manner is slouched in the chair, chewing on a cigar he has forgotten to light.

"I'm going to New York next week, Jim. This is the big one. If I get this contract, we'll have it all sewed up despite the expansion, and I'll take off four months for that round-the-world trip Helen and I have been dreaming about."

"If the work can spare you."

"Nuts to that. The work will get along without me. It did before, and it can do it again."

"And what if you don't get this contract?"

"Then we're between a rock and a hard place."

"So?"

"So Helen and I will take off for a month and go up to the Benjamins' cabin and just get ourselves closer together."

"That's not a bad consolation prize."

"No, it's not is it? Hmmm. I sure hope we get the contract, but it really doesn't seem a life-or-death matter any more. Am I getting soft or flabby?"

"Are you?"

"No, I don't think so. I just know that being an efficient business machine—'Larry Bellows, Mark One'—is not the highest achievement I want."

"What do you want, Larry?"

"I don't really know, Jim. Except I want a sense of more space in my life, of having time to savor things—good and bad things, of taking time to feel things and to talk about them with a few people who mean a lot to me."

"Will you give it to yourself, Larry? The space, the time, the savoring—will you let yourself have them at last?"

"Yes, I think I will now. I don't have to run so hard. And that brings me to something I've been reluctant to bring up."

"Mm-hmm."

"I think it's time I stopped coming here. No, wait, that's making time the determiner. Let me say it differently: I've gotten a lot out of coming here, Jim, and I care a lot about you, but now I'm ready to—I want to—go it on my own. Unless you see some strong reason to the contrary, this is my last time."

"I don't see any strong reason to the contrary, Larry."

"Yes. Hmmm. I thought you'd say that."

"You said a minute ago that you'd gotten a lot from coming here. Make a kind of summarizing statement, can you?"

"I don't know, Jim. . . . Hmmm. It's hard to summarize all I've been through here in this office, on this couch, with you." He looks into my eyes so steadily, so warmly, I grow self-conscious even as I feel the fullness climbing in my throat. "Well, let's see. Hmmm. I'll just say it as it comes. After all, I'm supposed to be pretty good at words, eh?" Smiling wryly. "We've come a long way . . . together. . . . Yes, that's important. I think you've been making the trip too. Right?" He pauses, looks deeply at me again, questioning. I nod quickly, feeling the deep satisfaction that he really sees me, *me*, at last.

"You read it right on, Larry. I've been in a lot of places in me while I have been with you. Good places, tough places. . . . "

"Yeah, I thought so." Pause. "I'm sorry this trip is over, but I'm glad too. More glad than sorry. Hmmm. Looking back, you know, looking back to when I first came into this room, well. . . . I can hardly believe how very frightened I was then. Yet, you know, that fear is still in me. Right now, I can sense that it's still there, waiting. When I'm at the office I can sometimes sense it. Especially when I get too worried about how I'll look to the people I'm dealing with. And other times . . . sometimes with the family. . . . No that's not the same thing. With the family it's the weight of those years, all those years I missed really being with them. Hmmm. That's not so much the fear as a kind of pain, a kind of . . . anguish, I guess you'd call it."

"Yes. Yes, I know, Larry. I know that in me too."

"Mm-hmmm. Expect you do." Pause. "I guess they'll—those feelings—will always be with me. At least some. But I can sense now that *I'*m the one who is having the fear . . . or the regret. *I* am the one who is worried about not looking good to others. Don't know how to say it, Jim. It's important, but the words just don't really catch the way I experience it. Hmmm. It's hard to convey what my insides feel like when I say that word *I,* like now when I'm trying to make it clear. Oh, I don't know, I. . . . Well, look, let's try it this way: I hope, I fear . . . uh . . . I want. . . . Hmmm. And I. . . . Most of all *I am.*"

Larry taught me one of the fundamentals of the nature of human identity: the critical significance of subjective experiencing to identity and awareness of life. When he first came to see me he had lost objective proof of his being, and he had no appreciation of his I-ness. Those ant bites that filled him with terror represented the disintegration of his sense of his own being. And neither without nor within himself could he find anything to restore his feeling of identity. The external evidences which had once seemed so substantial had dissolved, and he found no inner sense to replace them.

Lacking an inner sense of direction, Larry behaved according to the expectations he and others had of the object which he had been—a dynamic, aggressive head of a successful business. That was not enough for inner security in his own being. Nor was there any real vibrancy or assurance in what he was doing, whatever his success by commercial standards. Vital inner sureness of one's being could only come with experiencing his inward sense.

The crucial thing that Larry learned was that his achievements, his image in others' eyes, and his self-observation were insufficient to give him a solid feeling of his own being. Without his inner eye he found himself nothing. To get to an awareness of his being, he had to attend to his inner experiencing, to dis(un)cover his immediate presence in each moment. He had to experience his own nature as *process* rather than *content* or *substance*. When he was able to gain this awareness, he found an inner integration in which his sense of being, his wantings, his efforts, and his recognition of outcomes were experienced as all parts of the same wholeness—his own identity.

Larry had sought to deny his nothingness.[7] He tried to erect a sure wall of achievements between himself and the all-devouring void that continually consumed all that he experienced. When he was out of action following the accident, he came up against the terrorizing recognition that no secure sense of his own being existed in the very places in which he had most tried to build that identity. His past attainments melted like snow, dissolving the wall he had built, and falling away into nothingness. He continually felt an urgency to pile new attainments on the old to numb himself to their mist-like fading. When he was unable to take refuge in such wall-building, he was forced to seek some other meaning to his life.

Larry came to recognize that he was the process of his being; more accurately, Larry began moving toward it, even as he began to relinquish his vain efforts to create a substance-like identity. Fully incorporating awareness of being is a life-long undertaking and not a matter of a simple insight.

Larry discovered the nothingness which is inescapably at the center of our experienced being. The key word in that sentence is *experienced,* past tense. That which *has been* is no more, is no thing. Only in the process of *being* aware do we express our existence. Only when Larry relinquished the effort to *prove* he existed was he freed to be. He never replaced his former identity; he discovered instead that he could let go of the need for it if he was truly and subjectively alive in the moment. A line of Alan Watts' summarizes Larry's experience beautifully, "Where he expected to find the specific truth about himself he found freedom, but mistook it for mere nothingness."[8]

What made it so difficult for Larry to get in touch with his inner sense was the terror that gripped him whenever he began to allow himself to listen within himself. The sensation of falling, of evaporating, of becoming nothing was for Larry—and it is for many of us—a panic-evoking nightmare. When he could draw on his growing relationship with me, he could go into that agony, and only by going into and through it could he come to the direct experience of "still being" . . . the prototype, so to speak, for Larry's later insight that even if his company failed, he—Larry— "would still be around."[9]

Larry's therapy started out with his having to make a very fundamental choice. He had first come to see me expecting to spend a relatively brief time to "be treated" for the panics that were disabling him. Only after some hesitation did he decide to make a commitment to a more thoroughgoing examination of his living. This was a cornerstone decision: Larry chose to seriously consider what was happening *within* him in contrast to his earlier preoccupation with what was happening *externally* (his business and his achievements). The profound impact of the panics and all that brought them about had forced him to redefine what truly mattered in his life. It is doubtful whether, in the normal course of his life prior to the accident, Larry would ever have begun to treat his subjective life as a primary concern. Once he had begun to do so, however, it was inevitable that his whole way of being would change.

As Larry began to take his inner experiencing more seriously, he found he had to recognize processes within that subjectivity that ordinarily he paid little attention to. He began to listen to his fear and anger, rather than pushing them aside until they grew so strong they broke through his control. He discovered that his imagery and fantasy were not simply frivolous adornments of his thinking but were important ways to deepen and broaden his awareness of himself and to express what it was that was going on within him. He eventually came to accept disappointment and failure[10] as products of his own actions, rather than dismissing them as accidents or of no significance.

As Larry reclaimed these processes and experiences into his very being, his intuition of his life changed. What had seemed so empty became filled with living inner awareness. Without having to write his name on the river, he was his own aliveness.

Larry's experience in psychotherapy brings home to me four important recognitions about what it means to be more fully alive.

I am alive only in the process of my being.[11] *I cannot find my being in what I do, what I achieve, what titles I hold, what others think or say of me. Only in the instantaneous moment of being aware, of experiencing, choosing, and acting do I most truly exist. Therefore, I cannot see my own being, for I am the seeing and whatever I see cannot be me. I am the seeing, the moving, the awaring.*

If I am to have my life truly, I must be aware of my living, of the reality that my center is my experiencing, of the inescapable fact that unless I take my life seriously, it will slip away without my having it. *My inner sense is the key to open my awareness of my living.*

Taking my life seriously, I discover much of my being that I have valued too little but that I can come to appreciate. In doing so, I can enrich my being. So I will give attention to my emotions[12] *—all of them, including those I have formerly tried to shove aside, such as fear and anger—*to my fantasy and imagery, *and* to experiences I have tried to eject from my life *but which are part of every human being's story, such as disappointment and failure.*

If I allow my identity to become bound up with objective thing-ness, then I am exceedingly vulnerable to external circumstances and contingencies. Identity based on what I have done, how I have been seen, what others think of me, is past-bound identity. It can lead to staleness and repetitiousness in living. Only true process identity is alive in the moment and free to change and evolve with the flow of my life.

It is striking how names can convey such important but often subtle differences about people. When I think of "Laurence," I think of a well-dressed, smooth-mannered, conversationally skillful, successful businessman, wearing a hat. When I think of "Larry," I get a quite contrasting image of a sweaty, shirt-sleeved man, driving his heel into the remnants of a chair[13] and into the remnants of a pattern of life that he knew could no longer sustain him. That pattern of life had proven inadequate, insubstantial, and mocking to the long record of achievements and recognitions Larry had accumulated. He declared himself, thereby, no longer the prisoner, and he broke out of his deathly trap and away from the ant bites of nothingness.

When Larry first came into my office with his hat, his expensive cigar, his polished manner, and his hidden terror, he was untouchable. I had the feeling that if I reached out a hand to his arm or chest it would have encountered an invisible sheath of firm plastic rather than warm cloth or skin. He was so carefully designed and executed that he was unreachable. Within that neatly put together shell, a much smaller and quite panicked human being cowered.

Our months of work together helped Larry discover just how imprisoned he was in his impressive and impenetrable shielding. Then he could slowly begin to consider the previously incredible notion that he might be able to live without it. Bit by bit he began to relinquish what had once seemed so essential to survival. While he certainly had not dissolved it all by the time he left psychotherapy, he clearly had freed himself of much of its hampering weight.

And as that burden was reduced, Larry discovered that he could move more freely, could feel more deeply, could relate more genuinely, could listen to his inner sense, and could know his own being more richly. He found that the notion of life as process— which at first seemed too mist-like and unsatisfying—could open the doors of possibility and of immediacy of being. And so Larry came home to his own center.

I last heard from Larry several years ago. He was passing through town on a trip with his wife. He called to say "Hi!" and to tell me he had just read something of mine that meant a lot to him. His work was going well, he said, and he added, "And, Jim, I thought you'd understand what I meant if I told you two things: I'm taking more time off to read and just get in touch with myself. It feels good, and I seem to be recovering a part of me that got lost a long time ago."

"That does sound good, Larry. I'm really glad. And what was the second thing?"

"I threw my hat away."

✻ 3 ✻

JENNIFER
Responsibility and Choice

"Why did you do that?" Mother asks, and she seldom really means to inquire into your reasons. The question, most of us learn pretty early, actually is an indictment: "You've done something wrong again." Still, there is a measure of "why" in the question—if only we are quick enough to seize it. If we reply promptly, "Well, the rules said I should," or give some other answer that points away from ourselves, we may escape censure. Clearly it is no use to say, "Because I wanted to," or "I was just acting on impulse." That would just be asking for trouble. No, nothing that assigns the reason to something inside of us will help us out of the situation. Something external, something public, something somehow official—that would be the most acceptable reason.

It's the same with the word *responsible*. Most of us first bumped into it in such sentences as, "Who's responsible for this mess?" Not a comfortable word, to be sure, or one we want to link up to our insides. Again the best answers are outward pointing answers: "He did it," or "They made me," or—best of all—"I thought that's what I was supposed to do," which means "according to the rules" or to some authority. Authority is, of course, always out there, never in here, never in me.

And so we learn early that responsibility is apt to be a heavy burden. The idea that the word might signal something like an opportunity—for anything except trouble—only occurs to us much later.

Our earliest experiences with *responsibility* usually are such as to make us want to prove that we had no choice about what we did. We look for outside "reasons" to hang the unwelcome responsibility on: what others will think, how it's always been done, what the rules require in order to get rid of the unwelcome responsibility. This need to escape responsibility comes about because we have it all entangled with another concept, *blame*. These two, responsibility and blame, really do not overlap much at all. In fact, they point in opposite directions psychologically. Blame is a denial of one's subjective centering ("It's your fault that I. . . "). Even when I blame myself ("I'm selfish to have forgotten about that . . . "), I'm really assigning the cause to some supposed attribute (my "selfishness") rather than really accepting responsibility. Responsibility, on the other hand, stays focused on the act and its outcome ("Yes, I really choose to do that. I'm sorry that you feel badly about it. How can we work together to make it better for you?"). Thus, responsibility is forward-looking; it says that we still have the power within us to act further and produce better outcomes. In this sense, opportunity is the other face of responsibility.

When I am chiefly concerned about blame, I lose touch with my inner sense; when I claim responsibility, I assert that I have a vital role in my own living experience. I have learned from my patients that if I am to be fully alive and to know my own potency in my life, I must accept that *I always have responsibility for what I do*.[1]

Jennifer feels powerless in her life. She constantly struggles with what she sees as the burden of being responsible and with her compulsion to prove that she is innocent. She succeeds so well at the latter that she continually views herself as a victim and spends her energy on protesting,[2] on crying that she has been fouled by life. Her protests are cold comfort, and she comes to therapy because her feeling of powerlessness is costing her far too much of her aliveness.

This lady seemed to hold up a mirror to my own tendency to always try to cover my tracks and be prepared to explain any action that anyone might question. More than once I've found myself composing involved explanations in my mind to account for some minor misdeed—banging the tires into the curb when parking, being short with a caller on the phone—as though I would be called on to explain it. As Jennifer and I worked together, I was repeatedly struck with how this continual preoccupation with blame creates such a flood of self-criticism that it weakens, nearly to the point of collapse, the structure of a person's life.

February 14

The woman's voice on the phone is tight, urgent. "Dr. Bugental, I know you are busy; so I won't keep you long. But I must see you today! It is really important. Please trust me. Please see me today."

Schedule full except for my rest period. I keep promising myself I'm going to protect my breaks better. But she does sound desperate or as though she's under great pressure. Images of her committing suicide or doing some other drastic act if I put her off. Headline: "Psychologist Refuses Help; Patient Kills Self." But that wouldn't be fair. She's not my patient. I've never seen her. Why am I so self-centered as to worry about my public image when there's this woman crying out for help? All this and more races through me in a tenth of a second.

"Mrs. Stoddert, I can hear how important you feel this is; so let me level with you. My schedule is completely full today, and tomorrow, too, for that matter. I could see you Thursday at four, which is the next regular appointment hour open. . . . "

"No, please, listen. I must see you today."

"All right, I have time at two-fifteen, which is my usual break time. If you feel it is essential that we talk today, come in then."

"Thank you. Two-fifteen today. I'll be there."

She's here at two, as her early buzzer signals. I finish the hour with Hal, see him to the door, and then go to the waiting room. What sort of person will this be? The lady waiting for me is slightly taller than usual, has a nice figure, and is wearing brightly colored clothes that contrast with her gray face and disarrayed hair. She nods a quick response to my self-introduction and comes into the office with a no-nonsense directness. She takes a chair, lights a cigarette in a manner that tells me she is bracing herself against an inner tide of emotion.

"Thank you for seeing me today. I'm sorry to have intruded on your rest time. It is important though."

"I understand. Suppose you just tell me about it."

"I'll try." Pause. "I am thirty-three years old. My husband is thirty-nine. I have been married eight years. I . . . we have no children. My husband is an engineer in electronics at Levy Company. Actually he's in charge of an engineering group. I have a master's degree in educational administration and counseling and am Dean of Women at Sloss College. I've been there three years. My parents are dead. My husband's parents are both living, but his father had a stroke last year and may not be alive much longer."

She is talking in a forced, earnest fashion, enunciating carefully, pausing often. The impression is that she's reading from a list she has prepared inside of herself.

"Yes, and what is it that particularly seems to concern you today?"

"I'll get to that in a minute, Dr. Bugental. Please bear with me. I think it would help if I gave you background first. Is that all right?"

I nod agreement. If I just listen to the content of what she's saying, I get impatient—I didn't give up my break time to get a routine case history. But when I look at her and hear the unspoken strain in her, I realize she is already communicating much that may be important if I am to help her in any way. My God, the iron clamp she has on herself right now is fantastic in itself. Obviously she is bursting with some emotion, but she is not permitting it to interrupt her careful reading of her invisible data list.

"Thank you." Correct, formal. "As I said, we've been married eight years. Nearly nine. Our anniversary would be next month, the twenty-second. We have been, or at least so I thought, reasonably happy. As I have tried to think about our marriage, I believe we had the most difficult times when we had been married about five or six years. At that time—when we had been married six years, that is—at that time, we seriously discussed divorce, but we decided to stay together, partly because my husband insisted. I think I was more inclined to seek a divorce at that time than he was. I may be wrong."

"Yes, but it seems that way to you as you recall it now."

"Yes." Pause. "We are not religious people. We do go to a Protestant church on certain holidays. We are both in generally good health, at least physically that is. Are there other things you would like to know by way of background?"

"Mrs. Stoddert, let me put it this way. There is such an abundance of information you might give me that I don't know what to ask for. Only after I have a better idea of what concerns you can I suggest what further information we ought to think about together. Do you see?"

She looks troubled, uncertain. The iron grip seems less, and I think she's frightened right now, but it's hard to read her expression. She bites her lip, grimaces. Maybe I ought to explain more. "What I mean, Mrs. Stoddert, is that it's as though I were a librarian and you wanted some books; until I knew what subject you're interested in, I wouldn't know what part of the shelves or catalog to check."

"Yes, yes, I understand." Impatient, but disciplining herself again. "I'm sorry, I didn't mean to speak sharply. I'm simply having trouble knowing how to say what I need to say next."

"Why don't you just let it come out the way you find it inside of your thoughts, and then we can get more details as we go along?"

"Very well." Pause, catches her breath, getting set. "All right, then. . . . " Pause. "I think I am going to kill my husband." She sits back breathlessly, and I feel equally breathless.

Calmly, softly now. "Since you're here telling me about it, you must have some other thoughts about it too."

"Yes. But if I don't kill him, then I must divorce him. And if I do that, I'll kill myself."

"Those are hard choices. Take it slowly now, and just tell me about it in any way that comes. Don't push yourself to cover things in any particular way."

"Well, I'll try, but I don't want to waste your time and

mine. It would help if you'd ask me questions so I can give you the information you need more efficiently."

"When you say 'the information' I need, what do you have in mind? What do you want me to do?"

"Why to help me, of course."

"To help you what?"

"So that I won't kill my husband! Oh!" Suddenly she cries in quick convulsive sobs.

"You seem surprised to find out how much you don't want to kill him."

"Yes. Uh-huh." She finds it difficult to get her breath or to speak because of the dry, choking sobs that keep racking her, but she keeps trying.

"Wait a minute now. Don't try to talk. You're doing something far more important right now." She fights chokingly with herself. She doesn't let go to the weeping, and it doesn't let go of her. She's having a hard time breathing, although there are hardly any tears. She is so evidently at war with herself, and her body is the torn battlefield.

After several minutes of this struggle, I tell her to try to rest while I get her a cup of coffee. She is able to sip the drink slowly, and gradually the physical torment subsides. It has hardly done so when she lights a cigarette. Her first puff brings on a new siege of choking, which passes more quickly—and without the cigarette being put out.

"I'm sorry. I just couldn't get my breath."

"I understand. But what you just went through is important in itself. It expressed better than any amount of words how much in conflict with yourself you are."

"I suppose so. Thank you for the coffee." She's unimpressed by the idea of her nonverbal communication. "Now what would you like to know, and I'll try to keep better control of myself."

I'm tempted to help her see how quickly she dismisses her feelings and inner experience but decide against it now. She's still under too much inner pressure. She obviously needs to feel she has dealt in words with her violent impulses. Only then can she feel she has started to regain control. Control is clearly very important to her. "Tell me what happened recently to make you feel you want to kill your husband." How calmly we can say such terrible words!

"He told me Saturday—no. . . . What day is this?"

"This is Tuesday, the fourteenth."

"Thank you. He told me Sunday that he is having an affair with a woman I thought was a friend of both of us. She and her husband have been in our house many times, and we have been to their house. Now he says they have been carrying on this affair for several months."

"Hmmm."

"He has been with her—having sexual relations with her—once a week or oftener for two months or more. He says he cannot remember just exactly how long." She is reciting facts, reciting them intensely, but still reciting. Her emotion is unreadable—rage or panic or hatred or dread, I can't tell. Only intensity.

"I understand the shock, Mrs. Stoddert. What I need to know more about is how you came to the feeling that you would kill him."

"Just because the bastard deserves it! No, I don't want to get that way now. It's just that he is so unfair. So damned unfair! I mean, how would you feel, how would anybody feel? I'll never trust anyone again. I really feel all alone now. But that's not the point. It's just that he's got to be punished. I'm embarrassed to see my friends. I wonder who knows. But it doesn't matter. I have no friends. I can't believe people can be so selfish, so unfair!" She's expostulating, convinced that I, or anyone else, can see the necessity of retribution; yet even as she's letting this flood of feelings and ideas through, she's trying to be orderly and stick to some "point."

"You feel cut off from everyone now."

"Yes, of course. I don't know who knows about it. I suppose that doesn't matter, and I shouldn't feel that way, but I can't help it. I am so mad at him that I don't think very clearly. Please forgive me for getting so worked up." Pause. "What else would you like to know?" A massive effort to control herself.

"Mrs. Stoddert, I get the impression that you feel it is obvious why you would think of killing your husband—because of his affair. Candidly, it is not obvious to me, and I'd like to understand better why you feel that way."

"Yes, I know I'm not thinking straight, but that's why I needed your help. I might have gotten by till Thursday as you suggested, but I just didn't trust myself. I mean, I felt so wild. I'm not usually that way, except sometimes, of course. I suppose I'm not making much sense." Apologetic smile.

"That's okay. Just go ahead and talk it out however it comes to you."

"I don't like to do that. I wander around too much. It seems like it would be so much more efficient if you would ask me questions."

"What you call 'wandering around' is often the most direct and efficient way of expressing what is in your subconscious."

"Yes, I suppose so. But I don't like it. I shouldn't say that, I know. You're trying to help me. I mean, I know I'm supposed to help myself with your help, but. . . . Right now, I don't feel able to help myself much. I guess I really can. I mean, I don't want you to feel I'm incompetent or anything like that."

And so it goes. As the first pressure of her rage, humiliation, and fright at her own impulses passes, she becomes increasingly self-critical. Almost everything she says has to be amended or qualified in some way. She hardly seems aware of how she cripples her own thoughts and self-expression.

Toward the end of the hour, I return to the frightening impulses. "Mrs. Stoddert, our time is almost up, and. . . . "

"And I've just talked in circles, and you haven't had a chance to learn enough about me! I'm sorry! But I think you must have helped some. I really don't think I will kill my husband. That sounds so silly now. I really was frightened about it though. At least, I think I was. Maybe I was frightened that I would just give in to him. No, I'd never do that."

"Yes; well, I'm also concerned about your other impulse, to kill yourself. How do you feel about that now?"

"Oh, yes. Well, I don't think I'd do that now. I guess I might if something else happened or something. I don't know. I shouldn't say that. I don't think I'd do that. Anyway I think I feel you can help me, and so. . . . "

"I'll be glad to work with you on that feeling and any others, but I don't want to work with you or anyone under constant threat."

"No, no, I'm not threatening you. It was. . . . "

"I know, Mrs. Stoddert, that you did not intend to threaten me, but if we work together, it will matter a great deal to me if you feel impelled to do something violent to yourself or to your husband."

"Oh, no, I don't think now that I would do anything violent to him."

"All right, but there is another threat, and I don't want it hanging over our work either. That threat is the question as to whether you will do harm to yourself. I am equally concerned about it."

"I can't promise anything."

"Yes, you *can* promise two things: First, that you won't do anything to him or to yourself for at least a month while we talk things over; and second, that you won't do anything violent at any time without talking to me first. Those promises are absolutely essential if we are to work together."

"Well, I. . . . "

"If you can't decide right now, you can wait until you leave and give me a call after you've thought them over."

"No, no, that's all right. I can promise those things. At least I think I can."

"No, Mrs. Stoddert, I mean this very soberly, and you must hear it so. I will not work with you if you cannot make those promises to me. I will be glad, if you wish, to refer you to someone else who may not make such a requirement, but I want a relation of trust with you. Without those two assurances we would not have such a relation."

"Yes, I can see that. All right, I will promise you not to do anything violent to myself or my husband without talking to you first and. . . . Oh, yes, and not to do anything for at least a month. Is that right?"

"Yes, that's right. Thank you. Now, I think I can open up a time for us tomorrow at 3:15. Will you come then, please?"

And so we begin our work together. I don't often exact promises with such formality. In Mrs. Stoddert's instance it seems desirable and possible; although by the end of this first interview I doubt she has any deep impulse to kill her husband. I am less confident about the suicidal possibility.

I arrange to see Jennifer Stoddert each day this week. Because I take any threat to kill very seriously, I want to know her a lot better, and quickly. The subsequent visits confirm my impression that she is not about to act on her violent impulses, so the following week we begin a regular schedule of four visits a week.

February 28

In two weeks we have had nine interviews, and now Jennifer Stoddert's way of dealing with herself has become painfully clear. It is not surprising that she has such a punishing attitude toward others; she is even more unrelenting toward herself.

"I have so many things I need to talk about here. I wanted to make a list of them so I wouldn't forget, but I know you don't like me to write things down, and. . . . "

"Jennifer, if it helps to write things down, by all means do. I have asked you not to rely solely on a list of things to talk about when you're here because I'd like to help you get more in touch with. . . . "

"Oh, yes, I know. I shouldn't have said. . . . I mean, I know you don't ever tell me. . . . Well, I just was thinking that you thought it was better if I didn't have lists, sort of."

"It isn't that I'm against lists, Jennifer. I use them myself for some things, but. . . . "

"But I'm too dependent. I know it. Yes, I know that."

"Jennifer, it's hard for you to hear what I say to you because you have to know it already."

"Oh, no. I'm really glad to have you advise me, but I just didn't want to waste your—our—time, and. . . . "

"It seems to me that you'd feel you had failed some way if I told you that your understanding of what I said about writing things down was different than I intended."

"Oh, no. It would be perfectly all right. I mean, I'd be glad for you to show me where I misunderstood you. After all, that's why I'm here."

"Jennifer, I want you to pause just a minute now. Stop

talking, stop thinking about what to say, stop trying to do what I want. Just pause, and get your breath."

She looks troubled, starts to speak, catches herself, reaches for a cigarette.

"Wait a minute on lighting up, okay?"

"Oh, yes, of course. I. . . . "

"And wait to talk. You're still all revved up inside and not really with yourself." I'm talking slowly in a very deliberate manner trying to get a different mood to our conversation. "I know it's hard to wait when you have so much to say, but you really need to get your breath and let yourself get collected here."

We wait, but I'm not sure how much Jennifer is doing other than humoring me. She doesn't seem to know what I'm talking about. Let me try to help her another way. "Jennifer, I want you to listen to your own breathing. Don't say anything yet. Just pay attention to your breath. Feel it come into your nose and mouth, feel it in the back of your throat. . . . Wait, now, really let yourself go with my words. Feel it in your throat and then down into your chest and stomach. Then follow it back up. There, that's it. You're beginning to get it. Stay with it." A bit of the impatient strain is gone. She is trying to use my suggestion.

"Now, Jennifer, I want you to feel inside of yourself the same way as you are doing with your breath but this time feel for the way you were talking at me and trying to hear me a few minutes ago."

"Yes, I can see that. . . . "

"No, wait, a bit more. This is important to what we're trying to do. So hang on a minute more."

"Okay."

"Good. Now it felt to me when we started talking about your making lists of things for you to deal with here that you got kind of anxious, sort of very concerned to show that you understood what I wanted and were trying to do it. Can you feel that?"

"Yes, I think so. I just didn't want you to feel I wasn't paying attention or really understanding or. . . . "

"Yes, and Jennifer, it was so important to tell me that you understood before I could tell you again, wasn't it?"

"Well, maybe, I. . . . Well, yes, I guess so. . . . I mean, I didn't want to be. . . . I mean I didn't mean to interrupt you or. . . . "

"But if I told you again, then I wouldn't know that you really understood already. . . . "

"Yes! That's right. I didn't want you to tell me again because then you wouldn't know I'd understood before. . . . "

"And it is very important to you that I know you've listened to me and understood me very well."

"Oh, yes. Yes, I wouldn't want you to think I wasn't really listening and paying attention and. . . . "

"It sounds like that would be a very bad thing for you to be caught at—not paying attention when I talk to you."

"Well, yes, of course." Pause. "I . . . I guess so. Well, you don't want to have to repeat and go over things all the time. And I certainly should use whatever you tell me."

"Jennifer, wait, it's beginning to snowball." She quiets from the agitation that started to grip her. "Let me try to help you see a bit more."

"Yes, please do."

"I think you could sense a bit ago that it was really something about not paying attention that felt bad to you—not just that I might have to repeat myself. It was like you would be a bad or ungrateful child if you didn't pay careful attention to what I might say to you."

"Mmm. Yes, I think so. I mean, that doesn't make much sense, I know. But it was that way for a minute. I mean it was like you were my mother and would be mad at me if I weren't giving you good attention. That's silly, I know, and. . . . "

"And yet that's the way it used to be, isn't it?"

"Oh yes! She would get so cold if I didn't listen."

"So cold?"

"So cold, and then she'd say that obviously I had more important things to think about so she wouldn't trouble me by talking to me. Oh, I felt so awful. Here she had been so caring toward me, and then I didn't listen. I have always been so distractable. I don't know what is the matter with me."

"What would happen after she said she wouldn't trouble you anymore by talking to you?"

"Then she wouldn't speak to me at all."

"Not at all?"

"No. And sometimes it would go on for days. Until I would just cry and cry and beg her to forgive me and promise not to be distracted any more and to listen very carefully."

And so I get my first look at that sad, cold, distant woman who was Jennifer's mother, who always held out the promise of closeness if only Jennifer were good enough, but who never could really yield to the little girl who yearned for her. Often, in our hours together, the sense of Jennifer's mother is so strong I feel I can see and hear her in the room. Jennifer has so thoroughly taken into herself her mother's critical demandingness that repeatedly I have the impression of hearing Jennifer begin to speak and the mother instantly start to criticize.

Late in the hour I return to the matter of Jennifer's lists of topics for our sessions. "Our time is just about gone, Jennifer, and I want to do two more things today."

"Yes, of course." She settles herself attentively.

"I want to explain a bit more about the matter of your writing lists of things to talk about here. This time, try to let yourself hear me without worrying that I'm having to repeat myself. I haven't said this before, but I may say it again several times in the future, and that will not only be all right but part of what I can do here."

"Yes, well, all right."

"The most important reason I don't want you to depend only on lists about yourself is that they distract us from what is going on in you right at the moment. It's a very different thing to talk about some part of Jennifer that a list reminds us of than to explore something that is alive right now in your experience. You have had far too much of making yourself an object of rules and lists. Now we want you to discover your inner aliveness, just in each minute."

"Yes, I see. Well, I really am glad you explained that."

"Now, Jennifer, if I read you rightly, you kind of understand what I said, but it doesn't make too much sense right now and. . . . "

"Oh, no. I think I understand all right. It's just that I was wondering. . . . Well, I suppose it doesn't matter anyway."

"Why not try it out?"

"Well, I wonder how I'll ever tell you what's happening in my life, if I only talk about what's going on inside of me when I'm here."

"What comes to mind right now as an example?"

"Well, like the meeting Bert and I had with Ellen and her husband or what Bert says he wants. . . . Oh wait!" Delightedly. "I see! I'm thinking of them right now, aren't I?"

"That's it. You see, *you* are there, and you are someone we can trust. You will be there."

"Oh, that's. . . . " Abruptly her eyes are swimming. She looks confused but still pleased. "That's so nice. I mean to have someone say I can be trusted." She smiles again. For a minute she's silent, savoring the feeling. Then she clearly calls herself to attention. "Well, you said there were two things you wanted to tell me."

"No, the other was a question I wanted to ask and that you've already begun to answer: What would be some of the things on your list, and what is it you'd like to tell me about them?"

"Well, like Bert and Ellen and her husband. Oh, I get so mad when I just think of her . . . and of Bert . . . and of what they did. . . . Anyway," pulling herself together, "they're going to move to Fresno."

"Who?"

"Ellen and Dan. Good riddance, I say. She and people like her just. . . . Anyway, Bert and Ellen and Dan and I had a talk the other day, and I told Bert to clear out and go with them. But he said he didn't want to. And Ellen and Dan said they were going to go to Fresno, where Dan has a new job, and they were going to try to work things out between them. And I hope they can make it, but a woman who'd do that. . . . And I thought she was my friend. . . . But, I don't want to get into that now. Anyway, they'll be gone in a couple of weeks."

"And Bert?"

"I told him to move out. I couldn't stand having him around. He's been sleeping in the guestroom, but I didn't even want him in the house."

"You are still so mad, and. . . . "

"Well, I just don't think there's any excuse for what he did. I suppose I should be more forgiving, but. . . . "

"But you don't feel forgiving right now."

"No, I don't. That's not the right attitude, I know. I should be really cool and just say it doesn't matter, but it does matter. Oh, I don't want to get into those feelings again." Pause. "Anyway, Bert's moved out. But he keeps saying he wants to come back. Why does he say that? After what he's done. Oh, I don't know."

And so Jennifer struggles with her anger and her hurt and her sense of outrage.

In the next month or so, as Jennifer moves beyond exclusive preoccupation with her bitterness over Bert's affair, I begin to get a broadened picture of her and her life. She is an overly earnest woman with a great need to do things the right way and a relentless expectation that others should do the same. She is very involved in trying to be a responsible and yet humane administrator at the college, and she often has misgivings about her decisions. She seems to have few close friends; I suspect she is quite lonely, although I am not sure she will let herself know that. To do so, she would have to judge herself a failure, for the person she is supposed to be would never be lonely.

In the therapeutic hours I frequently find that I have two strong and quite contrasting feelings. I feel weary and impatient with her endless interruptions of her own lines of thinking, with her continual starts and stops that are the result of her relentless criticism of herself. Yet along with that impatience, I have feelings of sadness and sympathy. These come from my image of Jennifer as a woman who yearns to dance but who lurches on crippled legs. For under the frustrations of her continually trying to say and do everything exactly right, she is a gentle and warm person who genuinely wants to love and be loved. It's just that many, many years ago she learned she must win approval before she could win love. And approval from her mother was to be won only by rigidly disregarding her own inner life and forcing herself to meet externally set standards. Thus her inner sense, her I-ness, had to be ruthlessly denied.

May 15

After we have worked together three months, I see no real likelihood that Jennifer will do violence to Bert or herself. On the other hand, she is nearly as unrelenting as ever in her insistence on Bert's unfairness and blameworthiness, and she is little changed in her continual self-criticism. She is on the couch this afternoon telling me of yet another frustrating, futile conversation with Bert.

"He says such contradictory things. How can I ever trust him?"

"How do you mean, Jennifer?"

"He looks at me with such a sad look and says he really is sorry for how much he hurt me, and I think he means it. I mean, for a minute I think he means it. Well, I don't suppose I'm really convinced, but he seems so sincere. Maybe I just want to believe it. But I can't see why I'd want to ever believe anything he says again. Anyway, he looks. . . . But it's so hard to read looks. I may be just imagining it. I mean, it's so easy to be fooled, and I know. . . . "

"Jennifer." Wearily; we've done this so much. "Jennifer, you've chopped yourself up so much that I'm losing track of what you're telling me. You started to tell me the contradictory things Bert says, and you ended up contradicting yourself and then contradicting you own contradiction. Your critic inside of you is just merciless in what it does to you."

"I know. But I can't help it. Well, maybe I just don't really try to help it. I really hadn't known how much I did it until you began to point it out. . . . " She allows herself no excuses, not even explanations. I can see her stern, unrelenting mother in the way she treats herself.

"You can't trust yourself, obviously."

"Yes, I. . . . I mean, no, I guess I think I can't. It's hard to know. And I really wanted to tell you about Bert's lying to me." How she cuts herself up! It must be agony for her.

"Tell me."

"Well, he says he's sorry that I was so hurt by his affair with Ellen, and then he turns right around and says he can't really feel sorry for having had that affair! How can I believe someone who is as two-faced as that? How can I ever believe him or anyone again?"

"Jennifer, it's hard for you to see how he could feel positive about his experience with Ellen and still feel badly about its effect on you; is that it?"

"Yes! Yes, of course. What hurt me? His caring more for screwing Ellen than for my feelings! It still makes me so mad. And then he says he cares about my feelings! It's obvious he doesn't care a damn. Why does he still lie to me?"

"You need to insist that Bert's lying to you, I see."

"Why do you say that? I 'need to insist'? That's what he's doing, isn't it?"

"No."

"No? What do you mean? Are you trying to excuse him? Isn't it his fault I got hurt?"

"You really get angry if I don't agree at once with the way you see things."

"What do you mean? I just don't understand you. I know you're not trying to make me angry, but it seems you're telling me he's not to blame for hurting me."

"I didn't say that. I didn't say anything about blame. You are so concerned about blame, though, that you have to limit your ability to hear what he does say to you."

"I can hear what he says all right. He just is trying to have his cake and eat it too. He's trying to say it was all right to go to bed with Ellen because he's sorry I got hurt. Well, I just won't buy that! And you, you seem to say he's not to blame for it either. Well, who is to blame, if he's not? Am I? I suppose I'm to blame that Bert and Ellen went to bed together. Is that what you're trying to tell me?"

"You really are mad at me for not agreeing with you, aren't you?"

"Well, I wouldn't say *mad*—more disappointed. I mean, it's just so unfair. I don't mean you're unfair. I know you're trying to. . . . "

"Jennifer, when you're telling me what a bad guy Bert is, you don't criticize yourself and chop up what you're trying to say. But the minute you begin to talk about yourself and your own feelings, the old critic really tears you up."

"I don't know. Maybe so. I can't understand what you

mean very well, but what I want to know is, are you saying I'm to blame for Bert's going to bed with Ellen?" Angry, defiant.

"Well, are you?" Challenging.

"No! Of course not! What a terrible thing to say! Why should I . . . ?"

"Who said it?" Pressing, harsh.

"You did. And don't play any of your tricky games with me. Is. . . . " She's frantic, beside herself.

" Jennifer, will you please stop!"

"Stop what?" She will not meet me readily.

"Right now you are frantically running in all directions and totally confusing our communication." Exasperated.

"I'm doing what? You're the one to blame for our confusion. You blamed me for making Bert go to bed with that Ellen. Why do you blame me?"

"Blame, blame, blame! That's all that seems to matter to you, keeping score. Who's to blame. You don't seem to be very troubled about what's happening to your life, to your marriage, to your relation with me, and to your therapy. 'Let's just get the blame score right in that big scorebook in the sky.' What about something besides blame?" Hard, demanding.

"Now *you're* blaming me! It's so unfair! You're so unfair! You are to blame because we're all mixed up now. I hope you're satisfied."

"You sound just like you were accusing Bert." Suddenly I see it; will she?

"But you . . . you. . . . That's right! I am just like I was with Bert!"

"Who is to blame is so important to you." Kindly now; the sudden insight is painful and very fragile.

"It's the only thing I have." Close to tears. "He took everything else." And the tears come cascading.[3]

My feelings for Jennifer as she weeps are so contradictory. Her blind preoccupation with blame and fault is maddening, but at the same time it seems—just as she says—"the only thing" she has left. Of course, blame is not truly the only thing; but that's the point she can't let herself see as long as all acts and events have to be weighed in terms of who's to blame. If I can only help her find at least some sense of her responsibility in bringing about the situation in which Bert needed the relation with Ellen, then Jennifer can begin to feel she is something more than an innocent and impotent victim, then she can recognize that she is not without power and need not just devote herself to the futile bookkeeping of blame.

I hope Jennifer's tearful recognition of how much she clings to blaming will help her break out of her self-defeating preoccupation with being wronged, but it is soon clear that more is needed. Certainly that insight helps, but the first real breakthrough comes in a different area. Probably because she is less threatened and traumatized in her working situation than in her personal-marital one, she reaches a broadened perspective there first. The time is six months after the conversation in which she "heard" me blame her for Bert's defection. Meanwhile she has made some real gains in reducing her continual and destructive self-criticism. Those months were filled with the essential labor of Jennifer's struggle with her self-critical compulsion. Gradually, with many gains and many losses, she begins to change fundamentally her way of being in herself and relating to others. No quick, dramatic therapeutic maneuver can substitute for this painstaking, time-consuming, but crucial, process.

November 19

On this day, after some time on another matter, Jennifer tells me about an interview with a student at her college. When she finishes, I suggest that she say again the first thing she said in her summarizing statement to the student.

"As nearly as I can recall it was like this: 'I'm glad you told me why you felt you had to act that way, but I really have no choice. The rules are clear.' That's more or less what I told her." She seems restless, and her manner is defensive as though she expects me to criticize her.

"What are you saying, Jennifer, when you tell the student that? How would you phrase the basic message?"

"Oh, I wanted to tell her. . . . Wait! Let me think . . .

well. . . . " Pause. "Well, I guess basically I'm saying, It's tough, kid, but those are the breaks, and the rules don't say anything about good, bad, or indifferent reasons. They just say, 'You do so-and-so, then so-and-so happens to you.' It's nothing personal. . . . I guess that's the message. No, maybe it's. . . . Well, that's it, I guess."

"Did you hear how hard your voice got when you were paraphrasing your message and especially when you said, 'You do so-and-so, then so-and-so happens to you.'?"

"I didn't notice, but I'm not surprised." Dispirited tone. "I certainly don't like coming down heavy on people, especially on people who didn't mean to violate the rules or cause trouble."

"Then why do you?"

"Oh, don't you give me a hard time!" She sits up on the couch and looks at me. She is close to tears, but she is getting angry too. I don't respond. "You know very well that it isn't because I want to. The rules really are very clear about these things."

"So you're really superfluous."

"What do you mean?" Voice rising, protesting, angry now.

"Just what I said. You are superfluous. The rules have judged the student and assigned her punishment. You're just a middleman until they get a better computer that can apply the rules without your having to be there at all."

I wonder whether she will break out angrily at me, but instead her face becomes a mask of concentration as she tries to understand me. I don't want her to get lost in figuring out what I said. "Look, Jennifer, don't treat this as a riddle to solve. Think what you told the student. You were trying to be considerate, but what you really said was something like, 'My understanding—human understanding—of your situation is not really significant. If it were, my understanding would be helpful to you now. Instead, the rules are stronger than we are.' You don't like that way of saying it, Jennifer, but it seems to me that that's what it boils down to."

She is still silent, but now her face again shows traces of anger. She takes a long breath. "I suppose so. I don't see what you want me to do, though. What else could I say?"

"I don't know. But right now, let's just stay with what you did say, because I think it will help us to see what's bugging you and what's making you mad and yet kind of depressed too."

"I do feel kind of angry now, but I can't see why."

"You must feel pretty much as that student did. Although my logic seems accurate, you don't think what it leads to is fair."

"That's right! I don't like what you're saying, and I feel judged without being able to prove that it's not right. What can I do, go around ignoring the rules whenever I'd like to?"

"That's pretty much what you told the student next, isn't it? What you said to her was something like, 'If I made an exception for you because you had what seemed to you such good reasons, then I'd have to make exceptions for all the others who also think they have good reasons. Pretty soon the rules would be meaningless.' What's the underlying message this time?"

"Ooh! I don't like doing this." Grimacing.

"Give it a try."

"Well, I guess I was saying, 'I've got to be consistent. I can't play favorites.' "

"Who's your favorite?"

"Uh, well, I don't. . . . I mean. . . . You know what I mean. I can't administer the rules one way one time and another way another time."

"Why not?"

"Well, what would be the point of having rules?"

"You seem to be saying that the point of having rules is to avoid having human beings use judgment."

"No, I'm not. Well, sort of, but. . . . "

"I hear you telling the student something like this: 'Consistency is more important than human understanding. If I exercise choice and set the rule aside for you, then I'll lose the power of choice in the future. Precedent will take my place.' "

"Oh! I don't like that at all!" Pause, considering. "I don't believe that, or maybe I do, but don't want to face it. Yet in a way that's true. I feel angry with you and angry with myself and angry at the whole system. Maybe I shouldn't be a dean. Maybe I should. . . . "

"Wait, Jennifer, you don't like what you've been trained to think about people and rules and all these things. But now you just want to get away from the whole business. I don't think any of us can do that, and I know damn well you can't free yourself of the feelings that have been making you so miserable just by dumping this job."

"Well, I don't like what you're saying. I don't feel helped with my problem. I think you're making it all worse. Now I'll be more confused than ever the next time I have a disciplinary problem."

"I don't blame you for not liking it, Jennifer. Yet I think that you need to keep looking at the whole thing. Can you hang in and see this one through a bit more?"

"Of course." She is suddenly transformed into an efficient and impersonal college official.

"No, Jennifer, that's not hanging in. Now you've submerged your own feelings just as you find you have to do so often in your work. You're trying to make yourself an efficient machine here with me, just as you try to make yourself an efficient discipline-administering machine in your office. Shutting yourself off to do the external job there is part of why you have the feelings that trouble you so. Shutting yourself off here would only complicate things for you and keep us from being any help to you."

"Oh, damn it, Jim. I really don't know what to do. This whole thing we're doing really upsets me."

I keep quiet, waiting. Try to convey understanding and support by manner and posture, but avoid intruding words right now. This moment is an important choice point for Jennifer. She's gotten an intellectual insight into her dependence on rules. Can she, will she, incorporate that insight into herself at more than an intellectual level?

Jennifer is silent too, but the sense of a great deal going on within her is strong. Then she sighs, "Okay, let's give it a try. I think I said one more thing to Fran, to the student. It was something like, 'I'm sorry, but you have to be restricted to campus for the next month.' I put over to her that I didn't like punishing her in view of everything but that we were both parts of the whole system and had to fit in. Ughh!"

"Had to fit into the system."

"Yeah, yeah. I hear it. And, you know, that's it. That's just about it exactly. I wanted to put over that we are just parts of the big machine, kid, so we can't go trying to remake the machine that we're part of."

"How does it taste?"

"Awful! Lousy!" She curls her legs up under her, and her whole body seems so tight that it's like she's trying to make herself into a solid ball. Lots of tension; she's still working at it. "I don't know what I can do about it. Right now my head feels tight, and I think I'm getting a headache."

"Feels like you're bracing yourself for something or against something."

"Yeah, yeah, I don't know. . . . Maybe I don't like what we've been saying so much that. . . . I'm not with it yet; I can feel that. What the dickens am I supposed to do now? Look, Bert, I mean, Jim! Oh, wow! I just called you, 'Bert.' Did you hear that?"

"He broke the rules too."

"Yes. Yes, he sure did. And just about broke me too."

"And you wanted to throw the book at him too."

"How do you mean?"

"You wanted to kill him."

"Oh, not really. I mean, yes, I guess I did. For a bit, a little while. But he had it coming. I mean he really lied to me. He really did go screw that woman. And there ought to be some justice. It just isn't fair. Oh, hell, I don't know what I mean." She is trying to get the old self-righteousness going, but somehow it won't take hold.

"It's so hard to know about justice and fairness."

"Yes. Yes, it really is." Quietly, subdued, sunk into her thoughts.

Unknowingly, Jennifer has taken a huge step. In relating to me today, she's ventured forth without her habitual protective armor of projecting all responsibility and blame on to others. She's let me lead her into considering her own role in situations where previously she acted only as an intermediary between the rules and the offending students. She is risking thinking about the meanings she—Jennifer—gives to rules and decisions.[4] We're moving toward a recognition of her inner sense. And to top it all, she has tolerated my applying this same recognition to her traumatized relation with her husband. So easily, so readily might she have dropped back into her angry insistence on his blameworthiness, but she did not. She is low and sad as she leaves today, but there is promise in her inward turning.

November 21

"Something's wrong, or somehow I can't get things straight in my head. I mean, I can see now that I've been trying to make the rules do all the deciding. I guess that isn't quite right either. But, you know what I mean, I've been trying to get myself to be more consistent in applying them, and now. . . . Well, I don't know whether I mean 'consistent' at that, but. . . . " She stops, confused at once by what she is trying to express and by her renewed self-criticism.

"Something's wrong."

"Yes, something's wrong, but I don't know what it is." Pondering. I see the familiar mask of Jennifer-trying-to-solve-the-problem-of-Jennifer's-feelings come over her face.

"Now you're going to take Jennifer apart like a balky machine and try to make her work better."

She looks at me in exasperation. "Well, uh, I know I feel confused and. . . . "

"It feels like the only way out of your confusion is to make yourself into a problem to be solved. Yet you and I both know that the solutions you reach that way seldom work out in your life."

"Yes, I know that, but. . . . " Then Jennifer takes a step I've often urged on her, but this time she takes it on her own initiative. She has been sitting curled up on the couch. "Okay, let's try it a different way." She lies down and obviously is trying to get into a physically relaxed position. "Okay, now, let's see. I think of Katherine who came to see me today. She's in trouble for cutting chemistry lab too often. She wants me to help her get back in good standing with Professor Herndon, and she wants to avoid getting punished. She's full of good reasons, but what it all boils down to is that the chem lab comes at the same hour her boyfriend has free, and they've been making out in his car when she should be in the lab."

"So, what does it all mean to you?"

"Well, frankly, I sympathize with Katherine. I'd rather make out with a good-looking man than with a bunsen burner and test tube any day. But I can't let Katherine know that, of course, so. . . . "

"Why not?"

"Well, I mean, what kind of thing would that be for the Dean of Women to say?" She giggles briefly. "On the other hand, why not? Well, if I said anything like that, how could I ever enforce any discipline or anything? But, of course. . . . "

"Ummm?"

"Of course, I suppose I might. But what if she then decided to. . . . Oh, I don't know. If I don't preserve a certain amount of dignity, how will the students respect me? Well, it isn't respect, exactly, but it's that they've got to know that there are limits, and that I'll. . . . When I start thinking of how some of the faculty would react if they ever heard I'd told a student I'd rather make out. . . . " The little giggle again. "But the Dean of Students insists that we get tough when the violations are willful, and Katherine's sure were that. But I don't know what's wrong that I can't just. . . . I mean, at one time it all seemed so simple, but now. . . . I think I ought to go back to teaching or try something else. I'm not the right person to be in charge of discipline and things like that." Jennifer is squirming with the ebb and flow of her thoughts. And, as she pauses, she is up on her elbows staring somewhat angrily and with evident bafflement at the opposite wall.

"Jennifer, what sort of a person do you think should have the job of Dean of Women? Suppose you were specifying the qualifications. What would you think the person should have that you lack?"

"Well, one thing's for sure. She should have a less jumbled up head so she could hear the students without getting her feelings all involved and so she could make a decision which she knew gave consideration for the needs of the college as well as the problems of the students. The right gal wouldn't go home and feel like biting her husband's head off the way I do with Bert. I mean, 'did.' "

"She wouldn't be upset and confused the way you are."

"Well, like the ideal Dean would be more sure of what she was doing. I just let it mess me up all the time."

"Where you're messed up is someplace else, it basically is not in your work."

"Well, I sure know I'm miserable with this whole thing a lot of the time; so if you think I'm not, you can. . . . Oh, wait a minute. When I stop and feel about the messed up feeling, it's perfectly clear what bugs me. It's me!" She is silent, struck by her own recognition. I keep quiet too, but I'm sure my manner conveys confirmation.

"The feeling in me is that if I were not so messed up myself, I wouldn't get so upset about my work. I feel kind of guilty to be bringing all of my garbage to the office and letting it get in the way of treating the kids fairly or letting it screw up the Dean's plans or whatever. If I just could get myself straightened out. . . . " She trails off.

"If you could get yourself straightened out, what then?"

"Then I'd. . . . " She has been very inward, but now she rouses herself, sits up, and looks at me. "I don't know just what I was going to say."

"I think you were going to say that if you could get yourself straightened out, then you wouldn't feel distressed over some of these decisions you have to make. If you were straightened out, you'd be like your hypothetical Dean of Women, sailing through all problems without any distress."

Jennifer giggles. "She sounds pretty awful."

"But she is the image you hold up to yourself of the person you should be. She is the right person, and you judge yourself so very clearly to be the wrong one."

Sobering, intent. "Yes, yes, I do. I always feel that if only I were more like I should be, I wouldn't have all this shit going on inside of me all the time. I just know my mother was like that. She seemed so serene and untroubled. I hated her for it, and I loved and admired her for it. But nothing could ever really get to her."

"Including you?"

"Including me."[5] Sadly.

December 4

"Jim, I suppose you know that you've been a great help to me in my work. Now I have twice as much trouble making a decision." It is a week or so since the interview with Jennifer described above. She is lying in her characteristic posture on the couch with one trousered leg hooked over the back in such an unladylike contrast to the image of the formal Dean of Women that I smile to myself. Right now her sarcasm is her way of asking for help, without quite taking full responsibility for doing so.

"You seem pretty complacent about this increase in your troubles." Steady, but suggesting there's more.

The leg comes down and her voice changes, becomes more sober. "I'm not really complacent. At least I don't think I am." Her face works as she tries to examine her feelings. "Well, maybe, in a way. I think we are on the track of something that is in back of my irritability and headaches, and that progress makes me feel good. On the other hand, it really is a pain every time I have some student in because of some infraction of the rules."

"Sounds like there may be a connection between the headaches and what a pain it is to administer the rules." Musing, gentle.

"Yeah, I heard that too." She is alert and interested.

"I wonder if the rules don't make me think of my mother and all of her rules and. . . . "

"Jennifer, that sounds very possible." Interrupting. "But you've made yourself into a problem to be solved again. You've got a new theory, and you'll cross-examine your own life to try to prove it, and then you'll end up as frustrated as ever, not knowing if it is really accurate or if it just is a logical possibility."

"I suppose so. But doesn't it help to have at least some idea how things like the headaches come about?"

"Of course it helps, but you're confusing the abstract possibility of a particular pattern with what you may have actually lived through. Look, suppose you suddenly woke up one morning in San Francisco without being able to recall how you got there. Then because you see an airplane out of the window you assume you flew from Los Angeles. Of course, you may have done so, but you might have taken a train, driven your car, or even have gone by ship. Only your memory, your own inner experience, can confirm for you the sure recognition that you used one method instead of the others. No amount of rational deduction about the relative costs of each method, the time involved, or anything else, will give you the feeling of certainty that being in contact with your own inner experience will provide."

"That's all very true, I'm sure, but I just never know for sure what my inner experience is. I mean, sometimes I'm pretty clear, but most of the time it's like there's a lot of fog or something."

"Part of what makes that fog is all your theorizing about yourself; you let it take the place of really being inside of yourself."

"Maybe so. I wonder why I do that so much? It must have something to do with my mother always saying, 'Now why did you do that?' I thought I had to have a good reason for everything."

"Like right now."

"Oh! Yes, like right now."

The growth in Jennifer is becoming more pervasive now. She can let me help her as I point out the ways she has confused her own thinking, and she doesn't hear my comments as criticisms that she must defend herself against. She is beginning to value other dimensions of experience more than the negative virtue of being blameless, and she is starting to get the idea of consulting her inner sense.

January 15

Shortly after the above session, I suggest to Jennifer that she might gain from being in a psychotherapy group. She is rather dubious about it. "I'll go into the group if you like, but I really don't see what being with a lot of other people and hearing their troubles is going to do for me. I'm mixed up enough without having somebody else's problems added on to mine."

"The group is not a place to trade problems. It's a place for you to try out being who you are without hiding behind rules or anything else. It's a place for us to understand better what threatens you in being with other people and what we need to explore so you can be yourself more genuinely. Rather than arguing about it abstractly, why don't you go for a half-dozen times, and then we'll see how it feels to you?"

"Okay, if you think it'll help, I'll give it a try."

February 1

"Well, Jim, I went to your group last night . . . and I. . . . Well, I just think it's probably not the thing I need right now. I mean, I'm sure that. . . ."

"It seems hard to say your feelings about the group."

"No, it's just that. . . . Well, maybe so. Anyway, I don't think. . . ."

"It feels like you're really uncomfortable with what you're thinking or want to say."

"Well, you see, it's sort of. . . . Well, they seemed so kind of unhappy and mixed up. I mean, take Laurence for example. He's so upset by that fight with his wife, and . . . and Kate is so angry about everything, you know. And the other one . . . I mean the man who. . . . His name is 'Frank' or 'Hank,' I think."

"Frank."

"Yes, well, Frank seemed so far down. Well, he sounds like he might, I mean. . . . Well, they all seem to have such bad things happening to them, and. . . ."

"And?"

"And I suppose I ought to learn from them that my troubles aren't so bad and quit feeling so sorry for myself, but. . . ." Pause. "But anyway, I don't think I need to go back. Besides, I have so much trouble getting away from the campus at that time, and. . . ."

"Jennifer, so far I don't think you've really been able to level with me on your feelings about the group."

"Well, yes, I suppose so. You see, the thing is that I was kind of disappointed that you didn't say more and give the group guidance. We just seemed to wander all over without any plan. . . . And frankly, though I don't like to say it, I didn't think the others would be so . . . so . . . sick. I mean, those people have real troubles!"

"They seem so much worse off than you are?"

"Well, not exactly. I don't mean really that their troubles are so much worse. I mean, the thing between me and Bert and this problem I have in being so confused about my own thoughts and feelings. . . . Well, I suppose those things are not so different. But these people seem so broken or torn up or something. I mean, I didn't know people could get so bad off about things, if you see what I mean."

"I think I do, but why don't you tell me more so I can be sure."

"Well, like Frank, you know. I thought a lot about him last night after the meeting. I wondered if maybe I should say something and see if I could buck him up. He really sounded pretty bad. Weren't you worried about him? You know, the way he talked about wanting to just close his eyes on the freeway and all?"

"You found Frank's misery sticking in your thoughts, eh?"

"Oh, yes! I just wonder whether he got home all right. Oh, I suppose I'm being kind of ridiculous. You probably know what you're doing, and besides it's none of my business really."

"But it does kind of make you wonder, doesn't it, whether it was wise for me to let Frank go off alone that way?"

"Well, not really. You know Frank a lot better than I do, and I don't want to butt in on something where I have no business, you know. . . . "

"It seems to make you uncomfortable to express any doubts about me."

"Yeah, I guess it does. But that's not the main point anyway. The main thing is that I just don't think the group is the thing I need right now."

When a new person comes into a psychotherapy group, his frequent reaction is that the other people in the group are much sicker or much more disturbed than he and that the therapist has probably made a mistake in placing him in the group. This reaction is, of course, what Jennifer is expressing. She is actually responding to the manner in which group members talk about their subjective experiences. In most of our day-to-day lives, we express our inner emotions and impulses in front of others only under conditions of great stress or personal disruption. So Jennifer mistakes the greater openness of the group members as evidence of severe psychological disturbance. This point is brought out in the third group session Jennifer attends (for she does return to the group after she has aired her misgivings).

February 13

Frank is talking about his feelings of misery. "For a long time, I just felt constantly hopeless and like 'What the hell's the use?' Nothing mattered, and I'd just sit there feeling I was no damn good, and the world was no damn good, and why didn't I just blow the whole bit? But now, lately, I don't know quite why, but I get these restless feelings, and I can't sit still. I feel miserable as hell, and then I find I'm out of the house roaming around, but I don't know what I'm looking for. Or I'll be as angry as though I'd just been robbed, and I'm not sure why I'm so teed off. I don't know whether I'm getting better or worse, but something's sure going on."

As Frank stops talking, Jennifer darts a quick glance at me as though hoping to read whether these developments are a good or bad sign. Hal, who has rather taken Jennifer under his wing in the group, picks up her action. "What are you looking at Jim for, Jennifer? Did you think he'd give us a character reading on Frank?"

Jennifer is flustered and just a little miffed. "I didn't know I looked at him. I was just going to ask Frank what made him mad these times."

But Hal won't be put off this easily. "I think you're dodging, Jennifer, and trying to get our attention off of you and back on Frank."

"Well, maybe so. But I really would like to know, if I'm not being too nosy. . . . " Pause, quick breath, turn to me. "I mean, if you don't think it would be . . . uh, the wrong thing, I mean, not so good for . . . uh, for you to say. I mean, is what's happening with Frank something you want or . . . ? Oh, it's none of my business anyway. Skip it."

And so Jennifer struggles with her feelings, with her concern and fear, with her relatedness and separateness. She wonders whether

Frank is improving or getting worse. She's uncomfortable to be so concerned. She thinks she shouldn't be so "personal," and she pulls back from asking me for fear it might be wrong for Frank to hear my opinion. It is only slowly that she comes to see how much we are all involved in and with each other.

April 10

For a time Jennifer seems content to watch the other group members working through for themselves the whole difficult and very important matter of discovering one's own separateness and shared relatedness. For example, in a later meeting, Kate is tracing out some of her own background and how it has influenced her:

"My parents never taught me about feelings, I realize now. It was as though any proper person would naturally have the right feelings without having to be told."

"That's right, Kate," Louise joins in. "I find it so strange now to realize how unquestioningly I, and everyone else, seem to have judged people by their emotions but never thought to help people really learn about them. Why, only the other day I was talking with Dr. Ryan about the. . . . "

"Oh, for Christ's sake!" Frank bursts out. "You two dames give me a pain with your la-de-dah head tripping."

Laurence, who has been in the group only a short time longer than Jennifer, is troubled by Frank's discourtesy or by his anger; I can't tell which. "Laurence, you winced when Frank spoke just then. What happened?"

Laurence: "Uhm, well, I think I agreed that Louise and Kate were becoming quite abstract, but I wish Frank, uh. . . . " Turning to face Frank. "I wish you didn't find yourself constantly angered and so impolite to the ladies. I know I'm old-fashioned, but it does trouble me."

Hal: "Yeah, Frank, you've got too short a fuse, even though I think you're right."

Louise: "You really startled me, Frank, but I agree I did get off into the more rarified levels. All I really wanted to say was that I, like Kate, had little training in regard to my emotions. I learned more about what I ought *not* to feel than what I ought to."

Frank: "Aw, hell, Louise, I'm not mad at you. You're okay. It's just that I feel so lousy all the time." Risking a small smile toward Louise, toward whom he seems drawn like a truculent boy toward an admired aunt.

Louise: "You are no great advertisement for the emotions, Frank old boy. I always have been afraid of my feelings, thought they were some kind of time bomb ticking away inside that would blow up if I ever looked into them or let them out. And you look like what I was afraid would happen."

Frank: "So blow yourself up and have a ball."

Louise: "If I do, I'll make sure to splash all over you."

The group swirls on with Jennifer watching spellbound but largely silently. Obviously, she is astounded at the manner in which the others feel at liberty both to express their own feelings and to get involved with each other's emotions. It seems clear that she does not yet believe that she might be part of such interchanges, nor does she seem to feel very much inclination to move in that direction.

May 8

On more than one occasion, Jennifer fumbles toward asking me my views of Frank's condition. She obviously identifies a great deal with his agitation and wants to find out how serious it is without disclosing her personal concern. Indeed, I'm not sure just how fully she allows herself to be aware of that identification, since it would be very frightening to her in its implications. Frank, who has given her the nickname, "Jenny," acts as though he finds Jennifer's tentative questions a source of annoyance; yet slowly they seem to be building a measure of understanding.

After several group sessions, Jennifer becomes a central part of the interaction quite inadvertently. It comes about toward the latter part of the session when Louise is telling of her sense of loss.

Louise: "I'm nearly forty years old, and I feel like I've never really been alive. Sometimes when I think about that I'm angry and want to break things, but today it just all hit me, and I feel so damn sad. Nearly forty, and I have no man of my own."

Kate: "I don't want to pry, but have you had much experience with men?"

Louise: "It's okay, Kate, I don't mind talking about it. Maybe it will help. I date once in a while, used to more, but now there aren't many opportunities. Except the ones who just want a roll in the hay, and I want more than that."

Frank: "Have you ever. . . ? I mean, are you a. . . ?"

Laurence: "Oh, come on, Frank, don't be nosy."

Frank: "Aw shit, you're such an old maid, I just wanted to know. . . . "

Louise: "If I was a virgin? No, Frank, I'm not. I've had a little sexual experience, only one real affair and that didn't go anywhere. . . . "

Frank: "Why not?"

Louise: "He was married, and. . . . "

Jennifer's face suddenly grows intense. She stares at Louise as though piercing her with her eyes. She moves restlessly, a struggle is going on in her.

Frank: "When was that?"

Louise: "A couple of years ago. For awhile it was so very sweet. . . . "

Jennifer: "Did you. . . . I mean, I suppose it's none of my business, but. . . . Well, I just wondered. . . . " She is pulled back and forth, hardly able to let herself speak.

Louise: "It's all right, Jennifer, I don't mind talking about it now. What did you want to ask me?"

Jennifer: "Well, just. . . . I mean, was he married when you. . . ?"

Louise: "Yes, but. . . . "

Kate: "Louise, how long ago was this?"

Louise: "Oh, it seems like just yesterday some ways; but then other times it seems like ancient history. It's so strange that it can still hurt so much."

Hal: "It sounds like it was very sad—for it to end, I mean."

Louise : "Yes, I'm afraid it was. I thought for awhile that at last I'd found what I'd always wanted, but then. . . . I guess there was no hope for me all along."

Jennifer: "What right would you have to any hope—going to bed with a married man?" Angrily, leaning forward intently.

Louise: "I don't know. That isn't what I meant." Startled, drawing back.

Jennifer: "You just screw with them for the fun of it and to hell with the wife, is that it?" Eyes blazing, hands clenching, opening, clenching.

Louise: "No, no. I just meant. . . . I mean I was thinking about my life and. . . . "

Jennifer: "Just thinking about yourself and only yourself. You don't care about anybody else. Oh, you bitch, you, I'd like to teach you a lesson."

Frank: "For crying out loud, Jenny, Louise didn't say she didn't care about anybody else. What's teeing you off so?"

Kate: "I've a hunch you've been on the receiving end of something like this."

Hal: "Jennifer," trying to reach her, "I'm glad to see you in here with your feelings, but you sure are laying a trip on Louise."

Louise: Crying and looking bewildered. "Look, Jennifer, I don't know what this means to you, but don't dump your load on me. What you said hurts, but. . . . "

Jennifer: "Oh, it hurts does it? You're lucky I can't hurt you like I'd like to. You dirty bitch! You lying, evil woman. You don't care about anything but getting laid by someone else's husband. You're not enough of a woman to get a man of your own. No, you steal somebody else's. Oh, I hate being in the same room with you. . . . "

Kate: "Jennifer, my husband ran off with another woman too."

Jennifer: "I don't care. I don't care about anything. I just want to claw this bitch, and. . . . "

Jim: "Jennifer, you're accusing her of being selfish, but you just rejected Kate because you were so wound up in your own feeling."

Frank: "Jesus, Jenny, you're a hellcat. Louise isn't like you're saying. You ought to. . . . "

Jennifer: "Jim, you're right. I'm sorry, Kate. That was very selfish of me. But how can you sit there calmly and let this . . . this . . . this husband-thief talk with us?"

Kate: "Because I learned a sad lesson, Jennifer. No one stole my husband. The woman who 'took him,' as you would say, had my cooperation."

Jennifer: "I don't understand. Do you mean you wanted him to go off with her?"

Kate: "Not consciously, at least. It's just that I don't believe any person can steal another person. A husband isn't a pocketbook. I think I didn't give my husband what he needed, and so he was open to other possibilities."

Jennifer: "Well, maybe that's true for you, but I . . . I just hurt so much, and I get so mad. It was so unfair, so unfair."

Hal: "What was unfair?"

Jennifer: "He went to bed with my friend."

Hal: "What's unfair about that?"

Frank: "Hell, why don't you let her alone? Can't you see she's hurting?"

Jennifer: "No, I don't understand. Why doesn't everybody see that it's unfair? For him to go to bed with another woman? With my friend?"

Laurence: "Of course, I see it. It hurt you."

Hal: "But what's 'unfair' about it?"

Kate: "It's like the rules of the game have been broken. I know the feeling, Jennifer, but I wish you could see what you did to help bring it about."

Jennifer: "I didn't do anything."

Hal: "I don't buy that. It takes three to make an unfaithful husband. And I don't think you want to face that."

Frank: "You all make me sick, just giving her lectures."

Jennifer: "Yes, you make me sick too. All of you. You don't care anything about decency and fairness. You're all so unfair. You take this bitch's part. You think she's so fine because she fucks with someone else's husband. Well, let me tell you," turning to Louise, "you filthy pig, I wouldn't spit on you; I wouldn't even be in the same room as you except that. . . . "

Louise: Shrieking, "Oh!! Oh! You self-righteous bitch! I didn't do anything to you or your husband, and you're calling me everything nasty you can think of. Who do you think you are to talk to me that way?"

Hal: "It's good to see you come out of your 'I'm-no-good' place and fight for yourself, Louise."

Louise: "I guess I'm a slow learner, but now I'm really mad. Lady," to Jennifer, "you've got a whale of a nerve passing judgments like that. I don't blame your husband for wanting someone more understanding if that's the way you were with him."

Jennifer: "Oh, you tramp, don't you dare speak to me like that!"

Kate: "Jennifer, Jennifer, you can't do it. You can't. . . . "

Jennifer: "And you! Don't play such an all-wise mother with me. I don't know what you did to drive your husband away from you, but don't try to tell me I did the same thing. I was always faithful in my marriage. I played fair. I played fair!" Nearly screaming it, trying to make somebody hear her.

Jim: "You're feeling very much alone right now, Jennifer."

Jennifer: "Of course I am. This bunch of. . . . These people are all telling me it's my fault that Bert went to bed with Ellen. They're taking his side. And that's not fair. He's to blame. Bert's to blame."

Hal: "Jennifer, we're not saying that."

Jennifer: "Yes, you did. Don't try to back out of it." Frantic, furious, lashing out in all directions.

Frank: "Jenny, take it easy. You're off your nut right now."

Jennifer: "None of you cares about vows and faithfulness and marriage. You probably all screw anybody anytime. Well, I don't want any part of you. I think you stink!" To me, "And you, Jim, is this your idea of what would help me? I told you I shouldn't be with these people. I have values. I'm not just a rutting animal. I. . . . "

Louise: "You have values but you can't see people. You just pronounce judgment and want to administer punishment, all in your own self-righteous system."

Laurence: "Jennifer, that sounds harsh, what Louise said, but she's right. You do sound terribly self-righteous."

Jennifer: "Oh, don't honor and promises mean anything to you people? Doesn't it mean anything that Bert broke his promise? It's so unfair! You are so unfair! Everybody says I'm to blame. I didn't go to bed with Ellen or with anybody else. It's unfair! He had the fun, and now everybody takes his side and says I'm to blame."

Frank: "Wow! You really feel sorry for yourself, don't you?"

Hal: "It sounds like you'd like to do something like that yourself."

Louise: "She couldn't let herself want anything like that. The rules are more important."

Jennifer: "You're damned right they are. I have principles. Principles, do you hear? Something neither you nor anybody else here knows anything about."

Laurence: "And do you have any principles about judging people without having the evidence?"

Jennifer: "Oh, you're so sanctimonious and dignified, but you're probably just like the others. Have you screwed Louise yet? Why not? She's probably just itching to get another married man into the sack. Aren't you, Louise?"

Frank: "Jenny, you really can be a bitch when you want to be, can't you?"

Louise: "You sound pretty jealous to me, Jennifer; are you sure you don't want Laurence yourself?"

Jennifer: "Oh, you . . . you. . . . I don't go around spreading my legs for just anyone who comes along, the way you do."

Louise: "Listen, lady, don't judge me by your standards. You don't know anything about me. You just know what that sick mind of yours wants to imagine. And you must have a pretty filthy imagination."

Jennifer: "I don't have to be talked to that way by a slut. I'm going to leave, and go home and take a bath and try to clean off all the dirt that this group wallows in."

Hal: "Jennifer, you just want to lash out at everybody now. You don't care what you say or who you hurt or anything."

Jennifer: "Oh, I thought you were different, but. . . . "

Kate: "Jennifer, you really are acting totally self-righteous, and though I want to be on your side, I'm getting mad at you."

Jennifer: "Don't trouble yourself. I don't need you or anybody." She's frantic now, reaching for her purse, dropping it, spilling its contents, crying, screaming.

Louise: "What's the matter, can't you take it? You can dish it out, but you can't take it. When the going gets tough, you want to pull out, run for home. No wonder your husband wanted a real woman."

Laurence: "That's a low blow, Louise." Mediating, concerned for both.

Jennifer: "Piss on yoooouuu!" Screeching. "Oh, I hate you! I hate you! I'll scratch your eyes out." Coming out of her chair, heading for Louise.

Frank: "Whoa, Jenny." He grabs her, and they fall to the floor. She's spitting and clawing.

Frank: "God, you're strong."

Jennifer: "Let me go. I'll show her. I'll kill her. I'll kill her! Oh! Oh!" She hears herself, hears again the word *kill,* and suddenly she collapses. All the fight is gone. She lies limply in Frank's arms and sobs and sobs.

Frank holds her with surprising tenderness. The rest of the group sit slumped, exhausted by the storm of emotions which has swept over us all. Kate and Louise are weeping. Laurence is sunk into his chair, face buried in his hands. Hal seems to have taken refuge in looking at the others with concerned, evaluating eyes. I am suddenly so weary I feel I can hardly move. Although I've said little, I've been on the edge of my chair, ready to act if I felt it necessary, determined to try to let this play through if at all possible, sensing it was filled with meaning for nearly every one of us in the room.

Louise raises her head and speaks in a low voice to Jennifer:

"Jennifer, there have been times when I've called myself worse things than you called me, but I'd like you to know that it wasn't like you think. I mean, he was married, that's true. But he was separated, and at the time I was with him, he really thought it was all over in his marriage. It was only when his wife found out about us that she decided she wanted him after all. And I urged him to go back because I was so guilty. Now I wish I hadn't. They didn't make a go of it, and he went off someplace, and I've never seen him again."

Jennifer: "I'm sorry." Weeping.

People talk in brief, half-whispered sentences to each other, gathering up their things, hesitant to leave. Usually the group has a post-session without me after the end of the formal period. Tonight there'll be none. Everybody knows, without it being said, that we've exhausted ourselves emotionally for now.

I sit quietly, waiting to see how it is with Jennifer. She may want a chance to talk with me. Louise, weeping, pats Jennifer's shoulder, smiles wanly at me, and goes out. The others also leave as Frank and Jennifer slowly and somewhat self-consciously sit up from where they fell in that last moment of struggle. I think Jennifer has been hiding in Frank's embrace, not wanting to risk looking at the other people. Now she turns to me with a face drained of all emotion but inward pain. Her eyes are red and smeared with mascara.

"I'm here, Jennifer," I say, "if you want to talk now."

Her voice is creaky from her strained throat and much crying. "No, it's all right. I'll go home, and I have a time to see you tomorrow." She gets up and leaves quickly.

Frank looks at me questioningly.

"I don't know, Frank. I really don't. We'll have to trust her." Inwardly I'm struck with the reversal; once Jennifer worried about Frank.

"Okay, good night." He leaves, and I close up the offices, bone-weary.

May 9

The next day Jennifer is ten minutes late for her appointment, very unusual for her. I feel relieved when she does arrive.

She sits in the chair instead of going to the couch. She is subdued and doesn't look at me. Her face is strained, and her make-up is poorly applied.

"You look wrung out, Jennifer."

"I am." Barely audible. "I'm so ashamed."

"You seem to be judging yourself."

Pause. "Yes, I suppose I am. I judge everybody else, why not myself too?"

"Mmmm."

"I have something to tell you. I . . . I . . . I spent the night with Frank."

"Oh?"

"We didn't . . . we didn't have intercourse. But we . . . we . . . did sleep together. I mean, we slept in the same bed . . . without any clothes. Do you think I'm awful?"

"What do you think yourself?"

"I don't know." Weeping. "I don't know. I never did anything like that before. I wonder if Louise was right. Was I jealous? Did I want to . . . to be with a man? It felt so good to have him hold me. I haven't been with a man for . . . since Bert told me. . . . " Crying harder. "I don't know why we didn't make love. I wanted to. Frank wouldn't." The crying stops. "Do you think he didn't want me, just pitied me?"

"How hard it is for you to accept that maybe somebody just cares about you even though they don't do things your way."

"Oh!" Stung, pulling back.

"It hurts to hear that, doesn't it?" Kindly, insistently.

"Oh, yes." Tears starting. "I don't like you to say things like that. But it's true, I guess. Yes, it's true. I think Frank really does care for me too."

"And now you can let that in."

"Yes, and I care for him. I think he'd have liked to make love to me. I could tell, you know. . . . " Embarrassed.

"Yes, Jennifer."

"He just didn't want to do it that way. But, Jim. . . . "

"Umm?"

"I did. I wanted him to make love to me. And I'm still a married woman!"

"And it's against the rules for a married woman to want another man than her husband to make love to her?"

"Yes, I. . . . Well, no, not to just want it. But I would have. . . . And I'm still married to Bert. Even though he doesn't live at home now. We're still married."

"Still married."

"Yes, and I want to be married to him, to Bert. Yet I wanted Frank to. . . . Oh, I'm so mixed up!"

"Are you mixed up about what you want?"

"Well, yes. I mean, no. I mean I want to be with Bert, and I really did want to make love with Frank last night, and. . . . Oh, I've made such a mess of things. Do you think he'll hate me?" And I wonder whether she means Bert or Frank.

She cries broken-heartedly. Gradually, the crying eases, becomes more relieving. Although the end of our journey together is many months away, Jennifer is beginning to accept the unacceptable, herself.

Jennifer's early training taught her to disregard her own unique inner being and to devote every effort to learning the rules and following them faithfully. It was so important to her to get things right that at times she could barely talk to me. She tried to hold in mind every possible consideration and to take account of all implications of whatever she might say; thus she ended up scarcely being able to say anything. Her life was very like her speech. Each thing she undertook had to run a gauntlet of self-criticism and ended up, as often as not, undone or poorly realized. Insistence on perfection is a sure route to aborting human efforts and to drowning out inner awareness.

Within me—as within Jennifer and each of us—is a knowing that is the true core of my life. It is this deep sensing that, like a beating heart, imparts the vital quality to each moment of awareness. It pulses as it serves as my subjective sense of being. It is not necessarily infallible in some external or lasting sense, but it is the solidest sensing about my own life that I can have in this present moment.

Jennifer had lost a centering in her own life that would have given her some orientation of her own. She knew only those emotions—especially anger—that could grow strong enough to break through her dulled inner sensitivity. Thus, she was often the prey of blind impulses unguided by the rest of her inner concerns—her sympathy, her values, her caring for her husband, for example.

Jennifer was not unique in being blind to her own inner life. Under the onslaught of the mechanistic view of man and his work, we all have tended to devalue, disregard, and even bury this vital sense that can give us a solid base for meeting existence. We have tended to become the captives of that which is external, objective, and publicly logical, and thereby we have lost our own individuality and centeredness.

Jennifer attempted to deny her choicefulness. She looked for rules and principles to make her decisions for her. She sought always to be protected from any possible criticism. She reminded me of a hotly pursued fugitive who constantly dodges behind trees, rocks, whatever is available, so that she won't be a steady target. Jennifer constantly hid behind rules, what others had said, or almost anything she could think of to prevent being seen as acting solely in her own name.

For Jennifer, the recognition of responsibility was inextricably bound up with the need to assign blame or fault. If I explain my own actions and reactions totally in terms of another person, I am that other person's slave or robot. As always with such a perspective, the point of the game is to prove the other person wrong[6] and to insist on one's own helplessness. The game is a futile one in which the relationship between two people (now contestants) is the first casualty. Such a contest usually ends up with each person feeling the futility of his efforts but wrongly attributing that feeling to the obstinacy of the other rather than recognizing the true nature of the problem. When I win at this game, I end up feeling a victim, impotent and angry. When I lose, I feel shamed and angry. In short, it's a no-win situation; unfortunately, it's one in which all too many couples engage.[7]

When Jennifer could begin to accept responsibility in her relations with her husband (and he similarly quit trying to prove that she was at fault), they found that they could relate to each other as partners trying to create a satisfactory relation rather than as opponents trying to beat each other. By no means did they arrive at this new pattern overnight nor did they maintain it uniformly, but they did begin what might be thought of as a benign cycle which replaced their earlier vicious cycle of disagreement–accusation–blaming–hurt feelings–new disagreement–new accusations. . . .[8]

Jennifer has completed her therapy with me, but her professional problem is still with her. Therapy did not solve it. What therapy did do was very important though. It helped Jennifer recognize that it was appropriate for her to be troubled when she found herself in conflict between the rules on the one hand and an individual on the other. Jennifer had felt that something was wrong with her when she experienced this conflict. She had believed that if only she were as she should be, she wouldn't feel distress when she insisted that the rules must apply to an offending student or that she wouldn't feel misgivings when she decided to set the rules aside in another instance. She was unthinkingly certain that there was a right way to handle every case and that, if she were only the person she should be, she would know that right way. What therapy helped Jennifer to recognize was that she would never get to such a point; indeed that she should be suspicious if she ever found she was not concerned about her decisions. One of the most important things she brought to her work was her concern. This concern was her uniquely human contribution to what otherwise would have been a mechanical and impersonal process.

With misgivings about her feelings of concern reduced, Jennifer could do a better job of exercising that concern about a valid issue: How much could she respect the individual and still protect the group?

Jennifer brings home to me several significant aspects of being human and of trying to heighten awareness of the inner sense:

I am responsible for what I say and do. *If I try to avoid that responsibility, I end up feeling impotent and angry. I can use rules, laws, traditions, others' views, or anything else to help me make my choices, but only I can actually choose for me. When I am too frightened to be identified with my choices, I flee from them, and in flight I find I have lost the sense of my own identity and access to my inner sense.*

My concern about what I say and do is part of being human and being significant. Where I have no concern, where I have no uncertainty (and these are very nearly the same thing), then I have no real role in what goes on; then, I am only an observer. Concern is appropriate in decisions affecting human beings. *I would not want a doctor or a judge making decisions about me if he never was uncertain about his choices. I would not want to be such a person either—at least I would not when I am most vitally in my own being.*[9]

If I deal with others chiefly in terms of rules or of trying to keep a fair accounting of relationships, I lose the fullness of being with people. There is a quality to vital human connectedness that surpasses mechanical perfection and equality. *If I will meet a stranger half way, I want to be ready to go all the way for someone about whom I truly care.*[10]

When I need to be perfect, *to be beyond criticism, reproach, or even any error,* I seek an unreal goal. *I want to do well in many things, because doing well may add to the meaningfulness of the doing. But doing well for its own sake or only to seek safety is foredoomed and wasteful. Hardly anything is worth doing as well as possible.*

Relying on rules and regulations to make decisions, depending on abstract principles (e.g., "fairness"), and displacing responsibility onto others all contribute to suppressing our awareness of the inner sense *that we need in order to experience our lives' vitality.* My choices need to be in harmony with my subjective sense if they are to be valid for me.

I spoke earlier of Jennifer as a dancer whose legs were crippled. The image is more than a metaphor. She did love physical movement and told me more than once of the sense of being transported she felt when she could ease up on her hard demands on herself. As we drew to the end of our work together, I could see a difference in the way she held and moved her body. There is such a terrible weightiness in the need always to be right, always to be justified. How could anyone flow emotionally or physically with such a load to carry?[11]

When I speak of my life pulse, I think how centrally important to physical life is the unceasing rhythm of the heart, and I recognize that subjective life has its rhythm as well. If I let myself be quiet and open myself up to my inner sense and truly get my living in phase with it, there is a greater grace to my movements, a more harmonious quality to my voice, an increased musicality to my imagery. The inward sense is an aesthetic dynamic as well as an existential insight.

FRANK
Anger and Commitment

Much of human aliveness is expressed in our relations with each other. How we relate to the people in our lives is one of the most central characteristics of our personalities. Yet when we step back to get a full perspective on the human condition we find that we confront a paradox: Each man is at once *a part of* all other men and yet he is *apart from* all others. Just as much as each of us is related to every other person so also are we forever separate from every one of them. It is this simultaneous and seemingly contradictory duality that underlies all of our relations and that penetrates to the core of our vitality.[1]

Each person works out his own patterns of dealing with this paradox. There is no one correct resolution. For Henry David Thoreau, apartness seems to have been as needful as food and drink; yet in his own way, he was deeply concerned with others. For many other people—Franklin D. Roosevelt or F. Scott Fitzgerald, for example, relationships seem to be the very stuff of their lives, yet one can sense the aloneness that lies back of their immersion in others. Not only do different people work out different balances between the two sides of this human dilemma, each of us at different times may be drawn toward one or the other emphasis.

Adolescence is notably the time of gregariousness, and the solitary teenager may be considered a misfit. In later years, however, we are more tolerant of the person who seeks and values solitude; though even then the contemplations of a perfectly content loner may be broken in on by well-meaning friends who attempt "to draw him out."

It is important for all of us to learn to attend to our own inner sense in order to modulate how much and in what ways we are with others.[2] To be sure, there are the times when we may withdraw from others in hurt or anger or fear and yet dearly hope to be wooed out of our lonely place. This sort of self- and other-deception, however, subtly undermines even the most promising relationships. Nevertheless, it is often hard to come to a clear inner awareness that allows an optimum balance of life-affirming relations and life-enriching solitude. The shouts and commands of our society—of parents and teachers, of advertisements and supposedly scientific advisers, of friends and organizations of all kinds—threaten to drown out our inner knowing as they continually immerse us with instructions on how to be with or apart from others.

Frank is a man who found the "a-part-of" half of the paradox of human relationships too threatening. He might have made a good hermit or recluse in another age and in different living circumstances. As it was, he dwelt in the world of people, but he angrily rejected being at one with them. He clung to his separateness as a drowning man might clutch a log he found in the heaving waves. And Frank feared drowning in the demands, invitations, expectancies, and judgments of other people.

To keep oneself as separate as Frank sought to do is a full-time task. One must be ever-vigilant against the outer world, but at the same time one must ruthlessly put down one's own inner promptings toward others. There must be no place for recognizing loneliness, for experiencing caring, for hungering for intimacy. The best safeguard (and a hidden way of relating) is anger—continuous, unrelenting, easily triggered anger. Frank was, accordingly, an angry man.

June 4

It is the kind of hotel that used to be called "commercial" and today is recognized simply as "second rate." In Room 411, the traveling salesman—unlike the one in the stories—is not with a farmer's daughter but with a tough girl who grew up in the tenderloin district and is practicing a profession which has run in her family for three generations. At a point classically dedicated to the lighting of cigarettes, they find they have none to light. Both feel the need for nicotine nurturance insistently, so the salesman dials "3" on the phone and gets the bell captain. "Send a boy up to Room 411." The "boy" is a thirty-year-old semi-hippie who manages to trim his hair enough from time to time to get a job that requires little except compliance and endurance. He has rather more of the latter than of the former.

The salesman answers the door in a pair of slacks. His companion, deciding not to miss the chance to advertise, wears nothing but a smile that she hopes is sensual. The bellman is apparently equally bored by both of them; at least he is until the salesman, not quite visually alert due to an alcoholic aura, hands the bellman a ten-dollar bill, clearly mistaking it for a one. "Get me a pack of Winstons and keep the change." The bellman is quick to palm the bill, and he moves out of the room with more than his usual alacrity.

Later in the day, that same bellman is lying on the couch in my office, reciting his latest adventure. He is rather pungent, not having washed since leaving the hotel. His face and hands are dirty, and his whole manner lets me know that he rather hopes he is bugging me, which he is.

"So this schmuck has the desk send me up to his room. He's bombed out of his skull from that *Jack Daniels* I took him earlier, and there's some broad wandering around with nothing on but a pair of shoes. Anyway this guy hands me a bill and says to get him a pack of cigarettes and keep the change. He's so spaced out he doesn't even see it's a ten he's giving me; so I grab it quick and cover it in my hand. I get him his lousy butts and keep the change just like he said."

Frank settles himself more comfortably on the couch and pauses. He is clearly waiting for me to react to his latest fling at petty larceny. I keep quiet, partly, I suppose, out of simple contrariness. The set-up has been too obvious. It is also my feeling that Frank is using this account as some sort of smoke screen to divert our attention.

"Hell, why not?" Suddenly. "The creep was asking for it." So Frank is going to argue with me, whether I give him anything to argue with or not.

"What do you want, Frank?" My tone is weary, I know. Perhaps I am punishing him—he gets to me more than I realize.

"I don't want anything." His tone is angry, but it usually is. "I just am telling you everything I'm thinking about, like you said I should." To my knowledge, I've never told Frank to tell me everything he's thinking about, but that's not important either.

"You sound angry."

"I'm not angry. You guys always want people to be crying or angry or something. I'm just trying to tell you about my crummy job, and the freaks I have to deal with. Like this old character— Gandowsky, his name is—who lives at the hotel all the time . . . he's really not too bad . . . threatens to have me fired if I give him any more lip. I can't figure what I said that got him so hot, but he was ranting and raving at me and. . . . "

"Frank, I'm getting tired of the *Adventures of Frank Connelly, Boy Bellhop.*"

"Well, what do you want me to do? You tell me to talk to you about whatever's on my mind, and when I do, you tell me you're tired of what I'm saying."

"Look, Frank, I suppose I am riding you a bit. You ask for it in some way, and. . . . "

"How do I ask for it? Christ, I don't want your trip. I don't ask for anything like that."

"Okay, okay. I don't want to get into that now."

"So you just lay it on me and then say, 'forget it.' I don't get you."

"You're right, Frank. I can't just drop it like that." Wearily. "Okay, you always seem to be looking to be mistreated. I feel as though I have to watch everything I say doubly, or you'll find something in it that you can bitch about—like right now."

"What kind of thing is that? You tell me I'm right and turn around and tell me I make you up-tight because I'm wrong."

"Frank. . . ." Half-laughing, half-annoyed. "You're doing it right now. In terms of the words said, you're right again. But always being right that way is a pretty lonely business. It's playing for peanuts because you're only in touch with me at the most superficial level."

"I don't know what you mean. Sometimes I think you shrinks make it by getting a guy so mixed up he's gotta keep coming just to get unwound."

"Frank, I think that at one level you are often right, and at another you are full of shit, and I also think you know that in some part of your head."

"Every time you agree with me, you take it back right away. I just don't know what you expect. I feel it's like you said, that you enjoy riding me."

"I never said that I enjoy it! . . . Oh, skip it."

So Frank wins another round, and of course, Frank is losing too. Wherever he is, whatever the circumstances, whomever he is with, Frank has to play out being the mistreated, angry, disappointed butt. And it's a self-fulfilling system. Pretty soon, whoever's with Frank finds himself fitting in—nagging, needling, and nitpicking.

After Frank leaves I have a break in my schedule, so I get a cup of coffee and some cookies and sit in my office thinking about our conversation. Frank is a challenge to me. He is so different from most of the people I see, and I find a real desire to make contact with him in a way we haven't managed yet. But boy, can he be a pain in the neck! Ruefully, I recognize how often he catches me off base. And yet, it strikes me, he never seems to gloat in catching me. It's just the only way he knows to relate, I guess.

Strange that Frank should come to psychotherapy. It must be the endless reading he does. I know he always has one or more books with him when he comes for his appointments, and from incidental comments he's let drop, I gather he gets quite a lot of time to read on his job as well as burying himself in books in his free time. I'm kind of jealous of that. And yet, because Frank's life is so empty in most dimensions, I'm really glad he has the books. And now they've got him involved in psychotherapy.

How he pays for his therapy is amazing to me. He has some pension from his military service, but I doubt it's sufficient, and his bellhop job certainly doesn't make it possible. One day he mentioned some money he got at his father's death, but I have the impression that was relatively little.

Tough, frightened, gutsy, complaining, unwittingly humorous, and persistently hanging in—Frank is a delight, an exasperation, and a challenge. And somehow I'm coming to like him very genuinely.

June 11

Another day, and Frank is telling another of his stories. "I was at the library, and this character comes up to me and says, 'Why don't you take a bath, you bum?' So I told him to go fuck off, and he gets all red in the face and says he'll have me arrested. The library ladies are all going, 'Shush, shush,' and I just looked at him and told him where to shove it, and he went stamping out to the phone. For all I know, he was going to call the fuzz; I sure didn't wait around to see. Christ! What creeps there are everywhere. Who asked him to stick his nose into whether I take a bath or not?" Frank glowers angrily, and I smile inwardly at one of the continual fringe benefits of working with him: his unconscious sense of humor. I imagine it was indeed the "character's" *nose* that tipped him off to Frank's not bathing, but Frank is not aware of the humor. I've tried before to get him to see it but without success.

"So what do you think about the incident, Frank?"

"So what's to think about it?" Angry sounding. "They ought to lock some of these square nuts up. He shouldn't be running around loose."

"Yeah, I know. But what about it for you?"

"What do you mean, what about it for me? I told you. I think the guy's off his rocker."

"So he's off his rocker. So what?"

"So he's a menace."

"Okay, he's a menace. So what? Who cares?"

"I sure as hell don't."

"You sure as hell must. You've just spent nearly fifteen minutes telling me all about this guy you say you don't care about."

"I'm just doing what you told me to do."

"What's that?"

"Tell you whatever comes into my mind. You said that's what I was supposed to do and now when I do it, you bawl me out. Honestly, I. . . . "

"Frank! For crying out loud, let's try to get this straight. I did not tell you to tell me whatever comes into your mind. There's far too much, and too much of it is apt to be trivia. I've said before, and now I'm saying it again, tell me what concerns you, what really matters to you in your life, and while you're doing so, throw in anything that comes along whether it seems related or not. But start out, at least, talking about something that seems to be important in your feelings."

"First time you ever said that."

"Okay, okay. Now it's said. What do you feel concern about in your life right now?"

"Well, why do you always sound so much like you're just barely able to put up with me?" Whammo! I deserve it too.

"Frank, you've got me. It's a combination of things, some in you and some in me. The odd part is, I really like and enjoy you, but somehow I do come off at you in a continually chiding, exasperated way."

"I don't know why you say I do something to make you do that."

"It's happening right now, Frank. I feel cautious, like if I'm not careful how I answer that we'll get to wrangling over words, and the hour will be all used up."

"Oh, hell, I don't mean to lay a heavy trip on you. I just feel so lousy, and I have to work at such a stinking job all the time, and I get kind of all fucked up in my skull, you know, and then everybody I see just pisses me off. And so I get to thinking, 'What the hell! I'm not going to just let them kick me around.' And so I start fucking them over before they do it to me, and pretty soon I'm in here doing the same thing to you. It's nothing personal, you know."

"That's sort of like being hit by a six-wheel truck and then having the driver rush back and pick you up and say, 'Nothing personal.' . . . Oh, hell, Frank, that's just not so. I think I got carried away by my simile. You dish it out, but you seldom do seem to make it personal to me."

"You tell me I hit you like a truck and then you tell me I don't. I don't know what you mean."

"Frank, you're not that stupid. You know, at least at some level, very well what I mean. You're just making points off me right now because I let my guard down for a minute."

"Now why would I want to do that?"

"Because you don't know what to do except gripe and attack."

"Where do you get off telling me I gripe and attack? Almost everything I say you find fault with."

"That's true, I'm afraid. I know I'm constantly counter-punching and playing your game. I guess it's that I feel challenged by you and have to rise to the bait, as well as my conviction that you have more to you than this shit you're always dishing out, and so I'm trying to get to that 'more.' "

"That's a hell of a way to get me to change it, by dishing it out to me."

"Yeah, maybe so. I really do get confused trying to keep straight and. . . . "

"So why blame me all the time because you get confused?"

"You really ask for it, Frank." Letting my voice drop down, slow down; must quit lunging back each time he says something. Come on, to myself, let's quit boxing.

"Now, how the hell do I ask for it? Why would I do that? Do you think I like going around being shat on all the time?" He's not having any, not meeting me.

"I can't imagine that you like it, Frank. I can imagine that something in you keeps needing to provoke other people. I don't even have to imagine that. I can see you doing it, right here with me, and I'm sure you do it with others."

"What's all that supposed to mean? Whenever you guys want to make a point but can't do it directly, you tell the sucker he's got some unconscious motivation. That way. . . . "

"Oh, shee-it, Frank. You're doing it right now. I answer one question for you and get sandbagged from another direction. You just want to fight about everything that comes along."

"It's always something I'm doing. Well, if you had to eat as much crap everyday as I do, you'd. . . . "

"Frank, you'd rather bellyache about life than do something about it." I know my voice sounds weary, and I don't care.

"I really feel bad when you say that." But his voice is more complaining than unhappy. "I thought I was supposed to tell you what I was feeling, and it's so lousy for me that. . . . "

"Yes, I know. I know because you've told me over and over again. I know because you tell me with so much satisfaction. And now you feel I've treated you unfairly because you've just been doing what I tell you to do."

"Well, I know you're supposed to be trying to help me, and I imagine you're tired." The pouting, mistreated tone still. "I don't know. I suppose I just never have much of interest to tell you. It's all pretty much the same, and I wake up every morning with this blue, crappy sense of foreboding, and then I bring it all in here and dump it on you, except I never really get rid of it, and. . . . "

My voice is gentler as I interrupt. "Frank, I don't want all this to get dismissed as just my tiredness or your sad, repetitive life. I am tired, and maybe that makes me bitch back at you more. I'll take responsibility for that. But it is also true that somehow you have become so invested in telling your story of how badly life treats you that you do it routinely and with a griping manner that turns people off or makes them angry. You don't like to look at that, but it's so, and I think some part of you knows it."

Frank looks thoughtful. He is a hunched man, of average height and weight. He has a certain air of tight anger, which at times makes him seem hostile and at other times conveys the miserable isolation that more genuinely characterizes his life. "I can't help it if I'm unhappy."

"You seem to feel that I've accused you of wrongdoing, and you have to defend yourself."

"Well, you sure sounded accusing to me," he counters. And of course, I did.

"I'm 'accusing' you—if you wish—of needing your unhappiness, of holding on to your misery."

"Why would I do that? I don't like being unhappy. It isn't any fun seeing other people having all the jollies while I'm all alone and just going around the same shitty treadmill all the time."

"Did you ever consider what it would be like not to feel miserable?" Pushing, insisting.

"It would be a great relief." Flatly.

"No, Frank, you're just talking from the top of your head. Let yourself feel into it: How would it be if you didn't feel unhappy, if you had no sad, lonely feeling?"

Frank is quiet for a minute and seems to be letting himself consider the idea. Then suddenly his face is intense, and he bursts out angrily, "If I ever gave up my misery, I'd never be happy again!"

Somehow I don't feel like laughing, even though the astonishing and paradoxical insight Frank has just voiced really startles me. His statement is literally true; it is exactly where Frank is trapped in his life. In a way I feel awed by his unthinking honesty and by the implicit trust that let him say it so plainly.[3]

August 23

"I was reading this character, Chard-in—or however the hell you pronounce it—and. . . . " Frank is annoyed, as usual. He glares at me as though I'd personally insulted him, and the impulse is strong to respond in kind. Gradually, ever so gradually, I'm teaching myself to see beyond the surly mask.

"I'm not sure who you mean, Frank." He pronounces the name with a harsh "chaw" and a sound like "guard-in."

"Aw, that French priest, you know. He wrote *The Phenomenon of Man.*"

I'll be damned! "You mean Teilhard de Chardin?"

"Yeah, that's the one. Lousy French names. Anyway, I was reading his stuff on how he thinks a new man is going to develop, and. . . . You know, his theory?"

I'm stunned. I know Frank reads a lot, but somehow I

didn't realize that he reads profound things like this. "Yes, in a general way, Frank. I haven't read much of Teilhard, though." Had to show off that I knew the author is usually called by his given name, didn't I? I think I'm miffed that Frank, who got his high school diploma while he was in the army, seems to have read more than I have of this author whom I value.

"Well, anyway, I think he's full of crap. I mean it's a real pretty picture that man is evolving—you know, that evolution is working toward making a better species. But I just don't buy it. I think most people stink, and as far as I can see they're getting worse—not better. I suppose being a priest and all he's supposed to think God is making things better, but it sure don't look that way to me. Besides that though, I really dig his ideas about 'convergence' and 'divergence.' I mean, as I look at it, that's really the way things happen. Take the whole reactionary crap that's going on in this country right now. . . . "

And so Frank spins on. I don't know whether to stop him and get him back on himself more explicitly, or not. I think he's implicitly saying much more than he realizes about his hunger for ideas, for sharing thoughts, for wanting to know, and for wanting my approval. He's such a completely lonely guy that he probably has no one else he can talk with this way, and besides, I'm pretty sure this is a kind of peace offering, a demonstration that he can do something besides gripe and that he can deal with the kinds of ideas he thinks I am interested in. I'll ride along with it for a bit. He really has understood what he has read; in fact, he makes me resolve to do some more reading in Teilhard myself.

After awhile, Frank pauses. He has gotten caught up in his talk, and now he is suddenly self-conscious about his involvement. "Oh shit, I don't know why I'm wasting my time on this crap anyway. It's just a kind of intellectual jacking off. I just don't see anybody but creeps who think *Captain Marvel* is the highest form of literature, and. . . . "

"I really was interested in what you were saying, Frank."

"Yeah, great, but I don't come here and pay you to be interested in my blatting about a lot of stuff that doesn't make any difference in my life anyway."

"I don't think that's so."

"What do you mean? What the hell difference does it make on my lousy job whether I dig this screwy French priest's ideas about the future of human beings?"

"I think it would make a big difference in your life if you never read any such stuff."

"Yeah? I dunno. I might be better off if I just threw it all in the can and flushed it."

"You just want to fight me now because you're uncomfortable about getting wound up in those ideas."

"What's wrong with getting wound up in them?"

"You really need to kick up a dust now, eh?"

"I don't know what you mean by 'kick up a dust.' How come you're always telling me I'm doing something wrong?"

"Frank, I just don't want to get caught up in one of your— our—merry-go-rounds. I think at some level you know damn well you're just trying to divert our attention, and I also think we need to get beyond that crap."

"I don't know what all this 'at some level' stuff is, where I'm supposed to know that you're always right and I'm always wrong."

"You don't stop do you?"

"Stop what?"

And so it goes. He won't concede anything right now.

I won't press him. Today he's come out of his hermit's cave a long way. He's risked showing me something that really matters to him. He's risked being ridiculed or patronized as he ventures into a realm more within my competence than his. He's ventured to relate to me in other than an angry, defensive way. Of course, he needs to move slowly, cautiously, and to pull back in after a time.

October 3

"I'm working the shit shift now. Go on at eleven P.M., and go off at seven A.M. Most of the time, there's just me and the night clerk and the night engineer, and do we get the weirdos! I mean like last night. About eleven-thirty this old bag—and I mean she looked plenty hard up—came in and saw me sitting at the bell captain's desk reading. She comes up to me very polite, you know, and she says, 'Could I sit down in one of those chairs for a little while, sir?' She calls me *sir,* for crying out loud! So I don't pay too much attention because I'm busy reading, and I just say sure, be my guest. First thing I know, old shit-head Berman, the night clerk, dings his goddam bell. I put down my book and go over to the desk. 'Who's that old woman?' he says. 'Beats me,' I tell him. 'She's dirty, and her clothes are all wet, and she'll get the furniture messed up,' he says. So he has me go over and ask her if she is connected with anyone in the hotel, and of course she isn't, and then he tells me to tell her to get out. 'Christ's sake, it's raining like crazy outside,' I tell him. But he says get her a cab if she wants. Well, she doesn't want a cab. It's pretty plain she hasn't any bread. So I tell her I'm sorry but the boss says she's gotta go, and she says that's okay and thanks me. Imagine that, she thanks me."

"Sounds like something out of Dickens."

"Yeah, I guess so. I haven't read much of that stuff though."

"How'd you feel about it?"

"Oh, hell, it's no skin off my nose. Anyway, after a while, maybe about one-thirty, I'm all alone in the lobby while Berman goes for a break to jerk off or whatever the hell he does, and suddenly I see this face at one of the windows. Damned if it isn't the old dame again. I pretend not to see her, and she goes down around the corner toward the side entrance, and I figure, 'What the hell?' I beat it over to the side entrance and catch her as she's going by and tell her to come on in. Then I take her down to the furnace room and tell old Foley, the night engineer, to let her dry out and rest awhile. He says sure and gives her a cup of his awful coffee. Then I beat it back upstairs, but shit-head is already there. He wants to know where I've been, and I tell him I had to take a crap. He says he didn't see me in the employee john, and I say I went downstairs instead. So he mouths off about how I better stay out of the guest restrooms. Anyway, I guess Foley got the old dame out all right, because I didn't see her again."

"Why did you do it?"

"Do what?"

"Come on, Frank, let's use this and not play our sparring game."

"What 'sparring game'? I don't know what you mean."

"God damn it, Frank." Really mad and not caring if he knows it. "You're so stupid-ass set on not meeting me that you keep throwing away opportunities to work on the very worries that made you come in here in the first place."

"I don't see why you're mad at me just because I can't understand what you say."

"Wait, Frank. Let's both make an effort to understand each other this time. I know I jump you, but can you risk admitting that you keep dodging away from understanding me too?" Urgently, steadily, careful with the closeness. Frank absolutely needs to avoid getting drawn into a real relation with me, but he also hungers for it.

"I don't want to misunderstand you. I'd be a damn fool to. . . . "

"No, Frank, I don't think you consciously want to misunderstand me. But I do think you feel a need to keep a distance between us, and when I appeal to you to work with me, you get edgy." He's not fighting me as hard as sometimes. Come on, Jim, recognize that he's trying in his way; hear him.

"How do you mean 'edgy?' I mean, I kind of get your idea, but I'm not quite sure how you mean."

A big step! He started to use his old quibble about words but diluted it. "Well, maybe that's not quite the word. I get the feeling that when I try to be with you, it makes you uneasy, and then you need to pull away a bit."

"Yeah, maybe. I don't know. What did you mean when you said I was throwing away opportunities?"

He's really trying to meet me now. "I've forgotten just how I said it, Frank. I think I was trying to say that there's something more we could learn from a story like the one you just told me about the old lady. When we bicker with each other we lose that chance."

"What do you mean 'the story I told you?' I didn't make that up, you know."

Easy, easy. He's got to pull back some. "Yes, I know it's real. I didn't mean to question it. Frank, I think my asking you to work with me, even though that's what one part of you wants, really bugs you in another way. Can you tune in to that?"

"Yeah, well, I guess so." Pause. "How could we use the scene with the old lady? I don't see what's important about that."

Which way to go now? I'd like to stay with his dawning recognition that he needs to resist, but I don't want to seem to corner him. He'd have to pull out fast if he felt I was zeroing in on him. "I don't know for sure. Why don't you just free associate to that experience and see what it brings to your mind?"

"I thought you didn't go for this free association crap. You told me I shouldn't just say anything that came up in my thoughts." Wow! He can't resist a chance to try to catch me.

"You really find it hard to stay with simply talking with me. It seems like you just have to score a point whenever you see an opening."

"There you go accusing me again."

"Frank, I really don't want to get into that hassle with you now. The main thing was I could suddenly see how hard it is for you to risk being close with someone. It seems to get rough for you even to stay with a person on the same topic for a short while. I guess I had a glimpse of the tough battle you must be fighting inside all the time." Warmly, but without patronizing or effusing.

He is silent a minute; a rare thing in itself. Will he risk acknowledging my understanding? He looks stonily straight ahead, not at me but at the wall. "Shit, I guess that's just the crutch I have to bear."

I'm thunderstruck. Did he say it? Did he hear himself? "What did you say, Frank?"

"I said I guess I'm just stuck with it. Why?"

"No, the actual words. Did you . . . do you remember what you said?"

"What is this? For crying out loud, you get off on the screwiest things. Sure I know what I said. I said it was the cross I had to bear. You've heard that before."

"You said, 'That's the crutch I have to bear.' That's a marvelous rephrasing of the old saying, Frank."

"Naw, I didn't say that. What the hell would that mean?"

"What would it mean to you?"

"Beats the shit out of me. I suppose you're making some big thing about my using it as a crutch."

"What's 'it'?"

"Now you're playing with words. How come it's bad when I do it, but okay for you?" So he's not having any. Well, he risked a lot, and then his unconscious sent this message. Can't do it all in one day.

And the rest of the hour is a continuation of the same old struggle.

October 5

At our next session, I'm encouraged that we made real progress the previous time. After his usual morose entry, Frank himself brings up our prior conversation.

"Last time you said I threw away my opportunities here, and when I asked you what you meant, you said something about there being more in that deal with the old lady than I had said. Well, I thought about it, and I went over the whole thing, and I can't find anything more." Slowly, Bugental; as usual he's saying you were wrong, but he's also saying he heard you and tried to use what you said. Don't get caught in his defensive ploys.

"It didn't seem to have anything else in it that you could see, huh?"

"No, I mean I sort of went through the whole thing again in my mind, and I think I told you everything that was important about it, and I can't see any dramatic lessons to learn in it or anything." His talk is different—less profane, more substance. He's still putting bait out for me: that bit about "dramatic lessons" is strictly to get us off. Underneath, he must be really terrified of closeness.

"Well, maybe so. Now looking back on the whole thing with the old lady, what do you think was working in you to make you do what you did?" Is that too much? It's awkwardly phrased; I'm so anxious not to crowd him into flight.

"How do you mean, 'back on the whole thing'?" He's cautious too, but he's not pulling out yet.

"Just however it seems to you, Frank, that you decided to do what you did with the old lady."

"Aw, shit, it was raining buckets outside, and that fag, Berman, gives me a pain in the ass anyway. So I figure, what can it hurt to let the old bag dry off and get warm. I don't know why you want to make such a big deal out of it."

"Seems pretty matter of fact, eh?"

"Yeah, sure. Why? Do you see something else? I mean if you see some of those big opportunities you talk about, let's hear them." This man is like a person who has been burned all over. However I try to touch him in order to help him, it hurts, and the pain makes him pull away.

"No, I don't see anything big right now."

"Well, do you see anything more than I said?" Hmmm. That feels different. He's coming out toward me a bit.

"Not really, Frank. I guess the biggest thing I'm aware of is that you risked something for a complete stranger."

"Aw shit! What risk is that? The fucking job is a stink anyway. They can shove it up Berman any time for all I care."

"I think it makes you angry if I suggest you have any kind motives."

"What 'kind motives'? I don't give a damn for that old bag. For crying out loud, you're making a huge big deal out of piss-poor nothing."

"Wow! You sure need to turn on a lot of power to deny that rather mild hunch of mine."

"Look, just don't get the idea I give a damn for some dumb old dame or anything like that."

"That seems very important to you."

"Yeah, well . . . well, I think you better not get some screwed up idea of my motives if you're going to be any help to me."

"Okay, so the message is: Frank has no kind motives toward old dames. Is that it?" Uh-uh. Too much sarcasm. Shouldn't yield to the temptation. He really knows how to get to me.

"You're deliberately twisting what I said. That isn't the message, and you know it. I can have kind motives where it means something. Why the. . . . "

"You're right, Frank." Interrupting, urgently. "You're right. I did twist your meaning. I'm sorry. I think you just got to me a bit, and I hit back."

"Oh, shit, it's okay. Don't make a big deal out of it."

"Maybe you understand about. . . . No, I don't want to

do it that way. Frank, try to hear this, please: I started to make a parallel between the way I needed to twist your words a few minutes ago and the way, it seems to me, you need to twist mine at times. I started to do it in a subtle way that would have been kind of a dig. I don't want to do that. We've both done that too much, and I think we both would like to use our time more to work on the problems that are deeper for you. Can you dig what I'm saying, Frank?"

"Yeah, yeah, I get it." Pause. "You know I hate it when you get so intense and emotional. Why can't you just say things straight?"

"For a minute we met just then, but I think it was too much for you, and you had to find something to complain about to push me away."

"No, I just don't like all the melodrama that you seem to go in for."

"I feel kind of stung right now, and one part of me wants to hit back at you or to defend myself. Another part says, 'Frank needs to see melodrama in anything that involves emotional closeness.' "

"Why would I do that? I just don't like being talked to in big. . . . "

"Wait, Frank! Let me answer your question. I think you do need to push away any emotional sharing because you don't know much about it except in terms of hurt. The little I know about your early days says that you didn't get anything but hurt from your parents or your brothers and sisters. I guess I shouldn't say 'didn't get anything but hurt.' I don't know about that, but you've never told me much except for some of the hurtful times."

"I had some good things with my older sister, the one who kind of took care of me after my mother was put in the hospital."

"Will you tell me more about that? I really don't know much about how it was for you as a kid."

"Shitty, that's how. But there were some times. . . . "

Slowly, Frank begins to risk letting me know him. For several months we gradually move toward working together. Our main focus is on Frank's childhood, and it proves increasingly possible for him to tolerate a working together that is centered on the past. He seldom permits any show of present emotion, and I am careful not to crowd him. We are slowly building an alliance which we will need sorely when we finally come to deal with his current stresses and his anxiety about relating. Frank tells me of a trauma-ridden childhood, of repeated instances of feeling betrayed and abandoned by his parents, of his sense of desperation and futility. Concurrently, I come to appreciate the sheer guts of this man, who somehow keeps alive a small flame of hope, who reads endlessly, and ponders all alone on philosophy and psychology and ethics and religion. He has six college units earned in one burst of determination for self-improvement, a burst that abruptly ended when he realized that at his rate of progress it would take him nearly ten years to earn a bachelor's degree, and his goal was a doctorate. But still he reads, and barely understands, and reads and half understands, and reads and begins to think.

January 8

Frank enters with anger flowing off of him in waves like radiations from a hot engine. He drops in the big chair, stares bitterly at his usual spot on the wall.

"Well, I'm fucked! I mean but good. God damned self-righteous bastards! Shit! Shit! I don't know how I can keep coming here either. You're just as greedy for money as anybody else. I can hear you saying, 'Well, Frank, old boy, I'm sorry, but that's the way the cookie crumbles.' What the hell's it matter anyway? I don't think we're getting anywhere anyway. Oh, God damn it! I can't see. . . . "

"Hey, how's about filling me in?"

"I'm fired, canned, have been given the good old sack, am out on my ass, am informed that the great Cosmopolitan Hotel can stagger along without my services."

"How come?"

"Awghh! It makes me sick. Because Berman is a prick, that's how come. Because Gamble, the resident manager, is an even bigger prick, that's how come. Because. . . . "

"What happened?"

"Last night, about midnight, this guy and his gal check in, see. They only have one suitcase, and it isn't so heavy. I figure they just want to shack up. Nothing new about that. Except the doll is really something. I mean she is stacked. In the elevator, she takes off her raincoat, and all she had on was this thin dress, and I mean 'all.' And what she had was pure stuff, the real stuff, you know what I mean. I drooled seeing that dude take her into that room. He was one of those shirt-ad types, all good clean young American middle-class creep. They're both high on something, giggling, sneaking little touches, not giving a damn about me. So the big playboy gives me a lousy two-dollar tip and tells me to get lost, and he's reaching for her before I'm out the door, and she's dancing away and giggling.

"Well I went down to the bellman's station, and I couldn't read or anything, thinking about them up there balling. And it's been weeks since I had a piece. After about an hour, I get a call from their room to bring up some ice. So I take them up a bucket, and the dude is wearing a bathtowel and I can't catch a glimpse of the girl because he's in my way, not letting me in the door. I really wanted to see what she looked like without that dress, let me tell you.

"I go back down to my station, and nothing's happening for maybe another forty-five minutes or an hour. Then the elevator opens and the guy comes out, his clothes half on and his face in kind of a creepy daze. He's about as spaced out as anybody I ever saw. He gets across the lobby and goes out the door. I wonder if I ought to go after him or what. Berman, as usual, isn't at the desk.

"Then I get to thinking about that dame upstairs. First I'm thinking there she is all alone in that bed, and then suddenly I'm wondering if that creep did anything to her. I mean, he is so spaced he could have carved her up or something and never known it. The more I think about it, the more I get worked up, half wanting to go up in the hope I'll see some more of her without the dude there and half afraid what I'll find if I do go up.

"I think of waiting for Berman to come back and getting him to go, but the hell with him. If she's okay, I'd like to see her myself. I think of calling her room, but what good's that? So finally I just go up myself.

"I knock on her door, and there's no answer. I start to get kind of shaky, and knock again. Maybe I ought to get the pass key. Hell, no, I don't want to have to explain what I'm doing there if she's messed up. I knock again, and suddenly the door opens. There she is, standing there looking at me, leaning against the door because she's pretty near out herself, and she's mother-ass naked. Everything she advertised in the elevator is absolutely true. I mean she's got a body that doesn't quit. I guess I just stand there kind of dumb, staring at her. After a minute she pulls back, unsteady on those beautiful legs, and says to come on in.

"So I go in, and she kind of falls on the bed and looks at me but her eyes don't focus too good. Well, anyway, one thing leads to another, and pretty soon I'm as naked as she is and on the bed with her. I mean she was something. She kind of locked herself around me, and I didn't know stuff could be that good. Then just when everything is going great, the dude walks in! Christ! What a time for him to come back! The girl doesn't see him at first, but I do. He just stands there looking at us, and then he starts laughing. He laughs like he's going to bust, and I wish he would. Then the girl comes to and sees what's happening and tells me to get up. I do, and the dude tells me to grab my clothes and haul ass out of that room right now. I think about cold-conking him, but he doesn't look so spaced out now, and besides, it's hard to brawl with a fully dressed guy when you're bare ass. So I leave and get dressed in the hall.

"I don't know what the dude said to Berman on the phone, but when I get downstairs, there's old shit-head himself all drawn up like God Almighty. 'Get out of that uniform, and get out of this hotel,' he says. 'Your check will be mailed to you, but don't ever come back in here.' So I start to tell him what he could do with his crummy job, and he says he'll give me ten minutes to be out of the building, or he'll have the cops come for me. So that does it, and I haven't any job, and what the fuck do I care anyway."

"Wow, Frank! You had quite a night!"

For just a moment a smile flashes across his normally sullen features. Then he grunts. "Yeah, I guess so. But now what the hell am I going to do? You're going to want me to pay you, and I haven't any rich old aunt to bail me out, and jobs are hard to come by, and besides I'm tired of the shit-ass jobs that mostly I get."

"Frank, you've referred to my wanting to be paid several times. Let me be straight with you. Yes, I do want to be paid. Also,

I don't have the reserves to be able to carry much of an unpaid balance from you or anyone. So. . . . "

"Okay, already. I said I knew you wanted to be paid. Don't get up-tight and give me the big lecture."

"Keep your shirt on, Frank. Hmphh! . . . It just struck me that you had it off once too often last night. . . . "

"Very funny!" But he chuckles too. I think he's secretly delighted with his adventure.

"Anyway, what I wanted to say was, if you need to get behind some for a month or so, that would be okay, but I doubt that I could continue much beyond that. After you see what the situation is, fill me in, and we'll work out some clear plan so we'll both know where we are."

"Yeah, sure. Uh . . . hell, I should be able to find something anyway, so don't sweat it, huh? Besides I'll have unemployment coming in for a while."

"Right."

For nearly three months Frank looks for work in a desultory fashion. He alternates between fury with the whole employment system and all potential employers and dejection verging toward suicidal depression. He draws some unemployment compensation, and with it he manages to pay at least half of his account with me and to keep his dingy room. Eating regularly is a problem for him, and at times he goes to the midnight mission in the tenderloin district. Several times I think—although he never actually says so—that he steals food from supermarkets.

Meantime, we reduce the frequency of his interviews and decide that he will enter a therapy group.

January 9

When Frank enters the group, Hal takes one look at him, and his face locks into a grim expression that is the complement to Frank's own surly, defiant visage. It's hard to judge differences accurately when it comes to being ill-kempt or sloppy, but my impression is that Frank has chosen to do even less than usual to make himself "presentable" by usual social standards. Indeed, knowing

Frank, I probably should phrase that the other way around: I imagine Frank has done more than usual to announce by his appearance that he doesn't give a damn what anybody thinks about him—which is to say he cares so much that he can't risk being seen to care at all.

If Frank notices Hal's reaction, he gives no obvious cue. He nods rather curtly in response to introductions, and with evident difficulty, says his own name. Then he pulls his chair back a bit from the group's circle and slouches in it with elaborate casualness. As the group begins talking, he follows the conversational flow with apparent intensity of attention, turning his head continually to stare at each person who speaks. Somehow I feel as though he's putting on a performance rather than actually listening. I suspect Frank is so panicky inside that he can scarcely hear clearly, and I resolve not to press him unless he shows some signs of being ready to be helped into more active participation.

After forty minutes or so, there's a pause, and then Louise speaks directly to Frank for the first time.

Louise: "Have you been in therapy long, Frank?"

Frank: "No; I mean yes. I. . . . What the fuck's long? I started about a year ago. Why, what's it to you?"

Louise: "Oh, nothing, just curious. I've been coming about a year and a half."

Laurence: "You sounded pretty mad at her, Frank. Were you?"

Frank: Troubled, angry, frightened. "No, why should I be? Anyway, why make a federal case out of everything? Christ!"

Laurence: "Now you sound mad at me."

Frank looks off into a distant corner of the room, his face portraying bafflement at these strange creatures with whom he finds himself. Hal is watching him so intently his eyes seem to be riveted on Frank. There is a moment's awkward pause.

Ben: "You just sound pretty snotty to me."

Frank whirls to look at the other man: "Who asked you?"

Ben: "No one has to ask me. I just think you're a sour ball to anyone who talks to you, so I might as well get on your shit list right away."

Frank: "Big deal." His eyes go back to the distant corner.

Kate: "Frank, you do seem awfully angry at everyone. Is there some reason for that? I'm often angry myself, so I kind of feel sympathy for anyone who has those feelings."

Frank: "Who needs your pity?"

Ben: "Hey, you forgot to cuss her, tough guy."

Frank (to no one in particular): "What a creep!"

Laurence: "We all seem to make you mad, don't we?"

Ben: "He's just a ball of anger, that boy."

Louise: "Ben, why do you pick on him so much? What's he done to you?"

Ben: "Aw, Louise, you're just a bleeding heart. Can't you see he's a flower child who doesn't believe in washing or working or being reasonably civilized with other people? I know his type. He just gripes and collects unemployment checks the rest of us have to pay for."

Frank turns to look at Ben, obviously sizing him up. I have a hunch he's being goaded toward some kind of showdown, and I'm about to intervene when Hal, who has said nothing at all to this point, bursts out.

Hal: "For crying out loud! Ben, and the rest of you! Can't you see that this guy's scared stiff? Weren't we all scared the first time we were in the group? Why do we have to demand that he play our game right away? Ben, you were at least as scared as Frank the first time you were in this room, and I remember it."

I'm flabbergasted. I thought Hal was going to join in the attack, seeing in Frank the things that drive him crazy with his own son. Instead, he seems to have recognized the scared kid under the blustery exterior. The effect on the group is instantaneous.

Louise: "You're right, Hal. Frank, I'm sorry we were needling you."

Frank: "Yeah, well, you didn't. And besides, hell. . . . "

Ben: "Okay, so he's scared. So were we all. But we didn't talk so foulmouthed to everybody. Look, Frank, I don't like people who don't wash and who talk the way you do all the time. I won't pretend I do, but I'll admit that I came off pretty sudden on you."

Frank: "Don't do me any favors, you jerk."

Ben: "Watch it, buster, I don't take cute talk from punks."

Hal: "Stop it, you guys. Look, Frank, I know you're scared

but try to idle back on the cracks, will you? And you, Ben, we're here to try to use the group to deal with our hang-ups—not to act them out. If the two of you punch each other around, you'll only prevent yourselves and us from using the group for the reason we're here. Now talk all you want but quit acting like a couple of twelve year olds playing chicken with each other."

Hal's good sense—plus, probably, his size—seems to persuade Ben and Frank to cool their antagonism. Both make pro forma growls, but they readily let others in the group take over the conversation. I speculate to myself whether some more direct working-through of the hostility would have been more helpful and decide Frank just isn't ready for that yet. Ben is so judgmental that he needs help in recognizing the self-deception hidden in his self-righteousness, but now is not the time for that either. I feel a combination of chagrin at the neat way Hal handled the situation without any need of my intervention and relief that I didn't have to move in authoritatively. For the therapist to do so nearly always means that the group overgeneralizes about his intent, with the result that members are hesitant to confront each other for some time after.

February 2

Frank's fourth group session is the first in which he takes any real part in the discussion.

Laurence: "Frank, you haven't said very much since you've been with us. In fact I know almost nothing about you."

Louise: "Yes, that's right. I've been watching you, and I realize I don't have much of an idea what goes on in you. I get kind of shy and self-conscious the way you look at me—at us—but I can't decide whether you think we're freaks or what."

Frank: "Aw no, I don't think that. . . . I mean, I just don't have anything to say. I just kind of listen, you know. It's all kind of new to me, see, and when I. . . . " He stops, uncomfortable, not knowing what to say.

Laurence: "Frank, I wasn't trying to put pressure on you. I just would like to know more about you—if you want to say something, that is."

Frank: "Yeah, I dig. What do you want to know?" Surly tone.

Kate: "You sound like you're angry with Laurence."

Frank: "Hell, why should I be angry with him?"

Kate: "I don't know, but now it sounds like you're angry with me. Are you?"

Frank: "Oh, for Christ's sake, you keep pushing me, and, of course, I get teed off. Aw, I'm sorry, I shouldn't have said that."

Louise: "You don't have to apologize if you feel that way. I don't think Kate meant to push you though."

Kate: "Don't worry about it. I know how it is to be angry inside and to have it spill out all the time."

Frank: "I just feel lousy all the time, and I probably shouldn't even try to be with people and. . . . " Again he runs out of words, embarrassed by his self-disclosure.

Jennifer: "How do you mean, you feel lousy—physically or emotionally?"

Frank: "Uh, I dunno. . . . Both, I guess. Why?"

Jennifer: "I just wondered."

I feel a heightened alertness as I listen to Frank take his first hesitant, stumbling steps toward relating to others without relying on his anger to shield himself. I know I have to watch a tendency to be overprotective at this point, but he seems so vulnerable—that he could easily be frightened back into rejecting all possibility of being with people in any mutual way.

February 27

In his individual session Frank is busy with talk about a job interview he went to which involved a long trip across town and which turned out to be a disappointment. He is angry, bitter, and very distant from me. Yet he seems to be prolonging his account of this experience.

"Frank, I have the feeling you've said most of what you've wanted to say about that phony job, but that somehow you can't leave it and get onto anything else."

"What else is there?"

"I don't know, Frank, What else concerns you in your life right now? Other job prospects, the group, what you do with your time. . . . You pick it up wherever you think we can. . . . "

"Aw that group! I don't know what's the matter with those creeps. They're always on me. Always sweating it about me being mad at them. What kind of good is that supposed to do me? What do you think I am going to get out of that? Shit, I don't need any more people riding my ass."

"What's bugging you, Frank? The group doesn't get on you all that much."

"Yeah, well take that Laurence, he's a windy old creep who is always asking his nosy questions. 'Frank, I don't know anything about you.'" Mocking voice. "What business is it of his, anyway?"

"Maybe he'd simply like to get to know you a bit."

"Aw shit, that kind of bleeding-heart interest I can do without."

"You're determined to see it as an unpleasant intrusion, I see."

"And then there's that old dame, what's her name. You know the one who's always telling me how she's angry a lot just like me. So who asked her? Anyhow, I don't see her being so angry. And all the rest of them too. What am I supposed to get out of being in that kind of group anyway?"

"Is there anyone in the group you like or even feel a little bit positive about, Frank?"

"Oh sure, I mean, they're all kind of creepy, but then for a bunch of nuts who have to come to a shrink they're not so bad."

"It really bugs you when I ask about any positive feelings, doesn't it?"

"No, it doesn't bug me. What the hell? I have positive feelings sometimes just like anybody else. What do you think I am? You get the damnedest ideas sometimes. Why don't you. . . . "

"Okay, okay, Frank. So who do you feel any positive feelings for in that group?"

"Oh, they're all right. I mean, they're . . . uh . . . okay, you know. Except that smart-ass Ben. But the rest of them are . . . I mean, I guess any of them. . . . Uh. . . . Why? What does it matter?"

"Frank, I don't want to make you uncomfortable unnecessarily, because I know you're really trying to work with me now, but it really would be useful if you'd try to explore any positive feelings about the people in the group and see what comes into your thoughts as you do so."

"Yeah, yeah. Don't make a big deal about it. Well, uh. . . . Well, Hal—is that his name, the big beefy jock?"

"Uh-huh." *He can't even risk letting himself remember their names. Or maybe he can't risk my knowing they make enough of an impression on him so that he knows their names.*

"Yeah, well, he's a pretty good guy. Yeah, uh . . . and Louise, she's a. . . . I mean she . . . I guess she kind of reminds me of my older sister a little bit."

"The one who took care of you."

"Yeah, that one. And uh. . . . Well, I feel kind of sorry for the scared one. What's her name, Ginny?"

"Jennifer?"

"Yeah, that one. I mean, she seems so knocked out. I mean, don't get any wrong ideas or anything, but she. . . . Well, she. . . . Oh shit!"

"What's going on, Frank?"

"Oh Christ, I just know you're going to make a big fucking deal out of it if I say what I think about her."

"So you can't have your own feelings because of how I might react, eh?"

"Naw, I got my feelings, but you get so dramatic about everything. . . . "

"You are very anxious for me not to make very much out of how you feel about Jennifer, is that it?"

"Yeah."

"Okay, so how do you feel about her?"

"Well, I . . . I don't know. I mean, I think she's really kind of different or special or something. I mean, if she weren't married and all, I might. . . . Oh, shit, forget it. I like her. That's all."

"But that makes you very uncomfortable."

"No. It's just that you always. . . . All right, I guess it does."

Slowly, slowly, I tell myself. Frank has taken a big risk and trusted me a long way. He really expects that I'm going to laugh at him or criticize him or explain why he shouldn't have his feelings. That's been his whole history.

The hour ends shortly, and we don't deal further with his feelings about Jennifer, but it's clear that under the kind of rough way he pushes away her interest in him, Frank is hiding a strong response to her. And his letting himself have that response is another big risk he's taking.

April 24

On this day when I go to the waiting room in response to Frank's ring, I almost fail to recognize him. He is clean, neatly dressed in somewhat worn slacks and sweater, shoes not exactly shined but certainly cleaned, hair and beard trimmed to very presentable proportions. And he is very self-conscious. Neither of us says anything until he is seated in the office.

Frank lights a cigarette with undue concentration, making quite a business of getting it right and arranging an ashtray on the arm of his chair. Then he fixes his familiar spot on the opposite wall with a ferocious glare. I wait quietly. He stirs, draws deeply on the cigarette, busily taps the ash off, examines the burning end, draws on it again, taps it again.

"Shit!" What a wonderful word that is, capable of so many nuances. It is amazing how long we suppressed such a facile verbal instrument. Now, in a single syllable, Frank has conveyed intense feeling, exasperation with that feeling, and wanting me to break the silence.

"You look very different, Frank, but you sound pretty much the same."

"Yeah. I got a job."

"Good. At least I guess it is. Is it?"

"I feel like a damned fool. You know that, don't you? I mean the clothes and hair and all. I don't know why, but I do. And it pisses me off. I hate feeling this way."

"It really is a miserable feeling to feel so self-conscious about breaking out of a mold."

"What do you mean, 'breaking out of a mold?' What mold?" Pause. "Oh, skip it, I know what you mean. Shee-yit! I feel like I want to start bickering like we used to do."

"Yeah, it would kind of keep us busy and. . . . "

"Same time, I'm tired of wasting my time and money on that crap. Look, I got a job. You'd never believe it. Remember that old creep at the Cosmopolitan Hotel, the one who was threatening to have me fired for something I said to him? Gandowsky. Yeah, Ephraim Gandowsky. Anyway, I ran into him in the cafeteria, and the old guy was real friendly. 'How are you? What you been doing?' All that kind of crap. At first I was suspicious of him, but by God, he was on the level. So pretty soon we're gabbing like a couple of old biddies, and he's filling me in on all the shit about the hotel. Seems Berman got promoted and Hicks—he was the bell captain— got fired, and a lot of other stuff like that. Fact is, it turns out, Gandowsky complained because I was fired. Imagine that! He'd heard the story of how I got caught screwing with that chick, and he was all turned on by it. Made me tell the whole thing, and he got so excited, I thought he was going to come right there in the cafeteria. He just laughed like crazy. Then he asked me what I was doing, and when I told him I was stony broke, he said he'd give me a job. Seems he runs a big printing business over on Kenmore. Said I had to clean up a bit though, so here I am. Shee-yit! What a screwy deal, huh?"

"Sounds pretty good to me."

"Yeah, I'm not knocking it. You know he's a pretty good old guy. Told me I had to keep my hands off the women in his place though. But you know, I never figured him to be that way. I mean, I never figured he'd give a guy like me any kind of a break. Don't know what's in it for him. Maybe he wants me to tell him sexy stories. Don't think he's queer. He didn't act like it anyway."

"It's hard for you to understand why anybody might like you or want to do something for you."

"Aw, I don't know. I just wonder. . . . Hell, skip it. I don't dig what his trip is anyway. He's all. . . . "

"You really get uncomfortable anytime there's a hint of any closeness or emotion in relation to you."

"Oh, for Christ's sake, you keep telling me that! It's all a lot of shit anyway. You know it. Everybody's really only out to get whatever he can; so don't come on like the Salvation Army."

"You'd feel a lot better about getting in a fight with me rather than dealing with this miserable feeling inside of yourself."

"What miserable feeling?"

"The one you'd be aware of if you didn't jump up and down and wave your arms to distract yourself."

"I don't know what you mean. You get these screwy ideas about. . . . "

"Frank, I'm starting to get caught into the old game, and so are you. I want to pull out of it, and I think a good part of you does too."

"Yeah, I don't want to waste my time on that shit anymore."

"Me neither."

"But, playing it straight, what miserable feeling do you mean?"

"Just wait a minute, Frank, and see what it's like in your guts right now. What do you feel right in the middle of you, apart from our bickering, apart from the details of your new job, apart from anything else. What do you feel in you right now?"

He pauses, sinks down in his chair, shoves his hands in his pockets so that his shoulders hunch up around his ears. Frank has come a long way; he's really trying to work with me now. Be patient, I tell myself; you should make as much of a change in your own hang-ups, Jim.

"Jim, I don't know. It's hard to get a hold of. Mostly I feel kind of like a bellyache; only it doesn't really seem like it's my belly or a real physical ache, and yet it is too. I mean, I think I feel bad, but I don't know why. Jesus Christ! I just got a job and at better pay than I got at the fucking hotel, why should I feel bad?"

"Wait, Frank. Don't get off on that for a minute. You really were in touch with your guts for a minute. Just stay with that, can you?"

Silence again. Then he looks up at me, and it's like the first time Frank and I have ever really looked at each other. His face is completely naked, all the surly, defensive look gone. "I am just so God damned lonely I could shit."[4]

May 1

Frank's next appointment is notable for two things. He keeps busy almost the entire hour without mentioning his loneliness or anything close to it, and in the closing minutes—actually as he's getting to his feet to leave—he lowers his mask briefly once again.

"Oh yeah, well. . . . Well, there's no time for it now, but. . . . "

"But?"

"Oh, I had a dream about Jenny. Not important. Just hot for her bod, I guess." He starts for the door.

"You sure want to dismiss this quickly."

"Yeah, well, I know you've got somebody waiting and. . . . "

"And so you don't have to deal with the dream."

"Yeah, well, it really wasn't much. Or anyway I can't remember much of it. I was just kind of holding her, and she was letting me, and she seemed to like it, and. . . . " He pauses, hand on doorknob. I know we must end the hour, but I sense there's much more going on in Frank, so I wait silently.

"Jim, I really dig that woman. You know that? If I thought I had half a chance. . . . Oh shit! Gotta go." And he slams out of the door before I can say anything.

Frank is moving toward the very feelings he has taught himself for most of his life to avoid—emotional involvement with others. He is also risking letting me know about it, and I am warmly moved by that.

May 9

Frank comes into the consultation room slowly, almost reluctantly, not meeting my eyes. I wonder if he thinks I'm going to be mad at him for taking Jennifer home and to bed with him last night. I remember how warmly she spoke of his tenderness during her interview a few hours ago, and how surprised I was to hear that he refused to have intercourse with her although they slept naked together. I feel a warmth and a strange kind of pride in this frightened, angry man and the big step he took last night, but I doubt that he could recognize or tolerate those feelings of mine right now. Maybe some day. . . .

Again that spot on the wall gets one of Frank's grim stares. He makes a slow business of getting settled, lighting a cigarette, fixing the ashtray, the whole routine. Then he opens his mouth to speak his favorite word.

"Shee-yit."

"Hmmm?"

"Shit. Shit! Shit! That's all. Just plain shit!" He's angry.

"Wow! You really sound mad as hell. What's going on?"

"I don't know what the hell I'm doing here. I don't know why the flying fuck I ever came here in the first place. I don't think I've got a brain in my whole goddamn head, or I'd get the hell out right now."

I wait. Whatever's cooking with Frank is much deeper and more intense than anything I was expecting. He's hurting, and he's hurting deeply, but I haven't any idea why. So I wait.

"Ohhh, hell! Jim! Why didn't you tell me a long time ago to go back where I belong? What am I doing here? What am I doing with people like you and Hal and Louise and Laurence and. . . ?"

"And Jennifer?"

"All right, goddamn it, yes, and Jennifer. Poor Jenny! Jesus H. Christ, she hurts so damned much inside. Do you know how much she hurts? Oh, of course you do, but holy hell, what a double bitching life this is, isn't it? Poor Jenny! She told you, huh? Jim, I couldn't let her be alone. She was half out of her skull last night, believe me. I was scared for her. I just had to keep with her. I suppose you think it was shitty, huh?"

"What was shitty, Frank?"

"My taking her home and to bed. She told you, didn't she?"

"She told me. And she told me you wouldn't have intercourse with her and that you were very, very kind to her and really took care of her. Is that what I'm supposed to think was shitty?"

"Oh, Christ! What do you think I am? I couldn't fuck her with her all torn up like that. That would be like screwing a baby or something."

"It seems hard for you to accept that you acted in a really caring and helpful way."

"Oh, that's all crap, and you know it. I'd love to screw Jenny, and I may just do it. I just didn't think I wanted to last night."

"To quote you, 'shee-yit!' "

"You don't know how to say it right. I'll bet you never said 'shit' until recently."

"Frank, I think you're a very neat guy for what you gave Jennifer last night. Will you please hear that and quit the smokescreen?"

"What do you mean 'smokescreen'?"

"Uh-uh, we don't want to go back to that. We've left that behind."

"Yeah, you're right. But you know damn well it makes me uncomfortable when you say things like that; so how come you do it?"

"Like what?"

"Now you're playing that game."

"You're right. Okay, so I do know it makes you uncomfortable for people to see you as warm and caring, but Frank, I think it's time we dealt with that discomfort so you can get on with your life. I don't think you have to be hung up anymore—or at least not to the same extent—on the myth of being a tough guy who doesn't have feelings and doesn't need or care for anybody."

"Not so fast, Jim." He's really scared. His voice is as husky as though I'd pushed him to the edge of a precipice, as I guess I really have.

"Yeah, I hear you."

"Jim, for a minute I really could hear you then, all the way down to my feet. And you're right, but it scares the very shit out of me. Oh God, Jim, I'm really scared. I want to just run the hell out of here and just keep going and never stop. I want to forget all about what we've talked about and about all of the people in the group and especially about Jennifer." His voice trails off.

The hour is one of those magical times that can happen on occasion with some people and never happen at all with others, a time when a person finds himself open within and can know what he usually veils from himself, a time when I am trusted into the most private self of another, a sacred time. Toward the end of the hour, Frank surfaces.

"Jenny wanted to see me tonight. I told her I had to work. I don't, but I'm scared to see her."

"What scares you, Frank?"

"I'm scared for her. She really wants to go back to her husband, and if she gets hung up on me, she'll never forgive herself enough to make it with him."

"I see what you mean."

"So I guess I just won't call her or anything."

"But you'd like to."

"Yeah. Yes, I would."

"And that's the second thing that scares you."

"Yes, it is."

We sit silently for a minute, looking at the reality of Jennifer's and Frank's feelings, looking at the inevitability of his letting her go.

July 29

This day stands out for it is the first time I have seen Frank in a new suit, clean shaven, and taking a self-conscious pride in his appearance. He has been promoted at work, he says, and he has to live up to the new responsibility. I feel a moment's misgiving. Have I helped Frank become a neat cog in the materialistic machine? But he has news for me.

"I talked to old Mr. Gandowsky and told him I'd take this job for one year. He's going to pay me just as much as if I were permanent, but I'm going to live on about half of it and bank the rest. Then in September next year, I'm going to start back to college. Gandowsky says if I do a good job in this year, I can work half-time for him and that way I can keep going. I'm gonna go all the way, Jim."

"Frank, that really sounds great."

"Yeah. There's one thing more." He's clearly uncomfortable now.

"Uh-huh?"

"I want to get a doctorate, Jim."

"Yeah, I know. That sounds good."

"In clinical psychology, Jim." That's what's scaring him.

"Frank, I think that's just great, and it makes me feel very good that you want to come into my field."

"Yeah." Sigh. "I didn't know whether you'd feel that way or not. I hoped you would, but I thought maybe you'd laugh at the idea."

"I'm not laughing."

"Wow, I'm really glad you feel that way. I just decided I wanted to go for the whole shit and kaboodle!" And Frank's unconscious has the last say.

The inner sense has much to do with our relations with other people. When we are really tuned into it, we find that we have rich and varied reactions to people, that we are often better able to empathize with them, and that we can more readily make ourselves known to them. Conversely, other people are the most powerful sources of input into our lives—at least for most of us. How others react to us, whether they provide us with warm response, cool distance, hopeful promise, or the pain of disappointment can potently influence us in many conscious and unconscious ways.

Frank was so fearful of the power others might have over him that he tried to wall himself off from them. Although he would never have put it that way, he was trying to protect his inner awareness from what he clearly feared would be the overwhelming strength of others' influences.[5] Yet his effort miscarried. We cannot live solely in terms of inner awareness for that awareness is constantly interacting with the human world around us.

Frank needed not-to-please as strongly as some people need to please. In retrospect, I have a grudging admiration for the relentless quality of Frank's perverse skill in countering anything that might be directed his way. Of course, Frank was very lonely in the tight little one-passenger life he had constructed for himself. He stocked it with books and ideas and tried to subsist on the company of distant authors. But ideas have a way of growing and escaping the bounds individuals (or governments) try to put around them. And because of his reading, Frank came to therapy and to a new and wider living.

Frank attempted to deny the fact that he—as are all men—is at once apart from and yet a part of other people. He tried to be only apart from, but it is man's paradoxical condition that he is always both. Frank's denial grew out of a fear that if he ever let himself become a part of another, he would be absorbed, swallowed up. In time, he came to reinterpret the paradox of human relationship and to see that he could maintain his own identity and yet risk relationships, that he could attend with his inner sense and yet really hear others' voices. He had long felt that human relationships were only based on exploitation, were only those of subjects who used objects. He began to experience, first with me and then more generally, that relationships are essential elements of every person's subjecthood.

We are, each of us, in a very deep and real way, alone. No other person, no matter how loved and loving, no matter how much she or he has shared with us, no matter how open we have sought to be with her or him—no other person can enter fully with us into that deep inner realm of our aloneness. At times we experience that seclusion as a blessing, as a healing and protective solitude, as a source of our integrity as individuals and as separately existing beings. But there are other times as well—times when our separateness is a life-long prison sentence, when it is a dungeon cell from which we know we will never fully emerge. These are the times when we ache so deeply that all our bones hurt, when we yearn with all that is in us to bridge the gap between ourselves and others, to reach some special other fully and completely, and to let that other enter into our hearts without restraint. Then our aloneness is agonizing. Then our inner sense seems relentless in its insistence that still we are separate.

And so it is as well with the other half of the paradox of our being. We find ourselves drawn—sometimes, as with Frank, even against our will—into others' lives, others' feelings, others' experiences. We try to erect the wall of our separateness against such involvement again and again, only to see it crumble like sand embankments before the advancing tide. We dread the loss of our individual being into a cosmic, oceanic oneness.

Yet there are, on still other occasions, magical moments when we experience our community with others. Then we discover

that all men fear and hope, love and hate, lust and worship. Then
we rediscover our humanity, and our inner knowing confirms the
deep communion.

One of the foundation meanings of being human is that we
need two terms to characterize our relationship with another even
though that relationship is fundamentally a unity. We have to use
the somewhat clumsy phrase *separate-but-related* to describe what is
actually all one characteristic of our lives. When we are most at
odds with our own being, we experience these two phases as quite
distinct. Our relatedness gives us no solace in our aloneness, and our
solitariness only mocks our hopes of reaching out to others. When,
on the other hand, we are most authentic, we sometimes discover
how truly these aspects may merge. In the richest moments of union
between a man and a woman who truly love and trust each other,
there is a transcending of the paradox of separate-but-relatedness.
What most fulfills one is most fulfilling to the other. No longer is
there giver and receiver; no longer does the sense of self-and-other
constitute a gulf. Instead there is joy in the realization of individuality rediscovered in relation and confirmed by the full inner response of each partner.

Frank's sheer guts in hanging in with me through the long
months of our struggle to learn to work genuinely together was itself
a powerful learning experience. There are other aspects that stand
out for me:

I am, *as are all human beings,* at once separate from yet
related to others—*in fact to all else that exists. No man is an island,
but no man is identical with any other. I need to embrace the paradox. Frank feared the related-to half of the paradox and tried to live
only as separate from. It didn't—can't—work. I need to listen to
my inner sense and recognize my relatedness, taking it fully into my
being.*
*The experience of caring for another person is a powerful
one indeed. Frank had feared its power, but he came to risk caring
with me and, more strongly, caring for Jennifer. And then he
relinquished her in one of the most poignant ways caring can be expressed. I, too, have to recognize that* caring and choosing are in-

separably linked to relinquishing *and the sorrow of letting go. If I try to avoid the pain, I would have to dull my true inner knowing. Then I would miss the full meaning of my caring, the full range of my being human.*

I must care about taking the risk of making some commitment in life. *For a long time—beginning well before he came to psychotherapy—Frank had tried nihilism as a way to be safe. He rejected all values, all relationships, all commitments[6] of himself. He thought he was free, but actually he was starving emotionally, and he had to deny his inner voice. In therapy, he first began to risk commitment simply by coming regularly and by paying for his visits. Then he found he was making an investment in trying to grow out of his negativism. This led him to relate with others, and finally he was able to risk the commitment of regular work, a compromise in dress and manner, and long-term educational and vocational goals. Human beings have directionality. They are* intentional *always—at least in some way; for example, Frank's original intention to make no relations or commitments. If I am to be fully alive, I need to discover-create with my inner sense an intention and go some place (not necessarily in the sense of social or material achievements) in my life. And the whole trip is in the* going *more than in the* arriving.

Frank came to see me the other day. It has been nearly twelve years since that proud day when he announced his intention to become my colleague. By dint of amazingly hard work, he has completed his doctorate and internship in this time, and he has a wife—herself a graduate student—and a son. Knowing of these attainments from our correspondence, I found myself apprehensive before his arrival. As I had wondered years earlier, I would again: had I helped create a nice cog in the middle-class machine?

I was reassured first of all by Frank's truly ferocious beard when I met him in the waiting room. This is no tamed face, whatever else. He greeted me shyly, obviously watching to see how I would welcome him. We were both awkward, but soon we were able to begin to talk to each other. And as Frank talked, I knew that he hadn't lost his awareness of his inner center.

He's interested in working with kids who are on hard drugs.

He's contemptuous of much of the official line in dealing with such youth, and he's pretty sure that it will complicate rather than reduce the problem. He doesn't believe in being "soft," but he insists that kids must really be reached if they're going to change and that most so-called "tough" programs are actually evading the difficulty of dealing with the true problem. I'm impressed as I listen to him, and I say so. Then Frank becomes more hesitant and finally says, "Oh, shee-yit! Jim! You always have to make such a big fucking deal out of everything! I'm just doing my thing." And I relax, knowing Frank is still Frank.

✳ 5 ✳

LOUISE
Compliance and Independence

Deep in the night she stirs in my embrace, and I dimly awaken. My arm is numb from her loved weight. Gently, quietly, I try to pull it free, reluctantly parting from her warmth. She turns, still sleeping, murmurs my name and some vague syllables—loving sounds. I try to make out the precious words, but they slide into the abyss of her sleep. Suddenly that seems terribly, unredeemably tragic. Now wide awake, I know I am overreacting, but at the same moment I want to cry out, to stop time, to know the now forever lost reaching of her soul toward mine. How can we two, who have come through so much together, be so separate that I will never know those words?

Another night, another place, and I am reading the searching words of Allen Wheelis[1] as he examines our human guilt. He is recalling the horror of the Dacca racetrack when four suspected Pakastani Quislings were tortured to death before 5,000 cheering Bengalis. I am sickened. I don't want to remember what I pushed out of my thoughts when I first read of it in *Time* several years ago. And then the secret, the obscene, the persistent thoughts come: Did they do this to them? And that? My God! I don't want to think about it. How could I sit in those stands and watch? Could I have been one of the torturers? I don't want to know, but I do: I could have been in those bleachers screaming for the blood. I could have been down on the field, imagining more terrible ways to extract the last bit of anguish. I am brother to the torturer, to the killer.[2]

And I could have been one of those tied to the stakes, helplessly awaiting the next terrible inspiration. I know that kinship as well.

I am *a part of* all men (and of all that exists), just as I am a separate individual, *apart from* all other men (and the rest of being)'. The simultaneity, the actual unity, of these two contradictory realizations makes for a peculiar poignancy. Usually, I am aware of only one aspect—either the apart-from or the a-part-of; at such times, the other side is vague and academic.

But as a human, I can't cut this duality in two so neatly. I have to be aware of both if I am fully to experience my aliveness. Thus, in order to find fulfillment, I must have some very close relations, some more casual, and an openness to my shared humanity with people in general; at the same time, I must keep my center within myself and respect my own need for times of separateness. Only through his own inner sense can each of us find his balance among these ingredients.

For many of us, however, our early experiences do not teach us how to work out our own unique and meaningfully balanced diet of relations and solitude. The best-intentioned parents are threatened by their children's needs for separateness. Mothers and fathers insist that the pattern of relationships they have developed for themselves should be the one their children adopt. After having struggled to discover our own way of being, it is hard for us to accept that our children may have quite different patterns. But because each of us is an individual, with a separate I-ness, each of us does evolve an individual pattern. And it is from our experiences in early years that we learn the ways of relating that seem essential for survival.

As a small child, Frank learned to expect nothing but hurt from being close to others; thus, he emphasized the apart-from half of the paradox of human relations. He lived with as little involvement with others as he could manage and with no expectation of warmth or mutuality.

Louise, on the other hand, learned to emphasize the a-part-of half of the dilemma. Because she realized early how powerless and vulnerable she was on her own, she became skillful at winning approval and making sure others would always want her with them. But this flight from separateness cut deeply into Louise's sense of her own identity and damped her inward awareness.[3]

November 12

A subtle perfume of femininity emanates from the prim woman who sits in my big chair this afternoon. Not an actual perfume sensed with the nose and mouth, but a psychic essence exuding from her. Dress conservative but attractive; body not displayed, yet not completely denied. I'm intrigued, trying to identify what conveys sensual, erotic hints without using the obvious.

Meantime, while I'm playing with these speculations, this woman who gives off such a potent nonverbal message is talking earnestly and most unerotically. "After the accident, I was in leg casts for nearly a year and couldn't go to school. My mother, as she began to recover from her own injuries and from Dad's death, tried to teach me at home, and occasionally a visiting teacher came, but mostly I was on my own. It was such a lonely time. I remember I'd lie there and look out the window at the kids playing and wish I could go out and be with them. Then the evening would come, and I would start to get scared. Ever since the accident, I would get scared at dusk. I would ask my mother to stay with me, at least till it got dark, but she would have to go get supper and couldn't stay long."

"A lonely frightening time."

"Yes." A quick grateful smile. A little too grateful for such a simple response. Is that it? Does she overrespond? She does, but that isn't the erotic quality; in fact, in some ways it almost detracts from the invitingness.

"And then in the spring, Mother found out she had cancer. It seemed just too much. She tried to be brave, I know, but I could hear her crying in her room. I tried to keep her from knowing that I heard her, and I did my best to make her happy. She was in such pain, you know, and she just seemed to dwindle away. I think she just didn't have any reserves after the accident—it had used her up so. Right after Labor Day she died, and. . . . " She is weeping quietly. I feel for this woman, orphaned at eleven.

"Hard for anyone to take; especially hard for a young girl."

She nods, wipes her eyes, cries a bit more, looks up to me with a smile that surely would be called "game" in the novels of another generation. "I'm sorry to be such a baby."

"Really, that's scarcely the way I see you."

"That's very nice of you to say." Oh, blah! I find her too sweet, too proper. Where's the erotic perfume now? I'll be damned if it isn't still there. It's strange that somehow I can be put off by her somewhat cloying quality even as I'm wondering what it would be like to stroke her bare skin. That surprises me.

"I went to live with my mother's brother and his wife, Aunt Julie and Uncle Bennett. It wasn't good. Aunt Julie resented me. She tried to be understanding, I know, but at night I could hear them arguing and my name being said. Finally one evening. . . . " Crying again. So quietly.

"Evening, again."

"Yes, evening again. I suppose it's silly, but really I get the feeling that I've got to be on guard when the day is over. Even now I sometimes get frightened when I'm alone in my apartment as it's starting to get dark. And I really get almost terrified when I have to leave the office in winter just as it's about to be night."

"It's really not so surprising, is it?"

"No, I suppose not, but it is silly of me, don't you think?" An appealing smile that is clearly an invitation to say that of course it isn't silly. Makes me feel obstinate, like I want to say that she's right to think herself silly. Wow! This gal really gets to me in a variety of ways. I'll just be quiet for now.

"Well, anyway, one evening my uncle asked me to go for a walk with him. He looked very tense and sort of angry. He said he was really sorry but it just wasn't working out for me to live with them, that Aunt Julie was going through the menopause and so was very nervous. He was really sorry, but he had arranged for me to go live with a cousin of his in New Hampshire, on a farm there."

"How did you feel when he told you that?"

"Oh, just awful. I. . . . " Tears coming stronger now. "I

thought I had probably not helped Aunt Julie as much as I should have. I remember I asked him if he'd give me another chance, and I promised to be very good and help a lot. I was really scared. At least I had known Uncle Bennett and Aunt Julie before the accident, but I'd never even heard of these New Hampshire cousins. I begged, and I cried, and finally he said he'd talk to her again. And that night they had an awful fight. And I wanted to run away, but I was so scared, and I didn't know what to do." She cries in earnest now, and for the first time since she entered the room I don't feel the focus of her attention. Ah, that's part of the effect she has on me; I'm made to feel as though I'm the emotional center of her experience. It's really very intoxicating.

"You can feel again now how terrifying and lost you felt then."

"Oh, yes, yes." Her head comes up instantly, and the appealing look, now mixed with gratitude for my understanding, shines on me. I'm inclined to be sarcastic about the way she focuses on me, partly because in some subtle way I'm embarrassed by it and by my instant response to it. For I really am moved by her and her unspoken appeals and by her hurting and. . . . Yes, and by that erotic perfume which emanates from her.

"It only lasted about four months, I think it was. Anyway it was a terrible time for all of us. I probably should have just gone when he first told me. I kept trying to please Aunt Julie. I tried to help with the housework, but I never got it quite the way she liked it. I tried to not talk too much at meals, but then we would just sit in silence and that was terrible. I really tried, but. . . . So then I was sent to New Hampshire."

"How did that go?"

"Well, it was all right for a while. Mr. and Mrs. Colten were good people. They tried to make me feel at home, and they tried to teach me what they believed were the right things. They were an older couple. Their children were all grown with children of their own. Sometimes it was very nice with them. We had big family picnics and parties at the holidays, just like in the old stories, but then. . . ."

"Then?"

"Well, Mr. Colten was getting kind of old, I guess, and

I. . . . This is embarrassing to me." The sweet smile, but she really means it; not just a bid for reassurance this time.

"You find it hard to talk about what happened?"

"Yes, what I mean is, I'm sure he didn't mean any harm or anything. He really was a dear man."

"Mr. Colten."

"Yes, you see, I had matured while I was with Uncle Bennett and Aunt Julie, you know. I mean, I matured rather early and had a rather full figure even when I was twelve or thirteen. Oh, this is. . . . "

"You find it hard to talk about your body and your sexual maturing."

"I don't know why. I mean, I'm not a child. I'm thirty-seven years old, but I guess I am rather naive in some ways, or inexperienced. . . . " She drifts off, and now the genuine embarrassment is compounded with the subtle invitation, and it makes a potent combination.

"You are really very appealing in your embarrassment. Are you aware of that?"

Instant coloring and apparent dismay. "Oh! Oh, I didn't know. I mean, what did I do? I wasn't aware. . . . "

"Ms. Gowan, you didn't really do anything that extreme. You're much too concerned. I found it quite pleasant in fact, but I am interested in knowing how aware you are of the kind of impact you have on others."

"Oh, I'm sorry." More confusion now. She doesn't quite know what is expected now, and with Louise Gowan being pleasing is obviously of first priority. With the history she's telling me, that's not really surprising.

"What happened with Mr. Colten?"

"Oh! Oh, nothing really serious. I just gradually became aware that he would try to see me when I took a bath or that he was always trying to get me to go for walks alone with him. Once when I did, he took me down to the creek and said this was his old swimming hole. He got a big kick out of telling me that they used to swim nude in it, and he wanted me to take off my clothes and swim in it right then. He said he'd watch to be sure nobody came and that I was all right. I was very frightened, but he kept insisting, and so I started to do it finally. Then just as I got out of my dress and brassiere, Mrs. Colten came through the bushes shouting at us both. I think she thought I was trying to lure him on or something. I just cried and cried and tried to explain, but nobody would believe me. And the old man got all mixed up trying to protect me and himself and denying the whole thing, so that it just was terrible. Anyway, after about a week, they sent me back to Uncle Bennett."

"What were your feelings about that?"

"I don't know. I just felt kind of numb and terribly ashamed. I just didn't want to see anyone that had heard anything about the whole thing." She cries quietly, seeming to avoid letting our eyes meet. "Well, then, I couldn't stay there. So in a month or so, they arranged for me to live with an elderly lady and help take care of her in exchange for my board and room. That was Mrs. Davis, and I stayed with her until I was sixteen. Then I. . . . "

And so Louise tells of her troubled childhood. It is not hard to see why she wants so much to please. At nine she is seriously injured in an accident that kills her father; then before long her mother dies. Thereafter, she is constantly put in situations where she must be pleasing just so she can continue to live in what is temporarily her home.

Toward the end of the hour, after her account is completed and we have talked about plans for therapy, I decide to explore again the extent of her insight into her personal impact. "One thing that has impressed me as we talked, Ms. Gowan, is the extent to which you seem concerned with being pleasing and agreeable, to continually return to being happy, even though you tell of very unhappy events. It is useful if I know to what extent you're aware of this pattern in yourself."

"Oh, my, that embarrasses me." And she is genuinely embarrassed and yet coy in some very subtle way. It does come out erotic too. "Well, I think I know something of it. I have sometimes been aware that I want so much to. . . . I don't know how to say it. Well, I thought once after I'd seen a movie, 'I've had a Bette Davis life, but I cover it over with Shirley Temple.' "

And that says it very well, I think to myself, except I'd add "Shirley Temple and Marilyn Monroe."

Coming to know Louise over nearly a year's time, I feel the cloying sweetness less, but the erotic hint is nearly always there— as is the seeking to please. Her manner of focusing with unusual directness and intensity on my face and words is disturbing at times but powerful and intriguing at others.

Louise is the supervisor of social work trainees in a large community agency, and from what I can gather, she is effective and well liked. Yet she is becoming aware that she lacks inward vision and the sense of identity it brings. As she says, "I don't really know who I am. I almost would say, I don't know *if* I am. I mean, I am only sure I exist when I'm with someone, especially someone who needs me. Lately, since we've started talking, I find myself wondering, if nobody needed me, would I just disappear?"

She has become so aware of her dependence on others that she thinks of herself, by turns, as a hollow shell activated only by others and then as a "warming machine," valuable only as she gives to others but of no significance within herself.

October 18

"I keep thinking of Cynthia, the student I told you about last week." Louise is getting settled on the couch with practiced familiarity that contrasts with her first tentative and self-conscious trips on that strange conveyance. "I find I want to talk about her, and yet right at the same time, I don't want to even think about her, let alone bring the whole thing up." She adjusts the tissue on her pillow, smooths her modest skirt carefully over her legs. (Lately, I have the feeling that the skirts are shorter than they used to be, but I'm not sure.)

"What are you thinking about Cynthia?" I realize ruefully that I'm not sure which is Cynthia of the half-dozen student social workers Louise supervises. She has told me about several recently, but my attention is so much more on Louise's own manner that I am now uncertain whether Cynthia is the sexy one, or the one who was so furious at Louise, or the docile one with whom Louise makes some reluctant identification. I smile inwardly at my own unreal self-expectations that make me feel I ought to recall instantly everything Louise has told me; then I note that she is taking more time than usual to get settled today. It is as though her body won't relax and free her attention.

She adjusts her skirt again. "Oh, just that little adventure that Cynthia had with the medical student and the pictures he took." She half rises on one elbow and kicks off her shoes. Then she lies back and goes through the whole routine of getting settled again. "It's not important."

"You seem to be having trouble getting comfortable today."

"Oh, I'm all right now." Smiling. "I had a dream last night and sort of half woke up, but now I can't seem to remember anything about it. It was so vivid then that I was sure I would remember it, but. . . . It was so intense that it woke me up. I was trying to think on my way here what it was about, but. . . . " Her voice trails off.

"Louise, what about Cynthia?" Firmly. I remember which student Cynthia is now and think it might be useful to stay with this subject. Indeed, I have a hunch that the dream might be related. "What comes to mind now when I remind you of her again?"

"Well, just the little adventure she told me about, you know. I mean, I don't want to belittle it. She told me because she was so full of feelings and needed someone to talk to, but. . . . Oh, I don't know. I just seem to be rambling. You know, the incident I told you about, what happened with that young man. . . . "

She is obviously flustered and uncomfortable, struggling between a desire to dismiss the topic and the impulse to open it up.

"What happened with that young man?"

"Oh, you can be so exasperating! You know very well what happened, since I just told you last week." Pausing. Once again her hands busy themselves with her skirt, which seems not to cover her as fully as she wants. Her knees and a bit of her thighs are evident, but it is not a noteworthy display of leg by any means. I keep silent, and after a brief time she continues. "Well, I suppose you want me to say it. Cynthia went to this young man's apartment, and he persuaded her to pose for him. And eventually she posed nude for him, and then they uh . . . then they made love." She pauses again, and her left hand toys with the buttons of her blouse, a more frequent gesture lately.

She is waiting for me to comment, but I keep silent. "Well, I don't know why it persists in coming into my mind. I suppose I find it a little erotically stimulating, but it really doesn't amount to much. I also find it a little embarrassing to talk to you about these matters, as you know, but that's much better now. When I told you about . . . about the way I . . . uh . . . sometimes touch myself. . . . Oh, that's silly! I told you that I sometimes masturbate, and you're not my mother, and you're not Dr. Clifton [the Director of the agency where Louise works] so why do I get so uncomfortable. . . . Her fingers play with the buttons of her blouse as though opening them, but they do not actually do so.

"Louise, I think you're trying to level with me, and yet at the same time you're uncomfortable about letting me know how this experience of Cynthia's stirs you."

"Yes." Sighing. The hand is briefly at rest. "Yes, I suppose I am. It really is a kind of delightful story, I think. When I was Cynthia's age, I was so frightened of men and bodies and sexual feelings, I could never have done anything like that." Her voice is musing, as she dreamily reflects. Her hand is busy again, although it is apparent that she has no conscious awareness of it.

"Tell me in detail about Cynthia's experience, as you—you, Louise, not Cynthia—think about it."

"Oh, my! That really embarrasses me!" She laughs and colors a bit. The hand is still but not at rest. There is a brief pause, and I know she is debating with herself. "Why do you ask me to do that?" I say nothing. "I mean, I suppose you want me to think about sex or something like that, but. . . . " A pause; I still am quiet. "You know I was raised in homes where one just never spoke about such matters. Never! I knew the adults had bodies, but I never thought they did anything with them except wash them. Once I accidentally saw my father naked, and I turned and ran away, and I think he ran the other way. Now I know that all that is long ago, and I shouldn't still be so embarrassed and shy in this day, but. . . .

"It isn't as though I'm still a virginal spinster, and you know that I really got through a lot of my discomfort about bodies and sex when I had that affair with Ralph, but still. . . . It is just plain silly to feel so shy about talking to you about this little incident of Cynthia's, but. . . . "

"Louise." Tone kind but admonishing. "It isn't Cynthia's 'little incident,' as you keep calling it, that embarrasses you, it's what is stirred up in *you* that embarrasses you, and that you hesitate to let me see. I'm sure you could talk to me endlessly about Cynthia, if it were quite clear that it was only Cynthia we were talking about. But Louise and her feelings keep getting into the picture, and that's what is hard for you to accept."

She is quiet for a minute. Then, "Yes, I suppose so. It's certainly a very different matter to tell about someone else than to show you or let you know about me." Her hand is once again pantomiming unbuttoning her blouse, moving from one button to the next. "It's as though I am getting too personal or. . . ."

"Even now, Louise, you are earnestly discussing yourself and your feelings, but you are holding yourself apart from those feelings even as you speak. Can't you feel how some part of you is determined not to be immersed in what we're talking about?"

"Yes." The hand stops moving, and she is quite still. "Yes, I guess I am really reluctant to sink into the feelings I've been having since Cynthia talked to me. In fact, I know I've been dreading this moment ever since. One part of me wanted to just let go and imagine myself in Cynthia's place and really enjoy it and maybe even touch myself, but another part kept saying, 'You'll have to tell Jim everything you think and do, so be careful.' And I guess," laughing ruefully, "I'm still being careful."

I wait without commenting. She shifts uneasily, straightens her skirt over her legs. They really are rather attractive legs, I realize. At thirty-seven, Louise talks about herself as though her years of romantic possibilities are over, but she is far from the gray old lady that she portrays. I wonder what her body would be like nude. It is hard to discern the contours of her breasts because of the full blouses she wears. I wish that errant hand would get down to business and really unbutton those buttons instead of just teasing me.

"Well, since you won't rescue me by answering, I guess I'll try to tell you about Cynthia." Playful, teasing tone; a pause.

"Why don't you just try to tell it like you might have fantasized—as Louise's experience, not as Cynthia's?"

"Oh! I don't know whether I could do that!" She pauses. "It would be so . . . so . . . so naked. That's the right word. It would feel like being naked in front of you."

"Would that be a bad feeling?"

"Oh, my, you are making things difficult, aren't you?" She hesitates; her hand starts to adjust her skirt and then stops. "No, and yes! I mean mostly yes; or maybe . . . I don't know. It sounds nice, and it sounds very frightening."

"Your left hand has been trying to unbutton your blouse most of the hour today." As I say that, the hand has indeed pushed a button half through the buttonhole. Instantly, its movement is arrested. She lies very still. "Louise, look at it freshly for a moment, can you?" I wait while she gathers herself to hear me. "You have been trained, as was I, to feel that your body and the emotions and wantings it has are shameful and out of place in most circumstances. That training, well intended as it was, has cost us both many hours of misery and much disappointment and frustration. Now you're here to try to free yourself from such constraints when they are not truly meaningful and to discover when they are important so that you can make your own choices for your life. This is very much like other situations we have talked about in which you have had to choose who would direct your life—you or Mrs. Colten's voice in you."

She is attending with real earnestness now. "Yes, of course. It's the same thing in another way, isn't it? Once again—Mrs. Colten's rules and my trouble making choices on my own! I didn't think of that."

"And you didn't think of it for a variety of reasons, but one reason is that you learned shame about your body and its feelings. So it was simpler to avoid getting fully involved in what you were discussing with me here."

"Yes, I can feel that somehow I kept pulling back from letting go to it fully. It just seemed that you couldn't really mean for me to talk so intimately that I'd surely get . . . get warm. Oh, damn it, I'm no child. It was hard for me to face that you knew very well I'd get hot and horny if I told you about Cynthia's experience as my own. I felt ashamed to get aroused in front of you, and I wanted to discuss it academically. And I know that just doesn't work." She finishes with a resolute tone and a kind of angry determination to confront her fears. I find her very moving and attractive in this burst of courage.

"Unbutton your blouse, Louise!" Inwardly I gulp, and a part of me shouts in amazement, "What the hell are you doing, Bugental? Do you want to be hauled before the ethics committee or the courts or something?" But I keep my attention on the moment. This is risking big stakes, but trying to be proper now would be copping out on Louise and on myself.[4]

She has not spoken since I gave her the instruction. She is clearly confronting her own inner conflict of feelings. Then her hands come to the buttons and slowly and deliberately undo the first one, pause, then move to the second, unfasten it, and move to the third. She stops. "All of them?"

"It's your blouse. Those are your hands. You know now what we're trying to do. You decide." I wait.

The third and fourth buttons are unfastened and her blouse is undone to her waistband. Now she hesitates again, and I keep silent. There is only the tiniest glimpse of bra or skin because the blouse is still closed. I feel an impulse to tell her to open it, and I also feel a fear of crossing professional boundaries.

My thoughts race through my head as I watch Louise, her hands at the waistband of her skirt. I realize she is debating a further step—importantly, a step I haven't suggested. Then she opens her blouse wide and puts her arms at her sides with the hands palms up in a single quick and very appealing movement. Her simple white bra covers her full breasts quite as demurely as any bathing suit top and more so than many, but the gesture is so courageous for Louise with her whole background that I am at once filled with a warm, nearly tearful valuing of her and a strong sense of the erotic impact of her uncovering herself. Another woman might have stripped completely with less meaning and with less sexual investment. Louise's action is eloquent in itself. My mind applauds her courage; my body responds to her emotion.

"I want to cover myself up and run out of here." Voice taut, breath shallow. Silence. "I suddenly have the awful feeling that I've misinterpreted your meaning and have made a fool of myself. I'm losing all that nice warm feeling I had a moment ago, and I'm beginning to feel so chilled I may start to shake." Tears are starting from her eyes, and she is beginning to tremble.

"What you've just done is very frightening to you, Louise, because you've made a statement about yourself that you've feared to make before—except when you knew the other person was so involved that he could not stand apart and judge you. But now you are beginning to stand apart and judge yourself."

"Oh, it makes me so damn mad! I know you're not judging me, but in my head you're all the people who would be horrified if they could see me now." The tears still are coming, and she is struggling emotionally.

"Tell me what's happening inside of you right now." Voice tender, supportive.

"Oh, that's hard to do. . . . I'm doing so many things inside. . . . I'm trying to keep aware of where I am, and . . . and to keep aware of why I'm half-dressed here in front of you. . . . But it's all very slippery . . . and I keep wanting to run away from it all . . . like running away by being angry at you . . . or by being angry at me . . . or by giving in to feeling ridiculous . . . or ashamed. . . . And then I get angry about that. I really haven't done anything so awful. I'm sure you've seen a woman in her brassiere before, and really in today's world I'm certainly adequately covered! To make such a fuss about this is quite ridiculous in itself."

"Louise, you're not making a fuss about showing yourself to me in your brassiere. That's not keeping faith with yourself to put it that way. You're frightened by your *choosing* to do so. It's your letting me know that you feel sexy. It's your taking the responsibility to violate the taboos you learned from your earliest years. Those are the things that frighten you now."

"Yes, and that makes me even more mad. I feel like tearing off all my clothes and dancing down the street and saying 'Nuts!' to the whole stupid world."

"You'd really show them, eh?" Encouragingly. We begin chuckling. The mood changes, becomes less intense, and her hands pull her blouse together. "It seems less frightening now, Louise, but you evidently want to cover up too. What is that like inside of you?"

"I almost didn't realize I was pulling it together, but I felt kind of tense, like some part of me had been holding its breath ever since I opened it. I wonder why that is." She opens her blouse again, clearly trying to test the feeling. "That's funny; I don't get that feeling now."

"Louise, you still think of yourself in mechanical terms: 'Open blouse means certain kind of tension.' I don't think the blouse being open or closed, in itself, has much to do with it. What makes the difference is the feeling in you. When you feel you're risking something new and you are conflicted, then you feel tension. What you're doing physically is a by-product."

"Yes, of course, but I keep forgetting that." Meanwhile, her hands are closing the blouse. "There I go again. It's just like Mrs. Colten always telling me, 'Keep your skirt down. Don't sprawl and show your legs!' It seemed that was one of the main things in the whole world that distinguished nice girls from awful ones."

"Show me your legs, Louise!"

Instantly her animation fades, and she holds her breath. Then she cautiously takes hold of her skirt and raises it several inches till her thighs are perhaps half exposed. She seems to be poised and still breathless.

"They look very pretty, what I can see of them." Teasing. Now my own tensions mount. A quick thought of Louise telling someone about her therapist's unorthodox procedures; then I know that is neither likely nor important to the living person here with me and what she is trying to do. Also I have a warm, sexy feeling and enjoy her skirt tantalizingly creeping up another several inches.

"Is that the right place now?" Mocking tone, want her to show more. But I want her to take responsibility for how much she chooses to show. My tone serves both intents.

"Oh, I don't know!" Impatient. "You know as well as I do that there's no 'right place,' so why do you ask me such a question? It's wrong to do this at all. But it's silly to say that. I'm certainly not showing you anything you haven't seen before, and. . . . "

"That's where you're wrong." Abruptly, interrupting. "You keep reducing yourself to your mechanical actions, Louise, and if you mean I've seen women's legs before, that's certainly so, but. . . . "

"I know! I know, don't tell me. You haven't seen mine before."

"That's true, but that's not the point still."

"What is it then? Wait! What you haven't seen before is my choosing in this particular way to say 'here I am.' That's it, isn't it?"

"Yes, Louise, that's it." A feeling of completion and reassurance for venturing into these realms.

"Jim." She so seldom uses my name, I am warmed. "I'd like to take off all my clothes and show all of me to you. I don't think I can do that today, even though I'd like to. But maybe one day I will."

"I hear you, and I feel the same way." And the hour is over.[5]

October 20

Louise is very subdued when she comes back two days later. She avoids looking at me directly, settles herself on the couch with undue concentration, and then lies silently.

"What are you thinking?"

"Nothing. I mean, I'd rather not say."

"Can you say what it is that makes you hesitate to say what you're thinking?"

"I just want to get on to something important and not waste time on trivialities. I think I should talk with you about whether I'm going to try to go back to graduate school or continue working at the agency. It's getting close to time to apply for admission, if I'm going to do it. I've been thinking that I might be able to get some kind of fellowship or assistantship. Dr. Clifton would give me a strong recommendation, I'm pretty sure, and. . . . " She pauses, seeming to lose momentum. I say nothing, and in a minute she starts again.

"I mean, I think that at my age I ought to finish going to school. If I went to UCLA, I could probably get a doctorate in social work in about two years, maybe three. Then I'd be in a good position to teach someplace or maybe get to be the head of an agency, one of the smaller ones, and. . . . " Again she pauses. Clearly she is pushing herself to keep talking, but she seems to have little enthusiasm for the topic. Still I keep silent.

"I'm just not sure I want to spend two or three years at it,

you know. I mean, it's really worthwhile and all, but. . . . Well, anyway, I've got to make a decision pretty soon, and I wish. . . . "
She grinds to a stop.

"Louise." Quietly. She tenses as soon as she hears my voice. "Tell me what happened here the last time you were in."

"Oh, that was silly. Let's not waste time. I really do have to make a decision, and I really do need your help too. Do you think I could be ready to leave therapy by next September if I got admitted to a school in some other town?"

"You are very anxious to keep our attention away from what happened last time. You're trying to push yourself and me into this other matter, even though you have a hard time concentrating on it." Insistently, slight challenge.

"I don't want to talk about it. I behaved in a very silly fashion, as you well know. And you were certainly letting us get away from our concerns here too. So let's just. . . . "

I cut in sharply, "We did not get away from our concerns here. That's what you're trying to do today." I'm peeved with her denying what we shared, and I recognize that I'm also a bit guilty for my enjoyment of her. Thus, I'm anxious to prove that what we did is not a violation of her trust in me.

"I really do have to make some decision about graduate school, Jim; no matter what you say and no matter what happened the other day. So please help me pay attention to what's really important today."

"Louise, when you appeal to me that way, I'm really moved to go along with you. But when you say you want to pay attention to 'what's really important,' I know that is your feeling about our last session and not the nice safe topic of whether or not you will go to graduate school next fall."

Suddenly I am aware that she is crying quietly, making no immediate response. I feel a wave of tenderness and then a pang that our experiment with sexiness set her back. Even as I think this, I know it's not so, but again my guilt for enjoyment is displayed to me. (I must work this through further, especially if I am ever to encourage anyone else to violate taboos in ways that are also gratifying to me. Something in me reacts with shock! Do I plan to do *that* again?)

"I don't know what you want me to say about last time."
She is still crying quietly, but it is evident that she is trusting my
interpretation and trying to go along with me. I feel warmed by her
confidence and silently resolve that I'll never let her down. And I
realize I can let her down either by being too risky or by being too
conservative.

"Why don't you just tell me, as though I hadn't been here,
what happened during our last time together?"

"I'll try. I told you about how Cynthia's romantic, sexual
experience had aroused me. Then we noticed that I was restless
with my clothes and so we . . . and so I. . . . You suggested that
I. . . . Well, you know what happened. Why do I have to say it?"

"Louise, you can feel right now how very hard it is for you
to talk about what happened here. That is a simple fact. And that
simple fact points to the conflict within you. And that conflict is
what we need to find out a great deal more about right now while
it's raging inside of you."

"Well, I'm embarrassed, I guess, and kind of ashamed,
and. . . . "

"And . . . ?"

"Well, I don't ordinarily go around opening my clothes and
showing off my body to men."

"What's that got to do with anything?" Voice sharp again.

"Oh, I don't know. I'm just kind of upset, I guess."

"And you're angry with me a bit but somehow hesitate to
say that too."

"Well, yes, but I really have no good reason to be angry
with you. You didn't make me do anything. I did it. You didn't
do anything to me."

"I suggested you unbutton your blouse and lift your skirt."

"Oh, I know. But you. . . . "

"Louise, you're acting as though we—or you—committed a
great crime here the other day, and now you're being noble and
taking the blame."

"Oh, I know. I know I'm behaving very silly. That's why I
didn't want to even talk about it."

"Damn it! Louise! You persist in treating your emotional
response to our experience as a triviality to be gotten past as quickly

as possible. It is so very clear that you have a strong reaction to it and that it is interfering with your thinking and with your relationship to me. That is no triviality!"

Abruptly she lets out a great sigh. "I'm sorry, Jim. No, I don't mean that. I mean, it's a great relief to have you say that. I mean I really thought maybe you would be disgusted with me, that probably you hadn't meant for me to really do what I did the other day but were just testing me, and. . . . "

"Louise, you double-crossed yourself and expected me to do the same to you. Some part of you knows very well that we experienced a time of real closeness and intimacy Tuesday, and yet you are so afraid to trust that realization that you set out to deny it. When you don't keep faith with yourself that way, you mess up your own thinking and get your relation with me all fouled up too."

"I know. I think I do that to myself a lot of the time when I'm afraid someone else might find fault with me. I sort of jump over to their side and desert myself. It makes me so mad when I think about it now."

The rest of the session, Louise works well on her need to be pleasing to everyone. She learned early, she recognizes, that she could find a way of pleasing if she pushed her own feelings out of the way, if she closed off her inner sense.

Leaving, Louise gives me a quick hug at the door. She has done this before, but today's hug seems more sensual than I remember any previous embrace to have been.

December 5

The realization of how much she needs to be pleasing to everyone is very much in the focus of Louise's thoughts these days. She is astonished at how pervasive the pattern is, and she is intently working to free herself from it. She goes over exchanges with sales people, co-workers, and friends, finding in nearly every instance no real awareness of her own I-ness but rather a readiness to be controlled by the people with whom she is dealing. These repetitious sessions are wearing, but she knows how essential they are, for gradually she is getting much more aware of the difference between her own inner sense and the outer voices that play on her. Even that learning is not always encouraging, however.

"I remember a long time ago telling you I didn't know if there was any *me* apart from the person or thing that was trying to do everything for everybody that comes along. Well, I'm not kidding now, I really doubt there is anything else to me. In fact, sometimes I get a frightened feeling that all I am and all I'll ever be is some kind of nice doll that gives people whatever they ask."

"Do you do that with me?"

"No." Startled, quick, almost frightened reading of my face. "Oh, no, of course not."

"Is that a considered answer, or is it the answer that will be most pleasing, the right answer?"

"Oh, I . . . I don't know. You startled me. I mean, I wasn't thinking about here, with you."

"Why should you be different here?"

"Well, I . . . I wonder. . . . I mean, maybe I do sometimes. I. . . . "

"Maybe the right answer, the pleasing thing to say to me right now, is that you probably do it here sometimes."

"Oh, I wish you wouldn't do that. I really don't know what to say. I mean, I see what you mean, but. . . . "

"Louise, you are swirling around now because you're entirely outside of yourself. You are thinking about what I've said, and you're trying to see if it's right, but you're also trying to guess my intention and what I expect you to answer, and. . . . "

"Yes." She begins crying but keeps on intently. "Yes, I am doing those things, just like you said. I am trying to understand why you've suddenly brought the problem right into our talking together . . . so . . . Oh! I must do it here too. Oh, I hate that! I really hate it!"

"Are you really agreeing with me now or have you decided that would be the most pleasing to me?"

"Oh, I don't like it when you say that!" Tone now becoming harsh, anger emerging.

"Would I be pleased if you got angry?"

"Stop it! Stop that! I'm getting so confused. Stop, please stop."

"Louise, I don't want to make you feel badly, but you still haven't, as far as I can tell, taken time to feel within yourself about what your own thoughts and feelings are. You're still thinking about what I'm doing, and when you do that, you get tangled up in what I might want and expect."

"Yes, that's so. Wait! Let me think. Did I just agree with you because I really agree with you or because I wanted you to see me as understanding? Wait! Wait! Oh, I can't . . . I really can't tell the difference. After all, you're trying to help me, so why would you tell me something. . . . No, I can see where that's taking me. I don't know, Jim. I don't know!" The last is a wail, and the tears are streaming down her cheeks. She looks miserably unhappy.

"Louise." Voice quietly insistent. "Louise, tell me how it is inside of you now, right now while you're feeling so miserable."

"Oh, awful. I'm kind of whirling around inside. It's like I'm dizzy. Yes, like I can't get my balance. When you keep pressing me that way it's like I can't . . . I can't. . . . It's like the floor is tilting, and I'm falling, but then before I land, it tilts again another way, and I fall another way, and. . . . Oh, damn it, Jim! It makes me so mad!"

"Do you think that description of the way you feel is what I was looking for?"

"Huh? Oh! You're doing it some more. Well, frankly, right at this moment, I don't give a damn! Uh! Oh, my, oh!" She pauses, her face twists. She darts glances at me, pulls herself back. Suddenly she stands up, tears streaming down her face. "Oh, God!" Gasping. "I can't stand it! I want to run, to run right out of here. I want to run away from you and from myself."

"Tell me, Louise." Still quietly, quietly. Important to convey by my manner that what she is doing is all right, is necessary. Yet is that reinforcing the dependence? Don't think there's any other way. She has to go through this.

"For a minute I knew where I was. When I described the tilting and dizziness inside of me . . . I knew then. I didn't think what you might think of it, or me. Then when you asked, it felt good to tell you I didn't care what you thought. But I suddenly got so scared. I was sure you were going to be furious at me, and yet right at the same time I knew you wouldn't be. And still, at the same time, I thought you'd be pleased that I knew you wouldn't and then I thought you wouldn't like it if I thought you'd be pleased, and then. . . . And I started to feel like I was suffocating, and I had to stand up, and I wanted to run, and in a part of me I still do. Oh, please don't do that anymore, at least right now." She sinks down to sit on the couch.

"I hear you, Louise."

"But, Jim . . . Jim, I know sooner or later we've got to do it some more . . . a lot more. I hate it. I hate you when you make me so dizzy and frightened, but I want you to do it again, and again, and again!" She's very intense, angry, determined. My eyes swim suddenly with appreciation for her courage.

We have many sessions now in which we focus on Louise's continual need to be pleasing and the way it blocks access to her inner awareness. When we work with her feelings of needing to please me right in the moment of our talking together (as in the session I described above), Louise experiences great psychic pain and anxiety. This is important for her to go through if she is to free herself, but we have to modulate how much she can usefully take in one session. Still, gradually, she wins increasing access to her own inner center, to her inward vision.

To aid her in this struggle, I encourage Louise to join a therapy group, and with evident reluctance she does so. Once again, she seems compelled to be pleasing, and she quickly succeeds in winning over almost everyone in the group. Yet slowly, here too, she begins to relinquish this compulsion.

March 19

With the new year, another focus emerges in Louise's concern. At the social agency where she works, a new director is acting in a very authoritarian manner. I know this from colleagues as well as from Louise's own report.

"He is so cold and unrelating, Jim. It just seems so sad to have someone like that appointed right now, just when we were getting a good program going for the teenagers, and the whole agency was beginning to pull together as a team. If I never appreciated Dr. Clifton before he retired, I sure do now. Dr. Elliott is so suspicious and so sour toward the young people. He. . . . ''

"How does he feel about you, Louise?"

"I don't know. How would I know?"

I don't answer, just look at her steadily and confidently.

"Oh, I suppose I do have some idea. I mean, I've had several talks with him, and we have gotten along well enough. I wonder . . . I mean, when I say that, I wonder if I've just been pleasing him. Tuesday, he asked me to come in to see him, and he was very stern about one of the students sitting on the floor with a client. He had gone into the room—I don't know why—and found them on the floor, and he was determined that that sort of 'unprofessional conduct, Miss Gowan' will not happen again."

"What were they doing on the floor?"

"Just talking. I wondered if there was something more, but the student is a woman and so was the client, and Dr. Elliott didn't even suggest there was anything else wrong except that they were sitting on the floor instead of at the desk in chairs."

"What did you tell him?"

"I said I hadn't known about it, but that I didn't think it did any harm. He didn't like that—for a minute I wasn't pleasing him. But only for a minute. . . . '' Face falling. "Then I told him I'd talk to the student and see if there was any reason that she felt the floor was necessary for working with that client. Oh, darn. I really had to get back to pleasing him, didn't I?"

"I still don't know how you feel about a social worker seeing a client and both of them sitting on the floor."

"Oh, I don't see why it matters where they sit or anything else. If they want to sit on the floor, it's not important as far as I can see."

"But you can't say that to Dr. Elliott."

"Oh! Well, I suppose I could, but. . . . ''

"Will you please me if you say it to him?"

"Oh, darn you, Jim. I'm not trying to please you. I. . . . ''

"Well, that certainly pleases me that you're not."

"Oh, I wish you wouldn't do that! I get all mixed up. Now where was I?"

Although I'm not really trying to torment her, sometimes I

wonder if I'm motivated partly by a kind of teasing, flirtatious feeling. That's probably in the mix to some extent, but mainly I'm concerned about challenging her continual but unthinking compliance. The best time and place to do so is right when I sense it is happening in her relation with me.

April 2

The agency continues to be the scene of much of Louise's concern. A new medical consultant, recently divorced, asks Louise out for dinner, and they enjoy each other. Dr. Elliott becomes more demanding. Louise finds herself in the middle between him and her students over a number of seemingly minor infractions which the director evidently regards as violations of professional propriety.

"I've got to see Dr. Elliott again today." Louise's voice is resigned but disgusted.

"He must like your company. Almost every time you're here you tell me he's asked to see you."

"I'm not so sure anymore. I guess I still try to please him a lot—after all he's my boss—but on the other hand, I'm always trying to get my students out of his bad graces."

"What is it this time?"

"I don't know. He just said he wanted to discuss the student program in general. I'm kind of scared though. Honestly, he is so petty. He's put out rules against sitting on the floor, against any contacts with clients except in the waiting and consultation rooms— that may be okay, I'm not sure—against using our first names with clients, against almost anything that makes us a human place for people to come for help."

"How do the other staff members feel about it?"

"Oh, everybody's getting angry. I was telling Don the other night that. . . . "

"Who's Don?"

"Don Webber, the doctor I've been going out with lately."

"Um. What did you tell him?"

"I was saying that Dr. Elliott's effect on the staff so far is to make us more irritable with each other and yet to kind of draw us closer together too."

"How's it going with Don?"

"Oh, it's nice to be going with someone again. Do you know it's been almost two years since I've had more than a single date with someone?"

"How come?"

"I don't know." Her manner is evasive.

"What is it, Louise? The way you said, 'I don't know,' made it seem more like, 'I don't want to talk about it.' You seem uncomfortable."

"Well, yes, I suppose so. But how should I know why I don't get many dates?"

"You're the person who ought to know, if you want them."

"Maybe it's just that I don't believe in . . . uh . . . being intimate right away."

"Intimate?"

"Oh, you know, getting all sexually involved right on the first date. I mean, a lot of men seem to feel that you should at least pet a lot if not go to bed with them if they take you out."

"And you don't want to?"

"Not right away like that. I mean, I might like to be tender a little, but I really don't want to . . . to get more physically involved so soon."

"Do you mean you don't want to, or Mrs. Colten wouldn't like you if you did?"

"Well, maybe, she. . . . No, I think I mean I wouldn't like to. At least, not that fast with most of the men I know."

"How about with Don?"

"Well, he doesn't push me, and. . . . "

"And?"

"And so we are getting to know each other more gradually."

"How does that go with him?"

"Uh, it's nice. I mean, he's a very gentle and warm person. I really enjoy being with him."

"You sound very correct and formal."

"Well, I don't know why you want to know all of this."

"So why not ask me?"

"Well, why do you?"

"Are you asking me because I told you to or because you want to know?"

"Oh, darn it. I. . . . No, wait a minute. I. . . . All right I take my question back. I was embarrassed to tell you about Don and me, but I didn't want to say that. I think I know that it helps to talk about things that are embarrassing. So no question."

It's good to see Louise take charge of her own thoughts that way. I almost say so to her, but that could tend to reestablish the looking to me for approval. So I just wait.

"We haven't had sex. That's not so. We haven't had intercourse. But we do kiss and touch a lot, and oh, it is so nice. It has been so long. I don't know whether I'm in love with him or not, but I do love to be close and to touch and be touched. And he really is such a dear man, so kind, and so caring."

May 8

In this group session, Louise is trying to share some of her feelings of loneliness and her dread of growing old without ever having had a full life of her own. When she tells of her affair with Ralph, Jennifer hears only that Ralph was a married man and bitterly attacks Louise. For a woman who has organized her life around being pleasing to others, the experience is explosive. She is confused, tries at first to explain, but it is soon apparent that Jennifer is not to be reasoned with. Then Louise gets mad and starts fighting back. As concerned as I am for Jennifer, I find a kind of delight in seeing Louise forget to be proper and pleasing and stand up for herself instead.

May 11

Louise is clearly subdued and somewhat withdrawn when she enters. She gets settled on the couch quickly, and then sighs and lies without speaking for several minutes. I realize she is crying quietly; still neither of us says anything. Finally she reaches for a Kleenex and starts to talk in a barely audible voice.

"I'm having such a tug-of-war inside me that I just feel

bruised and sore. I really hurt like I had been pounded inside. I never realized it could be so painful."

"Can you tell me about it?"

"I'm so mixed up." Weeping more strongly. "I don't know how to say it all."

"Just as it comes. Don't try to sort it out yet."

"Well, after the group I thought. . . . Or at the end of the group, I thought I was going to be all right. I mean, I thought I knew where I was. I. . . . Then I got home and started to go to bed, and then all the awful things I'd said came back to me and . . . oh, I just wanted to die. I kept thinking of what I'd said to that poor woman who was hurting so much. And I thought you and the whole group must surely hate me. I didn't think I could ever come back here, and I knew I'd never dare go to the group again. And. . . . " She is silent, crying; sobs now starting to come.

"Mm-hmmm." Let her do it her own way.

"Then I thought I just had to call you, tell you I was sorry, find out how to get in touch with Jennifer, apologize to her. . . . I almost called you in the middle of the night. But when I thought about Jennifer, my feelings began to change, and . . . and then suddenly I was mad. I was so mad, and I thought of a whole lot more things I wished I'd said to her, and I knew I couldn't really tell her I was sorry. That would be a lie. But then I thought how you and the others probably would hate me for being so. . . . Oh, I don't know. Because right in the middle of everything, I . . . "

"You. . . . "

"I suddenly heard you asking me, 'Are you having the feelings I want you to have?' in that mocking tone of voice you use sometimes. And all of a sudden, I. . . . " She is silent, not crying.

"Mmm?"

"I said out loud to you, 'You can go to hell, Bugental! I'm mad, and I don't care who knows it.' And then I started laughing, right there in the dark in bed, I laughed out loud. But then you said—in my head, I mean—'Are you being angry because you know that will please me?' and I didn't know, and now. . . . "

"Now?"

"Now, do you know?" Surprised tone. "I feel better. I

mean, right now I do. I wish I didn't think at all about what you feel about all of this, but I do. And I hope you're not mad at me or disgusted with me. But I don't think you'll send me away even if you are, and. . . . "

"And. . . . "

"And, if you try to, I'll fight with you too! So there!" She turns and grins at me. I try to stop myself from grinning back, but I can't do it. So we laugh together.

Then I sober. "And so you've ended up pleasing me, eh?"

"Oh, darn you!"

May 18

Louise is increasingly preoccupied with the struggle with Dr. Elliott. His mandates are numerous and picayune. As she finds her own sense of strength, she is more able to take issue with him, but still she continues to be generally pleasing. As a result, she has so avoided any crises or showdowns.

Meanwhile, her relation with Don Webber is becoming more engrossing and more intimate. I feel at once a bit paternal (he'd better not hurt my child) and a bit jealous (I hope he knows how lucky he is to have such a desirable woman). I spend some time thinking about these recognitions, and I try to keep them conscious and in perspective.

Today Louise is really a delight to the male eye. Her skirts are much shorter than they used to be, and she is much less concerned to adjust them so carefully. Thus her legs are quite evident, and her new and brightly colored blouse accentuates her breasts much more than the garments she used to wear.

"You'll never guess what I did last night." She says it with too much gaiety, it seems to me. There's a forced quality.

"What did you do? That's obviously the appropriate question."

"Oh, you! Well, I should make you guess, but I won't. I went skinny-dipping with Don. What do you think of that?"

"Was it fun?"

"Oh, yes!" Nothing forced about that.

"Then I think it's great. Tell me about it."

"Well, we just drove down to the beach and found this wonderful place, and no one was around, and the moon was about half full, and we just looked at each other and said, 'Why not?' And so we peeled off our clothes and went swimming. It was just wonderful. The surf felt so good on my body. I don't see why anybody ever wears a bathing suit. Really I don't."

"Um hmm."

"See how far I've come?" Teasing.

"You've come a long way, baby! I think that's the appropriate line, isn't it?" Her mood of play is contagious.

"You know, I think I'm a little embarrassed to be so excited about what is probably a very ordinary thing to you and to most people."

"Sounds like you're starting to break faith with yourself."

"No! I mean, yes, I was starting to, but I'm not going to do that. It was fun for me last night, and it was new for me, and it was a big step."

"What else happened?"

"What do you mean? Oh, no, uh, no we didn't. I mean, well we kind of did, but not all the way."

"It seems so hard for you to talk about your body and your feelings. It's as though the words themselves are painful or contaminating in some way."

"I know. That's silly isn't it?"

"No, I don't think it's silly."

"There I go again. I sell myself out at the least word from you or anybody else. No, it's not silly. That's the way I was raised, but I'd like to change it."

"What else happened besides the skinny-dipping?"

"Well, we lay on the sand and. . . . And we petted. There. Oh, for heaven's sake, I seem to feel I have to be a blushing schoolgirl. We made love to each other. In every way just about except by having intercourse. I wouldn't do that because I'm not taking the pill now, and Don didn't have any protection."

"That's smart."

"But he's coming over tonight and. . . . "

"And. . . . "

"And I want to have intercourse with him."

"How's it feel to just say it out that way?"

"It feels great. Just great."

May 21

At our next session Louise enters looking intense and either very angry or very frightened—I can't tell which. She stalks to the couch, doesn't lie down, but sits on it, and looks up at me. I see her eyes are teary.

"What is it, Louise?" I find I'm wondering if Don has been cruel. Whoa, remember the jealous father is not a therapist.

"Dr. Elliott has put out some new regulations that are just too much, too strict, too old-fashioned. I'm so scared, Jim. I'm not going to go along with him this time. I'm tired of trying to smooth things out between him and the students and the other staff. Oh, I don't want to have trouble. It just scares me so. I mean, I keep thinking of running away. I know it's silly, but I can't help it."

"You're starting to break faith with yourself, Louise."

"That's right! I hadn't thought of that. Well, I'm not going to do that." Her head comes up, her jaw juts out. "I want to make a joke about myself getting mad, but I'm not going to. I am mad. I think Dr. Elliott's going to wreck a good program, a program I put a lot of effort into, and I'm going to fight him."

For a while she talks about this new-found determination, about the unreasonableness of the director's newest edicts (actually quite a startling attempt to turn the clock back, as I know from other sources), and about the fear she keeps feeling, which seems unreasonably strong.

"Jim, it's too much some way. I mean, I really find myself trembling inside when I think of telling him that I won't cooperate with these new regulations. It's as though he will literally kill me or do something else terrible. I know he might be able to get me fired. But I'm not sure he can even do that, at least not without an awful struggle. But this fear and trembling isn't just that I'll lose my job. It's much more, much, much more."

"Louise, lie down, and let everything slide for a bit now and just see what comes into your awareness. Don't look for anything specific. Just be open to whatever comes."

She swings her legs around and gets settled on the couch promptly. Her skirt nicely comes up to reveal much of her thighs, but she doesn't make more than a token gesture to pull it down. She really is delightful and sexually desirable to look at. Okay, I tell myself, now that you've enjoyed the view, let's get back to work.

Meantime, Louise has taken several deep, sort of shuddery breaths, and tears have started out of the corners of her eyes. Watching her, my mood changes, and I feel warm concern.

"Jim, I'm thinking of lying in bed with Don the other night. It was so sweet, so much what I've longed for for so long, so very long. I really don't give a damn about Dr. Elliott and his rules. I have been so lonely, so very lonely. It was so good to be with a good, warm, loving man. He was so kind, so kind, Jim. And it was so good to just make love without any restraint. I never knew it could be that way. Why have I waited so long? I am so glad we talked about sex and everything. I wasn't all tensed up, and I didn't just want to please him—but I did want to please him, and I did. I also discovered he wanted to please me! And that was so strange. He wanted to please me!"

"It's hard, even now, to think that someone wants to please you."

"Yes, and no. Both. I really am in love with Don, Jim." Her mood changes. "Are you jealous? I love you too, you know, but I'm *in* love with Don."

"I can hear that. And yes, Louise, I think I am a bit jealous, even though I'm a whole lot glad for you."

"Oh, that's nice." She is silent for a minute. Again her face changes. "Why does this darn fight with Dr. Elliott have to come along right now? I am so happy in so many ways, and then I think of him and I get that trembly feeling again."

"Just keep open and tell me whatever else comes along."

"I see my bedroom again. And that feels nice. And then I see clouds and a summery sky. Oh, it would be good to be outdoors and make love. Oh, that makes me think of New Hampshire and Mr. Colten. The poor old man! And poor Mrs. Colten too. I didn't know I'd ever feel that way about her."

"I wonder if there's any connection. You took your clothes off and enjoyed your body with a man the other night, and now you're going to get in trouble. That's what happened in New Hampshire."

"I don't remember enjoying myself there, but I see what you mean."

Too fast, Jim, too fast, I tell myself. She can't get it if you just push the idea at her that way. I know that. Why am I impatient? I think I must be more emotionally—and probably erotically—caught up with her right now than I'm letting myself know. Let's take it more slowly.

The rest of the session brings out nothing further, but she does explore her fear enough to feel that she is really determined to confront Dr. Elliott.

The confrontation was some weeks in coming. Dr. Elliott was out of town for a period, and then he was unavailable when he came back. Eventually, she insisted on seeing him and told him frankly that she could not cooperate with his new regulations. To her surprise, he did not rage at her. Instead, he told her to prepare a written statement of her position and that he would respond to it later.

June 18

"Do you remember how I told you once I'd like to undress all the way and show myself to you?"

I am startled and suddenly alert. If she intends to do that now, I'm not sure I should encourage it, but I also know I'd really enjoy having her do so. These months of following her erotic maturing with Don have been stimulating to me as a man who cares about Louise, as well as significant to me as her therapist. I content myself with a nod and a few words, "Yes, I remember."

"Well, uh, you know Don has this Polaroid camera, and we were fooling with it the other day, and he took some pictures of me. And, well, I thought maybe you'd like to see them. You know, this really embarrasses me, and I didn't think it would." Pause. "Do you want to see them?"

"Of course, Louise."

She hands me an envelope. I hold it, but make no move to open it. "What's happening in you right now, Louise?"

"Oh, darn you. I might know you'd make me recite!"

"You're being so very appealing and flirtatious that I think to myself, 'Oh, don't be such a spoil-sport; you know you want to see the pictures and she wants you to see them.' But Louise, I don't want to see them as much as I want to help you keep faith with yourself right now."

Suddenly sobered. "I know. I really am embarrassed. I can't take my eyes off that envelope in your hand, and I think I must be crazy. I can't be showing you pictures of me naked. The next thing. . . . And I want you to see them, but. . . . "

"The 'next thing. . . ?' "

"Heavens knows what will be next!" Laughing, flustered.

"What do you think might be next?" Smiling, insistent. I'm getting aroused by this game. She's teasing me; yet I don't think she is conscious of doing so.

"Who knows what will happen after you see the pictures of me naked?" Laughing, too much, forced. "You might get so wild you'd tear my clothes off." Abruptly the laughter stops. She's frightened, embarrassed.

"Tell me what's going on now, Louise." My own voice sober, still supportive, insistent. Want to put the fun back in, the tease, the implicit sexual chase, but even more I want to help her confront her fear.

"It just changed. I don't feel so funny, but. . . . "

"I think you frightened yourself when you said I might tear your clothes off."

"Yes. I don't know why I said that. I'm sorry."

"It sounds as though you feel you've done something bad."

"Well, I don't know. I just wish I hadn't said it."

"Louise, you're in flight from yourself and from me now. You've forgotten the happy, stimulated self you were a minute ago. You've forgotten who I am. You've forgotten what our relationship is. You're back to being a frightened schoolgirl, and you're making me into a punishing parent."

"No. Yes; I mean, yes. I don't know. I'm confused. Are you mad at me?"

"Your question even sounds like the child in you is speaking. How do you read me, Louise? Really look at me right now. Take charge of your life in the now. Can you?"

She looks into my face like someone peering through a fog. Her eyes are swimming, but she is bringing her awareness into the moment. Rather quickly, her expression changes. The smile starts in the corners of her mouth and breaks out into a delighted chortle. "Wow! I sure do it to myself, don't I?"

"Tell me."

"I mean knock myself out of what is going on right now. And then I feel like I'm a child again and back in the past. I can't believe how just a minute ago I was sure I would find anger or disgust in your face. I mean, I really expected to see you hating me."

"And now?"

"Now, I think you like me, and. . . . Oh! There I go again! I started to say that you liked looking at me, and right away the fear came in. I can't be so presumptuous. And besides, right there in your hand you have pictures that will prove how bad I am. Well! I just don't believe it. That *is* the past. Will you look at the pictures?"

"I'd like to." I open the envelope and suddenly feel my own erotic heat. Louise and I are so close emotionally as we struggle with her fears; and now, here she is quite naked in the pictures. The first shows her in silhouette, the curves of her body plain, but no detail. In the second, she is seated and so bent over her own legs that only the side of her body is displayed. Then she has draped some material over her so that her breasts are bared but her lower body is covered. Her breasts are full, and the nipples are erect. I pause and look up at her watching me intently, almost breathlessly. "You are a very lovely woman, Louise."

She draws in her breath sharply. "Oh, it's hard to stay here right now. I want to make a smart remark or to take the pictures back. Yet I really love watching you look at me. Do you know, Jim. . . . " She pauses, and suddenly I sense she is close to tears. "I've never before been proud of my body or really enjoyed it as a woman? Never!" She weeps quietly and then reaches out and takes my hand, squeezes it. "Thanks." Whispering. "I'm so glad I found my body before it was too late."

The last picture is a real delight. She is standing facing the camera and nothing covers her nudity. But it is her pose that is so great. Don caught her just as she spread her legs, threw her arms up over her head and stretched in a total body way that is so sensual and so unfeigned that just to look at her, I feel my own body want to twist and move in empathy. I look at her sitting across from me, and the wish is strong within me to see her just that same way in actuality. "That's really breathtaking, Louise. And, in all truth, it has a tremendous erotic impact for me." Ruefully, I recognize how formal my language is.

"Oh, I'm glad." She exhales.

"What are you thinking?"

"Just that I was kind of anxious still, and I was so relieved that you liked the pictures."

"That's a cop-out answer, Louise."

"Well, maybe. . . . "

"I expect you're thinking something like I was: How nice it would be for me to see you like that in reality rather than in a picture; how nice it would be for me to be with you in the way that picture suggests."

"Yes." Whispered. Head up again. "I'm glad you thought that, and I'm glad you said it."

We sit silently for several minutes, both busy with our own thoughts but still in communion. The buzzer signaling the arrival of my next patient and the end of Louise's hour catches us both by surprise. We stand; she comes toward me, and I hold her in a warm embrace. Her body yields against mine in a way it never has before, and my own pulse becomes more insistent. I would like to kiss her, and I know she is waiting for me to turn my head to her. For some reason, I hesitate and then decide against it. Giving her a little extra squeeze, I pull back and turn toward the door. "See you next Monday."

June 20

On Monday, Louise is a study in contrast as she comes in. Her face and manner are tight, strained, and unhappy. Her costume is bright, summery, and—for Louise—very revealing. She is wearing a halter dress with a rather deeply cut V in front and much bare skin in back. The dress is short and clings excitingly to her body, but her body is stiff and resistive to the dress. She sits on the couch, starts to take off her shoes as she usually does, pauses, and then lies down without doing so. She adjusts her skirt over her legs, and crosses her arms over her chest. She looks frightened and stubborn.

I decide just to be quiet and let her carry on with the fight that is obviously going on within her. She has scarcely acknowledged my presence and seems to be intently listening to an inner dialogue. Her arms tighten, then slowly relax; a tear appears at the corner of each eye and silently slides downward. More tears come, and there is some relaxing of her tightness. Probably five minutes have elapsed, and we have said nothing yet.

Finally, Louise sighs, unfolds her arms, and speaks sadly, "I am so messed up inside. I don't know how I can possibly tell you all that's been going on inside of me. Yet I'd like to. It feels like such a familiar battle, and damn it, it's been going on too long. I want to do something about it. Still I'm afraid to, I guess."

"Talk to me about it, Louise."

"It started after I was here last time. No, wait, don't ask me to tell you what happened last time. I'll do that myself. Last time I showed you some pictures that Don had taken of me. I was naked in the pictures. Wait! There's more." She pauses, determined to see this through herself, not wanting to be helped. "I enjoyed showing you the pictures. I think. . . . I mean, I believe you said. . . . I got the impression anyway that you liked seeing them too. I could be wrong, and you don't. . . . "

"You weren't wrong, Louise. I really enjoyed seeing the pictures of you nude."

"Yes." She sighs as though relieved of a weight. "Yes, I thought so, and then I was afraid I'd imagined it. Somehow I was so worked up I couldn't remember clearly all that happened. I kept thinking about it, and I would imagine that you were kind of . . . you know . . . well, aroused. Then I would tell myself that was just my imagination. No! Don't tell me. I want to do this my way right now. Then. . . . " The tears start flowing again, and this time she takes a Kleenex and dabs at them sadly. For a full minute, perhaps, she is silent. I am filled with a kind of love for her, seeing her courage, knowing how she is struggling with the threats and shame she has carried most of her life. She may indeed do it her way. I feel enriched to be able to be with her as she does so.

"Well, I kept remembering what you've been saying about keeping faith with myself. And it was awful hard. A lot of times I would find myself being Mrs. Colten or Aunt Julie, bawling myself out, shaming myself. Sometimes I would think you were probably awfully mad at me and would most likely tell me today that you couldn't work with me any more. Then I would get back with myself, and I'd try to be living today instead of in the past and. . . . "

Again she pauses as the tears flood her. This time she sobs quietly for a bit. "I don't know why it all hurts so much. But it really does. Maybe I do know. I think I've been realizing how much of my life has slipped by without me really being aware, with me just double-crossing myself again and again. And I'm nearly forty years old! Oh, I don't want to think about it, but I'm going to. I'm really going to think and think about it. I don't want any more of being dead and not with myself. And then today . . . or yesterday . . . or. . . . "

She is up against something different in herself now. I can feel that the tension that has been receding is now coming back.

"Today," she continues, her voice conveying the mobilization of her resolution. "Well, actually yesterday, I began thinking about coming in today, and I got this crazy idea, and. . . . "

"Louise," I begin.

"No, wait. Let me do it. I know. I'm starting to break faith with myself. It wasn't a crazy idea. But I sure think it was now. I mean, I really want to think it was crazy. I want to deny it and to deny the me who had the idea. I want to run away from that woman. I'm so afraid just to be her, just to be who I am. Oh! It really hurts. It's a physical pain in my chest and throat. Do you know that? It really is."

"It surprises you that your emotions can have such power, that your fear of being you can really tear at your body."

"Yes, yes, it does. Oh, I don't want to go on. I want to change the subject. I want to talk about the power of the emotions. I don't know why this is so scary. It's as though I'm convinced you'll destroy me or at least send me away if you know what I thought."

We are silent a moment. I have a strong impulse to help her, to point out that she is making me into her rejecting uncle, but she wants to do it on her own, and I am determined to respect that. Already I have found myself butting in when I didn't really need to. Why must I keep proving to myself and to my patients how much they need me?

Suddenly she gathers herself and speaks in a clear voice, "I thought today I would like to come here and take all my clothes off and show myself to you directly without using the cop-out of photographs." She stops speaking and seems to have gone empty inside. I wait, and she is silent also. At length she says in a softer voice, "Well, I've said it, and I had a hard time staying with myself. But I think I'm still here, and suddenly I see that you're here too. You know, in a way, I don't think I've seen you before this whole hour."

"I know."

"But I sure saw a lot of people sitting in that chair where you are. It's nice to have you there now."

"It's nice to be seen as me."

"Yes, I imagine it is. I'm beginning to see me as me, and I like that too."

Some part of me is protesting this talk. I want to remind her about undressing. I'd really like to see her naked. But another part of me is busy and protesting: "You can't let her do that! That's probably a violation of some law or at least the code of ethics. You'll get in trouble. What about her welfare? Are you looking for sexual kicks at her expense?"

"Jim, I want you to tell me frankly: If I did undress here, would it be hard for you? I mean, I don't want to make you hurt. . . . " She stops because I have begun to chuckle. A minute before, I was concerned about legalisms, and here she is concerned for me the person. Then her unwitting pun. My tension comes out in the laugh. She looks around at me in puzzlement.

"I'm sorry for interrupting you, Louise, but your unconscious just tickled me with a pun. You asked if your undressing would make it hard for me. I think the answer is 'probably so.' But that's. . . . "

"Oh! Oh, I see. Oh, that does embarrass me. But that's silly. Yes, I hope it does make it hard for you. Ooops! I'm not very sophisticated, and it kind of takes my breath away to talk this way. But it's fun too."

"Louise, I heard you expressing concern for me, and I don't want to let that get lost. If you did undress, I'm sure I would react to you and your nakedness and the whole situation. I wouldn't like to be unaffected by that. If you are worried that physically it might be painful for me, that really isn't a serious matter."

"I've always heard that men suffer if they get excited and then the girl doesn't . . . doesn't want to have intercourse."

"That's mostly male propaganda, Louise. If a man has an erection and finds it uncomfortable, he can certainly do something about it. He isn't helpless. Indeed men like to get excited by all sorts of sexual stimuli in circumstances where no completion is possible— sexy shows, magazines, and so on. But that's enough lecture. No, Louise, my concern about the possibility of your undressing here is not because of possible physical discomfort."

"But you're saying you are concerned."

"Yes, I am. Two ways. One, I know that many of my colleagues would strongly criticize me for letting you undress. We therapists have kept actions separate from words in therapy, especially any sexual actions, and it is scandalous for that dividing line to be crossed. I don't agree, but as we talk about your taking off your clothes, I find that concern in my mind."

"I wouldn't think of getting you in trouble! Let's just skip the whole thing. Besides. . . . "

"No, Louise, don't run away like that. You're giving a particular tradition power over your life just as you gave Mrs. Colten's teachings the power before. I'm affected by that tradition—in fact, I believe that it has some very important things in its favor—but I don't want to be blindly controlled by it. You and I need to think together and to be as aware as possible and to choose how we will act. Any pat answers from outside of ourselves are really cop-outs on our own responsibility and our own lives."

"I feel concerned about you though."

"That means a lot to me, Louise, but that's not the only consideration. I said I was concerned two ways about what would happen if you did take your clothes off. The second has to do with its meaning for you and for us right here. Have you thought about what might happen once you were naked here with me?"

Her quick intake of breath is answer enough. She looks at me startled, and then she bursts out laughing. "Now that's not a very gentlemanly question, doctor." We both are chuckling as she goes on. "Yes, I have, and I thought it was very nice."

"Put it in words."

"I had a little fantasy in which . . . ulp! Here it comes again. Golly! I sure have a bad time of it with saying things openly. Okay, here goes: I had a fantasy in which I undressed and then you held me—like you did when I left the other day—and then I undressed you, and . . . whew! This is hard to do when you're holding your breath. And then we lay on the couch and made love. Hmmmfff! There!" She let out her breath in a big exhalation.

"I hope it wasn't as skeletal a fantasy as you've just related." I smile at her. She is such a gutsy woman. Now that she's over the worst of her fearfulness, the erotic quality is back full force, and it is powerful indeed. I look at her in her little dress and imagine it coming off and the panties which it hides and which can be the only possible other garment she wears coming off too, and I am getting breathless. Come on, Jim, back to work!

"No, it wasn't, but I really don't want to spell it all out right now."

"Okay, but the point is this: What does happen after you are naked? I really find you attractive, Louise, and I can easily imagine it would be beautiful to make love with you. But for a whole host of reasons—some having to do with us here and your therapy and some quite outside of that and connected to other parts of my life—for all of those reasons, I would choose not to have intercourse with you now. So. . . . "

"Oh, I know that. I really didn't think that would happen. You asked, so I told you. No, what I wanted to do—and I'm kind of losing the feeling now—was just to be as naked here as I was in those pictures."

"It sounds very nice, Louise."

She is silent and motionless. Inside my own head, I feel surprisingly calm. I know I probably should have thought of many more points to raise. There's still the question of possible scandal if anyone found out. Oh, nuts, I'm tired of being careful and denying life. Louise is showing me a more courageous way. Sit back and enjoy her honesty and her body.

Slowly her hands come up behind her neck and work with fastenings under her hair. Still slowly, they come back down bringing the straps with them so that now she is peeling down the halter top of her dress. Hesitantly her hands move lower, and the tops of her breasts are bared. Then abruptly she stops and sucks in her breath as she clutches her hands to her chest.

We are both silent as she lies tensely, the tears rolling down her cheeks unheeded. Her whole body is so tense that it is on the verge of shaking convulsively. I find momentary disappointment as my excited anticipation is replaced by warm caring for what is obviously her pain.

"What is it, Louise?" My voice is a whisper.

"I'm sorry, Jim." More crying. "I'm really, really sorry." She cries with such clear sadness.

"Tell me."

"I'm sorry. I know how much you want to see me. I really can feel that. I've been feeling it since I showed you the pictures. And I want to . . . wanted to show you me. I have for a long time. Ever since the day I opened my blouse. And now. . . . " Again she cries. I wait. This isn't what I thought at all. I thought she was embarrassed at her sexual excitement, but I sense now she's weeping for me. For me!

"I still will undress. I mean, I really will, because I know you would like that, but I have to tell you—oh, darn it, I don't want to say this—I have to tell you. . . . "

"Tell me, Louise." Softly.

"I'd be doing it," whispering, "mostly to please you. Oh," aloud, "that's not all so. I'd enjoy doing it, but somehow, since I have Don—it wouldn't be the same. I mean, oh, I don't want to make you feel bad. I really care about you, Jim, you know that. I really love you. But not that way anymore. I mean, after I showed you the pictures the other day, I suddenly knew that it wasn't really for me anymore. Well, it was for me. I really get kind of excited; aroused, I mean. But then in another way, I guess, I was doing it

chiefly for you. Like I knew you'd like it. And I liked your liking it.
And now, now, I really would enjoy seeing you see me, seeing you
enjoy looking at me without any clothes on. It would be scary, but
it would be exciting too. And. . . . "

"And?"

"And, I want to do it for you . . . and for the looking at
you looking at me. . . . " Her hands start to pull the halter down
again.

"Wait, Louise." The hands stop, but no longer clutch to her.
The upper surfaces of her breasts are bared, and I feel again the
swelling wish to see her whole exciting body. "Wait, Louise. You're
saying something very important. Important to you and important
to me."

"I don't want you to think I don't care about you, Jim.
You've saved my life. I mean, I really would do anything for you.
And I really mean anything."

"I know, Louise, but I think you're in the middle of doing
something even more important than taking your clothes off for me.
You're right. I really would like to see you naked, but that isn't
what I want most. Right now, you are also offering me something
even more precious—your trust in me to be with you even if you
don't do what I want or what some part of me wants."

"I know it, Jim. I started to take off my dress, and suddenly
I knew that I wasn't keeping faith with you or with me. Before Don
and I became so close—I mean, both sexually and emotionally—I
would have loved to take all of my clothes off in front of you just for
me. I know, because I thought of it lots of times. But now, just now
when I started to take off my dress, I knew it really wasn't for me
but because I knew how much you would like it. I was making you
old Mr. Colten, I guess, and just trying to be pleasing. And I don't
want to do that to you or to me, Jim."

"And you knew that down under my sexual excitement I
really don't want that either, Louise. I really value your keeping
faith with me and with you."

After Louise leaves I sit for several minutes, feeling tired
and dispirited. She is so very right. I was so caught up in the delight
of her emerging sexuality, of her greater freedom with her body, of

her always powerful eroticism that I lost track of what was her motivation and what was my own. Ruefully, I appreciate Louise's courage in confronting me and recognize that we are entering the final phase of her therapy. There will not again be a possibility for that exciting woman to be naked with me, and I am sorry.[8]

June 22

Louise is subdued and rather hesitant as she comes in. She sits in the big chair rather than lying on the couch, and her face is very sober and inward as she gets settled.

"Jim, I'm having. . . . Ever since I left Monday, I've been having a battle inside of myself. I. . . . "

"Tell me."

"Oh, so many things. One minute I'm pulling away from myself and telling myself how presumptuous I was to. . . . And then I suddenly feel like I missed my chance to have something . . . something special with you. . . . Then I get mad at myself for thinking you'd . . . for wanting to. . . . Then I get straight for a minute in my head and think what a good thing Monday was, but right away I start to lose that, and. . . . "

"You've got a lot of different ways of seeing what happened here with us on Monday."

"Oh, yes! So many. . . . But . . . well, I wonder how you think about it too."

"I've thought a lot about it too, Louise. But I think the main one is a very deep appreciation for you and your guts and for your really keeping faith with yourself and with me."

"Sometimes I wish I hadn't."

"I know. So do I, at times. But mostly. . . . "

"Mostly I'm glad it went just that way."

And so the hour goes. We feel warm appreciation for each other, and we know that we have passed some point of no return. Louise is not only my patient. She is my friend who can give to me and not just seek to please me. However long our therapeutic work goes on, it will be importantly different from here on out.

After Louise goes, I feel reflective and glad that I have a

break before my next appointment. This frightened, desirable, conflicted, exciting child-woman has grown in this office to be a person of strength and self-direction. My own wantings might have obstructed that growth so easily, and perhaps they did in some ways. Still, in other ways, those very subjective seekings of mine were important to her growth. I could never have planned a strategy such as the one that unconsciously unfolded. For that matter, I could never have consciously planned the course that proved effective for Larry or Kate or any of the others who have grown in this room. Instead, looking at it in full perspective, I don't really know what went into our journeys together that didn't occur with Ben or Lillian or some of the others who never made the big breakthrough. Some of them profited from our work, but to a more limited extent. Why does the difference occur?

The thought of Louise comes back, and I bathe in a warm, sensuous, loving, satisfied feeling. Images of her: stiff and frightened at first, opening her blouse and pulling up her skirt, repentant and earnest and in flight, excited showing me the nude pictures—that one powerfully erotic nude picture—her gutsiness in confronting me the other day with her little dress half off, her growing inner quiet in speaking. Maybe I lost perspective for awhile with her—maybe I lose perspective more often with more people than I like to recognize—but something deep within Louise and within me could be trusted, and it came through.

July 26

Louise and Don have decided to live together. She is excited by the prospect, but she is also fearful. She recognizes that she is beginning to want to please Don so much that she has trouble finding her own feelings. We work with this familiar impulse rather directly, and she makes real gains even though she still finds it repeatedly present.

At work, Louise waits for Dr. Elliott's response to her written statement opposing his edicts. She has discovered that other staff members have prepared similar objections, and she looks forward with a mixture of excitement and fear to the confrontation everyone expects to occur. Then, abruptly, Dr. Elliott announces his resignation, and there is no direct denouement. Louise experiences frustration and relief, but she feels satisfaction that she was ready to fight for her position.

November 8

Louise and Don decide that they really are not compatible, so they part. She handles the ending of her romance well in that she is not overwhelmed, even though she experiences strong pain and disappointment.

January 10

Louise feels she has gone as far as she needs to in therapy at this time, and I concur. When she leaves, we both feel very loving and very sad. We have each grown and changed from our hours together.

June 11

I receive an invitation to Louise's marriage to Dr. Don Webber, with a note: "We find we'd rather fight and be together than be lonely and separate." This is one wedding where I'm going to kiss the bride as joyfully and fully as I know how.

Recalling Louise now brings me a sort of wry chagrin. All along, I knew the power of her femininity, and yet I still fell under its spell. In truth, I wouldn't be surprised if I would again, were the circumstances the same. It is a magical thing indeed—the warm, earthy magnetism of a sensual, sexual woman.

Actually, I needed to be accessible to the way Louise had developed of trying to influence her world, just as I needed to be accessible to Frank's angering tactics or to Larry's rationality.[7] In each instance, I would have been much less able to help my patient had I been totally unreachable. But in the same way, of course, I needed to stop short of being completely captured by the way Louise or Frank or Larry had of trying to influence their worlds.

Louise denied responsibility for herself and her own actions.

She learned early that she was powerless and that she had been cast into a world in which adults, themselves so very vulnerable (as demonstrated by her parents' deaths), clearly could move her about as they chose. The only route to safety seemed to be through being extremely pleasing to others. She scarcely experienced any inner awareness and rarely thought about what she herself wanted, since her need to be safe was so equated to the need to please. And she was indeed skillful at pleasing others.

Of course, *one cannot really deny his responsibility for his own way of acting and being.* Responsibility cannot be displaced, and to attempt to do so always ends with a disruption of the life of the person who tries it. I confronted Louise with her compulsive need to be pleasing and yet indicated that the only way she could please would be to be unpleasing; in so doing, I highlighted her confusion. The tactic brought out in the open the continuing but more implicit struggle within her.

It is significant that as long as Louise sought to deny her separate identity and her responsibility for her own life, she did not make deep and meaningful relationships with others.[8] When one is, as Louise was, oriented to live in terms of others, it is not possible to have any real intimacy with them. *Intimacy requires that there be at least two distinct people.* When one cannot be separate from the loved one, when one cannot afford to be different from the other, then there can only be a parasitical relation. With unconscious wisdom, Louise had avoided the kind of marriage in which she would have inevitably subordinated herself into a drudge wife and martyr mother. Her professional life allowed her to find others to serve and to give to, but those others were so numerous and so often changing that it was never necessary for her to completely annihilate her own inner life—an outcome which otherwise might have been all too likely. Thus, it naturally followed that as she began to affirm herself and her own individuality, she found herself entering into more emotionally involving relations, relations in which her own inner sense, as well as the wishes of others, had a part.

Louise had let her inner sense be submerged by other people's expectations of her. She had so little feeling of her own inner being that she genuinely doubted that she would exist at all if she were not in some way responding to others—especially to others' needs. Her expression of doubt was no figure of speech for Louise; she genuinely lacked the inner sense of being that can only come from dependably experiencing one's life in action. This experience—the immediate sensation of *I*-ness in process—is irreplaceable. She had tried to replace it with the voices of others, just as Larry had tried to replace it with the image he created for others to see. Neither Louise nor Larry found the substitution successful. Each of them experienced genuine feelings of terror from a persistent sensation of being empty. This emptiness arose from the lack of any centered, inner sense of identity.

Louise came to a new appreciation of her individuality and freedom of choice. No longer feeling they would cause her to be rejected, she began to become more a person in her own right. Her confrontation of the agency director led to no direct reversal on his part, but it gave Louise a new sense of her own dignity and personhood.[9] Her confrontation of me was even more important and represented a major change from her former compulsion to be pleasing. She gambled that she could keep an important relation with another person even though she reacted in a way different from what she thought he wanted. Although I do not have first-hand knowledge, I think the separation that Louise and Don went through before their marriage stemmed from her consciously or unconsciously testing whether she could be a separate person not dependent on him or his approval.

Certain recognitions stand out when I think about Louise's journey in therapy:

Louise confronted the paradox of human relationships just as Frank had, but she chose the contrasting emphasis. For Louise, safety seemed to reside in being a-part-of *others rather than in being* apart-from *them. She needed to please them, hide herself in them, and deny any differences from them. The consequence, predictably, was that she came to feel that she herself did not exist as a separate person. From Louise's experience, I learn for my own living how essential it is to discover my uniqueness, to let my inner awareness inform me of my own living and wanting as well as to be aware of my similarities to others.*

If I am to have a meaningful sense of my own being, I need to "keep faith" with my own life. *So many of us have learned to desert our own views, desires, or values when important or numerous others seem to favor a different position. When I set aside my own genuine awareness of an experience for some present satisfaction or seeming safety, I am alienating myself from my own center. I can only be me if I am willing to stand by my own being. But I also recognize that in order to do so effectively, I must be willing to see other perspectives as well.*

The folkways and morals we learned as children have grown out of human experience and are attempts to ease human relationships and to reduce human suffering. They deserve our respect. But blind obedience to traditional ways is not respect; it is subservience.[10] Each of us must redecide the major issues of how we will act and to what extent we will follow the approved ways and to what extent we will set them aside to be vital and authentic in following our own inner vision.

The feelings of my body are rich and valuable, *and when I let them be a part of my being, I am enriched.*[11] *In the past, I have mistaken social taboos for tests of my worth or for divine injunctions. They are neither. Valuing my sexuality, I want to take responsibility for giving it life, but life that is genuinely in harmony with my full inner awareness.*

There is a fine intoxication to the pulsing awareness that hotly fills consciousness when a man and a woman deeply experience themselves and each other, when they feel their bodies, their emotions, their promptings toward each other, and when each knows the other shares this heady sensation. At such moments we breathe a sense of endless possibility, a rich yearning toward the magic of touching, the music of caressing, the mystery of transcending separateness while yet celebrating it.

So much in our culture has tried to debase these moments of wonder and ecstasy, has called them cheap or dirty, has confounded them with possessiveness or rivalry, has seen them only in terms of the commonplace and the dreary. The truth is that such times are powerful, and that much of what is blessing or cursing in life may flow from them. But we are not hapless victims of some rampaging monster when feeling such emotions. We have choice, and there are many alternatives, not just a simple either-or. To enjoy such feelings does not dictate that they must be carried into ultimate action. Too many people seem to feel, in these supposedly sexually liberated times, that they must either avoid any sexual arousal or have a full sexual relation if they permit any excitement to come about. Such rationale is stupidity dressed up in the guise of candor or common sense. It is neither honest nor sensible.

The person who lives with full inner sense awareness will value the richness of moments of sexual-sensual aliveness, for they are usually times when he knows his life's pulse acutely. But if his inward sensing is truly open, he will also know that there are many other elements in his inner awareness. Among these will certainly be the other people of whom he is a part, his other concerns for himself, and very importantly, his feeling for the other person with whom he is now sharing this vibrant moment. When both the man and the woman in such a deep encounter are open within themselves and to each other, they will choose with awareness of their lives as a whole what actions will be most genuine and responsible. There is no one right path at such a time; each couple must meet the opportunities and the possibilities in his or her own ways.

These sorts of thoughts are stirred in me by recalling the delight I knew in Louise slowly opening her blouse and lifting her skirt for me, in looking at the photographs of her lovely nudity, in the first moments when I thought she was about to disrobe in front of me. I remember these times with real pleasure. I wish that we could have explored together even further. I am glad we chose the route we did.

Louise is not as sexy or as sweet these days—that is, not as overtly and insistently—but when I see her on occasion, she is still clearly the focus of others' attention, and the men present never fail to notice Louise. She is that very lovely person, a mature and very feminine woman.

❦ 6 ❦

HAL

Objectivity and Limitedness

The first great task of which we are conscious in our lives is "getting educated." Everybody and everything, it seems, makes it plain that this is a job of tremendous importance, worth tremendous amounts of time, money, effort, and sacrifice of other things. The very calendar seems to be rearranged by the school schedule so that September is really the first of the year, not January. "Educational" seems to be a word to work wonders on parents whether applied to toys, activities, TV programs, or sports ("physical education" is obviously good; "playing games" is a waste of time). So the message is very clear: All this education is to get us ready for the very difficult business of being adults, is organized to make sure we will know enough to be full-fledged persons, real people some day.

Yet there is a guilty secret! I know it, and most of the people who level with me admit it. The older we are, the greater the shame of our secret: We didn't make it. We didn't learn enough! Despite all the lavish structure of education, all the worthwhile experiences and careful teachings of all sorts of people, we don't really know enough to be adults even though we've made it past the magical twenty-first birthday.

Somehow we always expected that some day we would know

enough. We would be able to make decisions on informed bases; we would understand about the major areas of being alive—about marriage and parenthood, family finances, friends, sex and morals, politics and law, religion and death; and we would have reasoned and effective programs of action. We would know enough, we always thought, once we finished our education and were adults. And now here we are, acknowledged adults, and we do not by any means know enough.

How we deal with this incompleteness, this continual not knowing enough, is a key to how fully alive we feel. If I need to hide from myself how much I do not know and to pretend that I have reasoned and informed bases for whatever I do, then I must deny much of my awareness—both about myself and about the world in which I live. If I try to avoid the issues, I may take Jennifer's route of assigning responsibility to rules, or Louise's path of reliance on other people, or Frank's response of decrying any value, or I can use other ways to obscure my—and others'—recognition of my limitedness. But by doing so, I reduce my own vitality.

For Hal, getting educated was an on-going, never-ending, impossibly demanding obligation. He felt guilty for the incompleteness of his mastery of life, for not being ready to handle any situation that came along. Already extensively educated, he continually read and studied to try, at last, to know enough. He was doing a remarkable job at an impossible task.

Hal is a fellow psychologist but of a persuasion quite different from my own.[1] I knew him casually before he came to see me, and I found him personable and interesting. His training emphasized experimental psychology and objective, scientific methodology, and that school of thought held that behavior alone provides a sufficient basis for understanding human beings without recourse to the murky realms of subjectivity. Thus I am surprised and flattered when Hal asks to enter therapy with me. It pleases me that he chooses to work with me, but I am also challenged. Though I want very much to help him, I know myself well enough to know I need to be alert to see Hal, the person, rather than to react to his philosophic orientation.

March 26

Hal is big. He is big physically: at least six feet four and two hundred twenty-five pounds, I'd guess. He's big mentally: Phi Bete as an undergraduate at an ivy league school and a doctorate in psychology, also from a top university. Big too in his approach to life: private practice in psychology, group leader at growth centers, part-time assistant professor at a local college, committees and offices for the state psychological association, papers read at meetings and published in journals. And right at this moment his bafflement is big too.

"I don't understand. I thought you wanted me to tell you why I bawled Tim out this morning."

"No, Hal." Patiently; although we've been working together three months now, he doesn't really understand yet. "I asked you to see what thoughts or feelings you had about bawling him out. Wait, wait a minute." He's starting to respond too soon; he still doesn't get it. "Look, Hal, let me lead your awareness for just a minute, okay?"

"Sure."

"Okay, picture this morning at breakfast. Try to get the feel of how that image is in you now. You can't go back there in fact, but you can get in touch with how you feel now as you remember what happened. Just get that feel; don't give me an account or explanation; just the feel. Visualize Tim, your son, and his hair that bugs you so. Now you'll find something going on inside of you. Let it happen. What are the things happening in you *right now?*"

"Well, I told him to get a haircut yesterday. He said he would. He took the money. He knew I wanted it shorter. I don't think I'm unreasonable. I know how the kids wear their hair. For crying out loud, I'm not that square! I've got a beard myself. I just wanted it to look less like the wild man from Borneo. And he walks in with it in a fright wig, an Afro, or whatever the hell you call it! Jesus Christ! He looks like the village idiot! So I let him have it. I told him I wasn't going to have a freak living in my house and. . . . "

He still doesn't have the idea.[2] He doesn't see that there is literally a whole world of difference between thinking *about* himself and being aware *in* himself. In some way, I need to help Hal move from the world in which Hal is a troubling object, a puzzle to be solved, to the world in which Hal is simply himself, doing or not doing what he wants to the extent the world around him makes possible. Like so many of us, Hal is much more familiar with the objective world than with the subjective world. We are all, to at least some degree, wanderers, lost from the Eden of unself-conscious spontaneity of being.

"Hal, you're still recalling and thinking about this person who happens to be you. You're still not inside of yourself."

"I know what's inside of me. I'm mad as hell at that kid. That's what is inside of me. He just seems to watch for every chance to bug me, and it makes me so damned mad that he knows just how to push my buttons to tee me off. . . . "

"He knows how to push your buttons to make you furious, but you don't seem to know how to push your own buttons to act more the way you want to." For there is also another side to the story. Hal is engaged in a continuing and painful war with his teenaged son. This morning's battle is but one skirmish. Yet Hal is not only furious with his son.

"Jim, I don't know what happens when I try to talk to that kid. I just find myself in a rage before I know it. I start out telling myself I've got to be calm, reasonable, see it from his side, and in two sentences I'm shouting and threatening." Hal is torn by his love for and his fury at his seventeen-year-old son. The son, Tim, challenges Hal in every way he can. The fight over his hair is only one issue among many. Tim wants to drop out of school as soon as he graduates from high school—if he graduates; he's been absent so much and is so indifferent to his studies that he may not make it. Tim has been into pot and probably other psychedelics. Tim doesn't believe in capitalism, the American way of life, the traditional home and family, or success. Tim, in short, seems to refute everything that Hal has expended his life on. Except words. Both Tim and Hal are endless talkers and arguers, which for a long time was a bond between them, a bond that has now broken down into endless verbal combat. And from this combat, Tim emerges the victor (at least he doesn't overtly show his wounds), whereas Hal's emotional agony is increasing.

"You're really hurting right now, Hal."

"Yeah, yeah, I know. But damn it, what gets into me? If that kid came to me as a client. . . . Well, hell, I've got one right now. Kid named Harry Denton, just about Tim's age, and he sure has the same screwy ideas Tim has. I listen to Harry, and I don't blow my stack. Why can't I listen to Tim that way, work with him, be more patient? Oh, I know the books all say you shouldn't work with your own family and friends, but. . . . "

"That's the nub of it, isn't it? You have the model of the way you are with Harry Denton, and you just can't do the same thing with Tim."

"Yeah, it just doesn't make sense to me. I mean Tim's really not any worse than Harry. I can stand back and see that. Tim's not even as funny looking with that God-awful hair of his and all. Now I don't expect that I'll be as calm with Tim as I am with Harry. It isn't that, but. . . . "

"Hal, wait a minute. It sounds like you're handling this off the top of your head. Are you sure you don't expect that of yourself, that you'll respond as calmly and wisely to Tim as you do to Harry?"

"What do you mean, am I sure? Yeah, I guess so. Besides it doesn't really matter what I might like to do; it's what I keep doing that gives me all the trouble. If I only wouldn't blow my cool so. . . . "

"Hal, you're not really in touch with yourself at all right now. Instead you're hammering away at a problem named Hal Steinman and telling me not to distract you by asking about how Hal Steinman feels inside."

"Yeah, I suppose so, but I really don't see what good it would do to go into all that psychoanalytic stuff and talk about my toilet training and so on."

Under the guise of sarcasm, Hal is trying to lead me away from pressing him for his subjective awareness. I don't think he knows how little real access he has to his inner feelings and thoughts. The "psychoanalytic" reference is his half-deliberate attempt to lure me into one of our recurrent arguments about the role of the unconscious in bringing about the conflicts and disruptive emotions we all have. It is significant that although Hal's own orientation in psychology emphasizes behavior more than inner experience, he chooses to come to me for therapy, knowing I hold a different view. Now I want to justify that confidence by not taking the bait of intellectual discussion.

"No deal, Hal." Let him sense my irritation with his gambit, but my basic support at the same time, if I can. "You really are trying to keep us from focusing on what's going on inside of you."

"Ah, yes, Doctor Freud, it is the mysterious unconscious, is it not?"

"Look, do you want to play games, or do you want to work on why you pop off so quickly at Tim?"

"Okay, okay. So you're in charge. Tell me what to do, and I'll be good and do it." He is overly docile, mockingly acquiescent.

"Hal, for Christ's sake, what the hell's going on? You're just dodging and squirming every way to keep from settling down to work."

"Hell, Jim, I don't know. I just feel kind of out of it. I know you're trying to help, but it just feels like you want to take such a long way around, and I really don't understand what you want me to do now."

"I know, Hal, but I think that's a very important point in itself: you don't understand what I'm asking you to do. That, to my mind, is part of what is giving you the problem. You don't know what's going on inside of you, so you constantly find yourself acting in ways you really don't want to. You are a black box to yourself, and things you don't like keep coming out of that box. So, I'm saying, let's look into the box."

"That would make sense if I really didn't know what was going on inside. But I know. I know I want Tim to look decent, to study, to finish high school and try to go to college, to. . . . "

"Wait a minute! You're off and running, telling me all about what you want Tim to do. You've only said 'I want . . . ' *about* yourself. We're trying to talk about what goes on *inside* of Hal."

"All right, I'll tell you what goes on inside of Hal. He gets

damn mad. That's what. Mad that that kid doesn't have the common courtesy to. . . . "

"Hold it! Hal, you know and I know that you can go on the
entire hour telling me about Tim and what he does. You've done
it a half dozen times in the past month here. And what's different?"

"Not a damn thing! So what do you propose?"

"I'm trying to help you sense the difference between focusing on Tim and what he does and getting in touch with your own
inner experience. Now I know you have trouble understanding that
difference, but it's very important, and so far I don't think you've
really tried to get with it." Patiently, but impatiently too. He's a
bulldozer, and sometimes I've got to be a Sherman tank to get him
to hear.

"Still not doing it, eh?"

"Still not. . . . I think some part of you knows damn well
you're not."

"Now why would I want to do that? I just think. . . . "

"Hal! Damn it! You're about to go off on another line. I
think it's just frightening as all hell to you to be told—and to half
believe—that there's something you don't know how to do. You're
just running in every direction to keep from settling down and really
listening to yourself or to me."

"All right! What do you want me to do?" Angry, challenged.

"Let's start with you using the couch. Wait! I can see you
getting wound up to give me a speech about psychoanalysis and so
on. Skip it. I want to get you into an unfamiliar situation and hopefully get you to try to be in touch with yourself in unfamiliar ways.
So let's start using the couch."

"I thought you guys just used these things with good-looking
females. I don't know whether I can trust you." Grumbling, getting
up, lying down stifly, obviously not liking it.

"That's okay. You're not my type."

"Okay, so here I am on your damn couch. Now can we get
on to this thing about my blowing my top at Tim and. . . . "

"No! First off, when you use the couch, it's usually well to
shut up. I commend that to you right now. Shut up!" Pause. "Now,
listen, Hal, and really try to hear me. We've been battering at each

other, and that's okay, but now I really want to be very serious with you, and I want you to open yourself up as much as possible to understand not just my words but the intentions behind them. Okay?"

"Yeah." He sort of squirms, uncomfortable in his jacket, getting settled, but he's really going to try. "Yeah, sure, I just like to give you a hard time."

"Hal, I know that much of the time you feel that you're being kind of playfully troublesome with me, and I certainly enter into that. We both enjoy it as a kind of game between us. But, Hal, there's another part to that. You really don't know much about your inner experiencing, and that troubles you. You don't feel as much in control as you'd like to, as you need to be. So by making it seem like a game, you can tell yourself and me that you truly are in control and could stop the game if you really wanted to. Hal, here's the point: I don't think you can stop the game."

"Oh, come on. I mean, I certainly don't have to joke it up all the time."

"No, that's true. But the game is not just the joking."

"What is it then?"

"The game you have to play is that you have to convince yourself that *you* are in charge of your life and of what you do. Thus, you must act as if it's only a minor exception that you have trouble being as you would like to be with Tim or that you can't really get with what I'm asking you to do here."

"I don't know. . . . I wonder if. . . . " He trails off, musing.

"Hal, look, let's try to work together now. Let me take a minute to give you kind of a fresh picture of what it is I think you need to do. Then, give yourself a chance to try it. I don't want to make you feel tested, but I do want to challenge you to give yourself the best possible chance to get more deeply in touch. Okay?"

"Okay."

"Good. Now here's the idea: Most of the time we're dealing with things, people, situations outside of ourselves. When we come to think about ourselves, we do it the same way—objectively—as though we were objects to be dealt with too. For many situations that works well enough. But it doesn't work worth a damn when we're trying to understand why we feel or do as we do or when we're trying to change our feelings and the actions that flow from them. Like you trying to understand why you have such a short fuse with Tim. If you came up with the right explanation—whatever that might mean—it still wouldn't help you change unless you got in touch inside of yourself. So we need a different way of thinking than the objective. That different way is when we *listen to* ourselves, instead of figuring out things *about* ourselves. Hal, you really don't know much about how to listen inside of yourself. And I think, at some level, you sense that and are threatened by it. You like to be competent. More than that, you absolutely need to be competent. And you are most of the time. But this is one place you're not. And you don't like that, and you don't like to know it. Now, I'm going to stop talking in a couple of seconds, and I want you to lie there silently and just let my words and your own thoughts sort of mix together. Don't try to report on them. Don't try to solve anything. Don't try to reply to me directly. As much as possible, don't *try* to do anything. Just lie there, and then when you feel ready, just talk to me about how it is inside of you—remember, *inside* of you. Okay, now I'll stop talking."

I sit back. Wow, I sure gave him a lecture! Didn't mean to say so much. Just kept thinking of other things I wanted to add in. Still do. Wish I had suggested he start with bodily awareness. Think he'd find that easier in some ways. He's being very quiet. I think he's really listening to this approach for the first time. He's so damned effective in his intelligent, personable way. The therapy he does probably is overly rational, but undoubtedly it gets a lot of impact just from the kind of guy he is and the way he comes across to people. He probably is threatened by the apparent passivity of what I'm urging him to do. Should have said that.

He's certainly taking long enough to start talking. Did I make him think he couldn't talk until he'd come up with something new? Wait! Could he be asleep? Oh, no! He couldn't do that!

He could and is.

After Hal leaves I reflect for a few minutes on our conversation. His going to sleep, I'm pretty sure, expresses his unconscious resistance to my urging him toward an area of inner experience that he has long avoided and denied. In this denial, Hal is like a great many people in our educated, middle-class culture. We have been taught to disbelieve in the whole inner world of intentions, emotions, imagination, and wantings. Incredibly, we have come to believe that these inner feelings are ephemeral and inconsequential, that these—the very stuff of our living, immediate being—are not to be given as much attention as that which is external and public. Hal, who invests so much in being competent and knowledgeable, senses that he would be lost and wandering if he once entered into that unfamiliar inner world which is his own being.

June 19

Several months have passed since the soporific session, and during much of this time I've been confronting Hal over and over with his avoidance of his own subjectivity. Gradually, he has come to recognize that this is indeed a blind area for him, and now he is trying to gain access to it. Today's session is like many others during this time. Hal greets me in his friendly way in the waiting room, comes in and takes the chair. He still resists the couch except when I insist that he use it. I've been less inclined to urge it since the day he went to sleep. In the chair, Hal smiles at me rather shyly in contrast to his good humor in the waiting room. He waits a minute.

"What are you thinking just now?" Can he listen in to himself?

"Oh, I . . . I was wondering if you were going to say something to me."

"No, I'd just like to know what your concerns within yourself are."

"Well, I worry a lot about Alice. She's dating this new guy a lot now, and I have a hunch she's not a virgin anymore. I mean, I'm not a prudish father and all that, but I hope she knows how to take care of herself. I feel like I ought to do something, but I don't know what. She just seems to go her own way. I asked June if she'd given Alice all the information, you know, and June said Alice probably could teach her things. I guess there's not much you can do when a girl is nearly nineteen, and yet you kind of feel you ought to. . . . "

"Hal, you're talking about a 'you' who would worry. Is it

hard to say these things in the first person?" Some way I suspect that Hal has come prepared with this "concern about Alice," and thus it sounds impersonal and distant.

"Oh, yeah. No, it's not hard to say in the first person. I worry a lot about Alice. She's a really good kid, and I wouldn't want her hurt. See? First person."

"Right. Tell me about how you worry, Hal. Can you just sort of do it out loud and let me listen in?"

"Okay. Well, I just think she's such a good girl, and really she is so young, you know. And I'd hate for her to get hurt in any way. And uh . . . she's got a good figure; I imagine all the guys are wanting to get to her. I guess that's about it. That's what I think inside."

"Hal, it sounds like you are beginning to get more in touch with what's going on inside, but I imagine there's a great deal more. For example, I wonder if you had any thoughts about how you had raised her, what you'd taught her about sex, how free she might feel to talk to you if she were concerned, what she might be like as a sexual woman, what you might do to someone who did hurt her, and so on and on."

"Oh, yeah, sure, all those things. I do think about all those things. I really think she knows she can talk to us anytime about anything. And of course, I would really want to get anybody who hurt her."

"Hal, we're still missing some; although I think we're getting closer. Each of those ideas I suggested might lead you into a whole chapter of thoughts and feelings. Those were like the chapter headings. Each has a whole lot of ideas and feelings that belong with it. Just now you picked up two of them like they were questions and gave them quick answers. That's only the beginning, not the end, of exploring your concerns."

"Jim, I know you're trying to help me, but I just don't think I'm the introspective type. I mean you analytic guys go squirreling around in all that kind of stuff, and I suppose with some people it does a lot of good. But I don't know; for me I'm not sure it's the thing. I need to deal with the problem more straight on."

"What problem are you thinking of when you say that?"

"Well, just any one."

"No, pick one. What problem is it that you want to deal with more straight on?" Insistently. I'm challenged; face it.

"Oh, like how I still can't really keep cool when I talk with Tim. I know it's been a little better lately, but I expect it'll blow wide open any day now. Nothing's really changed."

"Okay, so say what the problem is there."

"Uh, well. I can see where you're headed. The problem is me, and you know it damn well. And so do I. Why can't I keep my cool?"

"Okay, so what's your answer? Why can't you keep your cool when you talk with Tim?"

"Oh, shit, Jim, I don't know."

"What's the head-on way of tackling that problem?" Rubbing it in.

"Finding out the reason I keep blowing my stack and changing it."

"How do you do that?"

"Try to figure it out. Try to apply reason."

"Okay, let's do it. Figure it out, apply reason right now. Let me listen in."

"Oh, you know it won't work, and so do I. I've tried a thousand times. I just don't get anywhere." Chuckle. "I sure teed you off though."

"Yes, you did. I think it's another example of how you avoid recognizing something you don't do well and yet need to do and do now."

"Hey! You know? I can kind of get a sense of that. I mean I know I really wanted to get away from that feeling of being up a blind alley."

"Good, Hal. You really are beginning to get more in touch with what's going on inside of you. See if you can follow it up."

"Uh, yeah. Well, I didn't like feeling that I was stuck, and uh . . . you kept pushing, and I kind of wanted to take the pressure off, you know. I didn't really mean to mislead you, you know. I guess that's about it."

"Can you feel the difference now, Hal? Most of what you just told me is certainly reasonable, but it doesn't come as much from your immediate experience as from what you know or think about yourself."

"Well, yes, I suppose so." Dubiously.

And that's as far as we'll get today. He got a quick glimpse into the processes going on within himself, but it was too unfamiliar, and he hasn't really come to value it yet.

June 21

When we talk again later in the week, Hal's blocking of his own inner experience becomes even clearer to him. It comes about when he's telling of yet another blowup with Tim.

"Jim, I just don't understand myself. I mean, I said to myself when Tim and I started talking about his school work, I said, 'Now, take it easy, you know you won't get anyplace by shouting at him. Take it slow. Pretend he's somebody else's kid.' I really went through all that in my head when we first began to talk, you know?"

"You were really trying, Hal. Really trying to give yourself good advice. But. . . . "

"Yeah, and two sentences later I'm shouting at him, threatening him. I mean, I hardly waited to hear him say anything. I don't know what gets into me."

"Hal, you tried to handle the situation by using two lies to yourself, and it didn't work."

"What do you mean, 'two lies'? I didn't lie about it." Aggrieved.

"You told yourself to treat Tim as if he weren't your son. That's one, and. . . . "

"Oh, come on, Jim, you know. . . . "

"I know what you were trying to do, Hal. I'm not blaming you, but I'm trying to show you how you try to trick yourself into doing what you want because you're not directly in yourself, from the inside."

"Yeah, but I've tried and tried, you know that, and. . . . What's the second lie?"

"The second was talking to yourself as if you were another

person. Now putting the two lies together, it looks like you're not with yourself. If you have to lie to a person, then it's clear you're not in a very good relation with him. Right? And that's certainly so, if that person is yourself."

"Yeah, yeah. I can kind of see what you mean. It's clear enough when you make it between me and someone else, of course. But it's different when I try to think about my relation with myself."

"That's because basically you're a unity, but you learned—like I did—to separate yourself from your inner living. That's the whole point of what we're trying to do, trying to help you get back inside of your real unity."

"I get you there, and I'm for that. But how do I get there?"

"Hal, let's just step back from all this for a few minutes. I want you to try something. At first it may seem pointless, but give it a chance. Okay?"

"Right."

"Tell me just as simply and directly as you can right now what you think probably happens inside of you to make you get so mad at Tim. How come, do you think, this happens again and again despite your feeling that you don't want it to happen and despite your intention not to let it happen?"

"Hell, I don't know." Disgusted, morose; disappointed in my question.

"Well, I know that's true in one sense, but in another way it's not so. Somewhere in you, you do know a lot more than you will let yourself be aware of right now."

"I've told you everything I can think of." Protesting, unfairly accused.

"That's true, Hal, but now I want you to take a little time and see what comes to your mind spontaneously right now. This time don't think of *things*. Just let yourself be aware of how you feel about yourself and Tim right now as you're sitting here."

"Want me to try the couch again?" Half-grin, but serious.

"Might be a good idea."

He peels off his coat, gets settled on the couch rather readily. He told me some time ago that he thinks he heard all I said to him that day he fell asleep, that only during the silence after I stopped talking did he doze off. Now for a moment he is silent, wriggling into a more comfortable position.

"Now, ask me again."

"What comes to mind right now as you think about yourself and your relation with Tim?"

"Just the same things I've told you before."

"Say them again, if they really and spontaneously come to mind right now."

"Oh, Jim, I don't like to be stubborn, but I've tried this again and again, and it just doesn't do any good." Dispirited, edging on impatience. "I don't know why he makes me so mad. I can't really talk with him at all."

"Well," persisting, encouraging, "just give it a try now. And maybe I can tune in with you and see better how it goes when you try to think about it."

"Okay." Dubiously, resignedly. "Well, I just think to myself what might be the reason I. . . . "

"No, wait, Hal, don't tell me about it. Just do it right now. Think out loud so I can hear what it's like inside of you as you work on it. Just let me listen in, but you think your own thoughts for yourself."

"Well, I wonder if maybe we've got one of those Oedipal things going and I resent Tim as another male in the house, but that seems nonsense to me. Then . . . uh . . . I think probably I never had a chance to go through my own adolescent rebellion . . . because of the war and all, and so I resent Tim's doing it. But if so, I don't get any big flash of light or ringing bells or anything." Pause. "And then I think I'll go read some more of Erikson and see if I can come up with a better idea, but I'm really not very optimistic."

"Hal, you're still standing off and looking at yourself as if you were another person and you had to think up possible explanations for what he, this strange person, does."

"Yeah, I suppose so. I don't know." Troubled, not so sure. "Well, I wonder what the hell's the matter with me. I know that I'm going to drive Tim utterly away or cause one of us to do something really bad if I can't get a hold on myself pretty soon. I get so damn frustrated with myself I'd like to kick my own ass for the way I act sometimes, and. . . . "

"Hal," interrupting, urgently, "when you're not treating yourself like a puzzle to be figured out, you're acting like a tough drill sergeant cussing out a dumb recruit. Don't you ever just think your own thoughts for yourself on your own side?"

"Well, yes, I guess so." Really troubled now, sensing the problem more than he has before; anxious to do well. "I mean, sometimes I feel really sad and kind of sorry for myself. I try not to dwell on that. It doesn't do any good, and I really can't waste the time."

"Wow! Hal, if you're not a dumb recruit to be cussed out, you're a poor inept slob to be pitied. You really don't have much chance just to be Hal, the person in the midst of his own life, trying to work things out as best he can, and feeling a lot about the people in his family and their lives. No wonder it's so hard for you to change things the way you want!"

"Ugh! I don't like that. I mean, I think I really understand what you said this time, but I sure don't like your pitying me."

"Pitying you!" Anger not feigned but probably not as strong as I'm letting it through. "You dumb jock, I'm not pitying you. But I surely can feel a lot of fellow feeling for you. That's a damn hard place you're in, whether you know it or like it, or not. I know because I'm often there myself."

He's silent some time, digesting this. Then his voice is subdued. "I read you. And thanks."

July 6

Hal enters the on-going therapy group, and he is instantly one of the central figures. His physical size joined with his ready wit and friendliness make him liked by all the members. As I watch Hal, however, I am aware that he is always responding to or aiding someone else. Hal, himself, rarely is the topic of discussion.

July 27

This is the fourth time Hal has attended the group. To-night's session is following the pattern set on the first night, and so I decide to try to help the group be aware that they are not really getting to know Hal, and at the same time I want to confront Hal with the realization that he is not using the group to explore himself. An opportunity comes as Hal is talking to Ben and Laurence.

Hal: "So the way I see it, Laurence, you and Ben are really saying the same thing, but you're saying it in two different ways. You talk about the principles, and Ben—well, old Ben's the practical type—so he's talking about particular applications. I don't know. Maybe I'm wrong, but it seems that way to me."

Laurence: "Well, yes, I . . . I suppose you're right, Hal, but. . . . "

Ben: "Of course, he's right. You just hate to admit it, and. . . . "

Laurence: "No, no. I just was thinking it over. Yes, I'm sure you were accurate there. Appreciate your pointing it out."

Jim: "Ben and Laurence, let me switch your attention for a minute. Hal's just resolved the argument you two were having. How do you feel right now about Hal?"

Ben: "Oh, he's all right. I mean, I'm glad he pointed it out. Maybe Laurence will quit feeling he has all the answers all the time."

Laurence: "Well, Hal has made a very interesting point, and it really seems to me. . . . Well, hmmm, yes, it was most helpful."

Jim: "The thing I notice about what both of you are saying is that you're not really reacting to Hal. You are thinking about what he said and about each other. That seems to be Hal's role in the group. He says helpful things and then rides away—Hi-ho Silver!—before anybody gets around to thinking about that person Hal."

Ben: "Hey! Yeah! That's right. I don't have much of any idea about him." Turning to Hal. "How about it, big man. What gives with you?"

Ellen: "Hey, Hal, can I be Tonto?"

Hal: Slightly flustered. "No fooling, I don't know what you mean, Jim. I just got interested in what Laurence and Ben were kicking around and suddenly it hit me that they were kind of missing each other and. . . . "

Jim: "Hal, I'm sure it seemed that way, but that's not the point. The point is you're everybody's helper, but we seldom hear much of anything about you, yourself. A little while ago when Ellen was crying, you were right there helping her tell about the bad thing she was in with her guy. . . . "

Ellen: "Yes, but he really did help me."

Hal: "Well, you know, I really felt bad about how Ellen was hurting, and I thought I was showing that, and. . . . "

Kate: "You were, Hal, and I could see a lot of caring in the way you were talking to her. I know I felt very warmly toward you for it. But I really don't know anything about what it meant to you, inside of you. . . . "

Laurence: "Yes, that's so. I hadn't noticed it, but you really never do say much about yourself. I'd really like to know more about you."

Hal: "Oh, sure, I'd be glad to let you know more about me. There just isn't a whole lot to say. I mean, you can ask me any questions or anything. . . . "

And so in a jovial way, Hal opens up the possibility of the group gaining information about him, but he doesn't seem to know how to bring his own inner experiencing into the sessions.

August 30

A month later, after a number of sessions in which Hal's sensitivity to his own subjective life is increasing, he is working more directly for inner awareness.

"Jim, I think I have a better idea nowadays than ever before about the business of being inside of myself, but it still keeps getting away from me. I just wish I could hang on to it better."

"Hang on to 'it,' you say; like hanging on to a thing, an object."

"Yeah, and. . . . Well, okay, hang on to my . . . to the idea . . . to my understanding about being inside, being subjective or whatever. I just don't know how to say it, but the idea is. . . . "

"Hal, I don't want to make a big deal about words, but I think there's an important reason that you talk about hanging on to an 'it,' like a tangible thing. I think you—and I—learned to make objects of ourselves. When we try to get those objects to behave differently, our language is the language of objects, of 'its' and 'things' not of 'I' and 'me' and so on."

"Sure, I can see that, but how do I change it . . . uh, how do I change my way of talking? I don't know how to do it."

"I think when we really know what we want to do and when we really are in ourselves, there's no 'how to' at all. We just know what we want, and we do it."

"That sounds great, but I can't imagine it."

"Of course you can; just think for a minute. How do you sing 'Home on the Range'? There's no 'how to' whatsoever. You know what you want to do, and you do it. How do you tell somebody about an idea you're all excited about? You just know you want to put the idea over and out it comes. You may, if you have trouble with some part of it, stop and look more objectively at the process of talking, but for the most part you're just in your excitement and pouring out the idea without any 'how to.' Isn't that the way it is?"

"Yeah." Slowly, considering. "Yeah, I can see that, but somehow it doesn't seem like quite the same thing. I mean. . . .I mean, when I go to sing 'Home on the Range,' I already know the tune and the words, but . . . on the other hand, if I'm telling somebody about an idea, I don't know the words in advance, but I do . . . I do know the general shape of the idea; yet. . . . "

"You're right, of course, Hal, that the process is not exactly the same as singing a familiar song, but take a different example. Right now you're exploring in yourself, trying to feel how it is inside of you and to check that against what I had suggested. Right?"

"Yeah, yeah!" Brightening. "That's right. Right now, I'm exploring inside, like you said."

"And you didn't need any 'how to' to do that."

"No, I didn't." Excitement at getting the idea. "Hum! I'd like to be able to do that in other areas too."

"Why not?"

"Well, let's give it a try. The place I'd really like to get into is the whole damn snarl with Tim." Pause. "Boy, I just lost the excitement as soon as I thought of that. Yeah, but I would like to try to get into myself more on that one."

"Fair enough. Why don't you just think out loud about how you feel in relating to Tim these days?"

"Yeah, well, like always, one of the first things I think of is how impatient I am with him compared to how I am with other people."

"Hal, I think it's still true that you expect yourself to be as objective and effective with Tim as though he was a patient of yours rather than your son."

"Maybe, maybe. I would have said I gave that up some time ago, but now I'm not so sure. Wait, let me feel into it more carefully." He sits rather tensely, body not really relaxed into the big chair, his good-looking features drawn into the funny squinty expression he now gets when he's trying to reach down inside himself. His voice is lower and slightly more relaxed when he looks up. "I'm not sure, Jim; I really can't tell what I expect of myself. There are too many ideas and feelings buzzing around inside of me right now. Maybe I ought to use the couch and try to get deeper into this." He gets up and takes off his jacket, loosens his tie and collar, and then lies down on the couch. I marvel as I have before at the natural grace of his movements. He is a born athlete, a former college football end, and he still has that intrinsic coordination in the simplest physical action.

As he gets on the couch he continues talking: "I feel impatient with this business of trying to get into myself. I want to grab this problem and twist its neck off and. . . . I suppose I'm saying I want to grab Tim, but I sure don't really want to hurt that boy. Or do I? Not really. I know I don't really. Now, let's see, I was trying to figure out what I expect of myself when I'm trying to talk to him. Well, the first thing I think of is his hair. No, wait, I'm trying to get into my expectations, not how I see him. Well. . . . "

"Hal, wait a minute. You're not really on the couch yet. Take time to let all of yourself get lying down. Quit working at yourself. You need to *listen* to your inner thoughts and feelings, not quiz them with a rubber hose in your hand. Now, shut up a minute, and try to. . . . No, don't 'try to' anything. That's just the trouble. See if you can let yourself quit pushing and become open to discover your own awareness."

"Okay, but that's hard for me." He shuts his eyes, gives off a huge sigh, and abruptly begins to weep. I'm utterly astonished, and my guess is that he is too. The tears just start welling out of him. It's startling to see this huge man lying here crying so silently but with such deep pain. He doesn't fight it, doesn't do anything. He just lies there and weeps. Watching him, I find I want to weep too.

After what seems a very long time, Hal lets out a great sigh, moves around a bit, and reaches for the Kleenex I have put beside him on the couch. "I don't think I've cried in years. I haven't ever cried like that, at least as far as I can remember. And the funny thing is, I don't really know what I was—am—crying about." The tears are back. Again we're silent for a bit.

Again Hal dries his eyes. "It feels good to cry, and yet it feels so very, very sad. I start to run a list of possibilities in front of myself. What you one time called giving myself a multiple choice quiz. But somehow I don't want to. Don't want to figure it out. I'm tired. Tired of figuring things out. I just feel bad, really bad. That's all I know right now." Again tears and a pause.

"I keep seeing Tim's face. Only I think—yes, it's a younger picture of him. When he was fourteen or fifteen, I guess. No, maybe even younger. Eleven or twelve probably. He was such a wonderful kid. We had such great times camping and fishing together. Oh, God damn it." He's weeping more strongly now.

"Such a wonderful kid," I say as he slacks off again.

"You can say that again. You should have known him, Jim. He was a great guy. I had such dreams of how we'd be together. You know, I never really had a buddy growing up. After I got to college and became a big jock, sure. Lots of friends. Some of them really close, but not when I was a kid. Not when I was a big clumsy kid. Tim would have laughed if he could have seen what an oaf his old man was. No, he wouldn't have either. He was always so considerate. I mean really considerate, not just doing the Boy Scout thing. I remember one time he. . . . "

And so Hal comes home to his own center. He reminisces

about his son and his own earlier years. He begins to explore with inward vision the meanings that he has so long withheld from himself.

Being in one's own center seems such a simple thing. Aren't all of us? Except for some people who are screwed up emotionally or in their heads? So it would seem, but actually it just isn't so. Most of us, like Hal, are more accustomed to treating ourselves as though we were separate from our own experiencing center. In this way, we sometimes hold off unwanted feelings—like the sadness that Hal is experiencing now. Treating ourselves as objects seems to be a way to avoid thoughts and impulses—sexual and hostile ones, for example—that seem too much for us to tolerate in our conscious awareness. We can fool ourselves that we are free of such rejected thoughts and feelings, but that's just what we are doing—fooling ourselves.

The cost of fooling himself in this way shows up in Hal's pain-filled and frustrating relation to his son. Because Hal's emotions and actions accord so poorly with his conscious intentions, he continually makes the relationship worse rather than better. When we move out of our own centers and treat ourselves as strangers, we lose access to the very sources through which we can have charge of our lives. We become back-seat drivers complaining about the route we're taking, but we never take the wheel ourselves.

November 25

Nearly four months have gone by since Hal made contact with his own subjectivity on the day he wept. As important as that breakthrough was for Hal and as dramatic as it was in our mutual experience, it only was the beginning. Determinedly and repeatedly, Hal tried to get in touch with his inner sense, finding himself lost and not able to hear it, and then winning through to it again. Over and over, Hal has to follow this sequence until he finally has more dependable access to his own awareness. He is much more able to talk from his center these days, but increasingly, what he finds there seems sad and futile.

"I don't know, Jim. At first, after I got this deeper awareness of what was going on in me, I felt kind of up. I think I was hopeful that now we would solve all the problems. Well, I've got to admit that I'm better with Tim. I don't blow off as often or as extremely. And, of course, he's different too. I don't know whether he would have been no matter what I did, or what. Let's just say that it's less violent between us. We still aren't really together though; and that makes me sad."

"You'd like to have that old closeness back, eh?"

"You know it. But those days are gone, and no use crying over. . . . Well, no, I won't say that." It's a forlorn joke, and we smile thinly about it.

"Where are your thoughts now, Hal? Your face just changed."

"Not much of a one to play poker, am I?" Again that wry smile, as though he is looking at something within himself that is so unhappy that he can only muster a surface response to the talk. "I was thinking about Mrs. Kanowsky, the one I was telling you about last week. Always she wants answers. She has so many problems, and each one is life-or-death. And for each one, I'm supposed to know what she should do."

"That's a heavy order."

"You better believe it! So I blew up at her yesterday. Told her she was expecting me to play God or all-wise father and take over her life. I'm afraid I was pretty rough with her. But, you know, I really am getting fed up with the way she—and a lot of others too—won't take any responsibility for their own lives. They want to dump everything on me. Anyway, I think it was for her own good. I hope so."

"You sound pretty down, not so much angry as depressed."

"Yes." Pause. "Yes, I guess that's so. I have a lot of unhappy thoughts these days. There's so much to do, and it seems like I get further behind all the time. I used to have a lot of zest for my work; now I don't know where it's gone, but it's sure as hell gone. I wake up in the morning and wish I could go back to sleep."

"Are you carrying more of a load than you used to?"

"No, about the same. I've been doing some reading lately. But I'm going to quit it."

"What do you mean?"

"Oh, like last night. I spent most of the night reading

Grozet's new book, you know, *Modern Practice in Intensive Psycho-therapy*. And it's a good enough book, but really he's just saying the same old things. I finished about two-thirty in the morning with a headache and a flat feeling. Grozet talks like he's got it all worked out, but I wonder. What would he really do with a confirmed passive-dependent like Mrs. Kanowsky?"

"Do you often read that late?"

"Used to in college, but not so much lately."

"You must have been looking for something."

"No, or I guess I mean, yes. I'm kind of dissatisfied with the way I run my practice. I thought of consulting you for supervision, but it would get too sticky with me in therapy at the same time."

"Uh-huh."

"And besides. . . . Well, I hate to say this, because you've really done a lot for me. But. . . . "

"That 'but' really seems to trouble you."

"Yeah, well, the thing is I really feel like you've helped me change a lot, and it certainly is better with Tim now and. . . . "

"There's still a big 'but' coming, and you seem to hesitate to deliver it."

"Yes, well, it's just that while I'm sure a lot more in touch with myself, and that's a good thing, but I'm not sure the place I'm in or coming to is so good. I mean, it's not your fault. It's just that I really am so low lately, and. . . . "

"And it feels like that's not going to change."

"Yeah, I guess it does."

The buzzer sounds and Hal starts to get up. It's a bad time for an interruption. "Hal, I know this was hard for you to say. I really want us to come back to it."

"Yeah, sure, Jim, don't worry about it. Probably just a momentary thing." He's gone, and I'm frustrated. Is he in a bad place? Did helping him break through to his subjective center really push him into this depression? How down is he?

Long buried feelings and thoughts—held imprisoned by our fear of fully knowing and being ourselves—emerge into the light of full consciousness in unexpected ways. Some are painful, some are furious, and some are filled with bitter futility. Some people who have seen these contorted survivors of our inner concentration camps counsel against their liberation. It is better not to know; let well enough alone, they argue. But life is itself partial and halting when we dare not confront the very stuff of our own being. Hal's pain and his sense of pointlessness are frightening to him, and to me, but I have the conviction that the only resolution that will give Hal his own vitality is to be found through genuinely confronting and reincorporating his inner alive awareness.

December 18

It turns out to be several months before Hal again brings up his restlessness with his work. "Maybe I ought to go back to the Post-Graduate Center and get some really top-notch training in group therapy. I often think I'm not making enough use of my groups. When I read what they're doing at the Center, it sounds like they may be onto something. You know the papers that have been coming out lately. . . . "

Listening to Hal now, I can sense the driven quality of his searching, the books and journals endlessly combed, the institutes and lectures faithfully attended. And still the incompleteness and frustration. Still he is miserable as he thinks of the work that he self-sacrificingly prepared himself for over so many years and that now takes most of his waking hours in one way or another. It's not surprising that late in the session he says:

"And so I've been thinking of going into full-time research or teaching, or sometimes. . . . I've been having these thoughts that . . . well, maybe if I got into teaching, you know. I mean, I've got a pretty good place at the college, and I think I could get on full-time there, and then maybe. . . . It might be pretty nice teaching a moderate class load and having some time left for thinking and. . . . "

"Hal, what's going on with you? You can't seem to let your thoughts go. You keep running dry or cutting off or something."

"No; I mean, I don't know. I guess I'm just kind of unsure or something. I mean, I kind of wonder whether. . . . " He drifts off, leaving it incomplete.

"Is there something you're reluctant to say?"

"Huh? Uh, no; well, not really. I am doing a lot of wandering around. Anyway, I wasn't really serious about it; so there's no use wasting time on it. Besides I'd really like to think with you about this idea of going into full-time teaching. I know you used to. . . . "

But his manner prompts me to cut in again: "I have the impression, Hal, that you're quite uncomfortable with this idea you don't want to talk about, even though you say you're not serious about it."

Now the pause is very long before he answers. He is obviously struggling with himself, and when he does speak, his words come out slowly and with much strain. "All right. I'll level with you, but I want you to know this is just one of those fantasy-thoughts that everyone gets. I've just thought of stopping, that's all. There's nothing to it, really."

"Stopping, Hal?" Persistently.

There's an edge of irritation—or is it desperation?—in his voice when he replies. "Yes, stopping, you know. Just stopping. Stopping practice, stopping psychology, stopping—uh—anything."

"Anything?"

His voice is very faint this time. The fight seems gone as quickly as it flared up: "Anything or everything—stopping living."

It is very quiet in my office.

My inner thoughts are strangely relaxed. It is not that I doubt the sincerity of Hal's suicidal impulse. When I think about that, I am on the verge of anxiety about it. He means it. He might well do it. I can't dismiss that. No, the curious relaxation is one of closure. In some way in the past five or six weeks, I've felt the presence of some threat in him again and again, and yet I never could discover what it was nor even find suitable leads in what he told me so that I could work with my intuition. Now it's out in the open. Hal thinks of killing himself. And he thinks very seriously about it.

I have been silent, busy with my own thoughts. Hal rouses himself now.

"I don't mean to threaten you, Jim. I'm not about to do

anything right now. If it ever happens, I'll not mess you up . . .
or my family . . . or anybody else, if I can help it. I know what it
can mean to a therapist if a patient suicides. In fact, I didn't want
to tell you. You were just too fast picking up the cues."

"Maybe you were slow in covering the cues because you
wanted me to know."

"Well, yeah, that could be, but. . . . "

"It's a pretty lonely place you're in."

"Yes, it is. But I can handle it." His chin is trembling, but
he's struggling to keep the calm, sad facade he's had all along.

"For some reason you need to suppress your loneliness and
pain even now."

"Jim, Jim, it won't do any good. I know, man, I know. Get
all the emotions out, eh? Yes, it does help, but only if there's something more going for the person. It's too late, or I'm too confused,
or something. I don't know what I'm saying. It's just no use, no
use." Now the tears push through his tight eyes. Abruptly he re-
laxes and sits limply, letting the pain have its way with him. He
makes no effort to reach for the Kleenex close to his hand, but
simply cries quietly without any sobbing, his big frame slumped, his
face drained of expression.

December 20

Two days later, on a Thursday, he is still in a sad mood. He
is not really depressed; rather, he feels resigned. His manner is
such a contrast to the holiday season. It is subtly ominous to be with
him.

"Hal, what's it like inside? Your outside looks distantly sad."

"That's sort of the way it seems inside too. I feel like I've
had it, like I am just waiting now. Waiting for something."

"Waiting. . . . "

"I don't know. Maybe something that will let me go. And I
don't even know what I mean by that. Something that will
release me. Maybe to do it, to end things. Maybe, something that
will release me from the need to do it. I don't know. I don't know,
Jim. I just have to wait."

"I'll wait with you."

"Yeah, I know you will. And that means a lot to me."

"And to me." We're silent together for a space.[3]

January 15

Another day and his mood is more restless, angry.

"Do you ever wonder why you got into this stupid business? Well, I do. I was just asking for it. Just asking for everybody to dump on me. Mrs. Kanowsky wants to know who should make the decisions about money in the family. Should she or should Herman have the last word? Come on, Doctor, what's the answer? Don't they teach that in graduate school? Then Mr. Bayward asks me with tears in his eyes—asks *me*, mind you—what can he do to help his teenage son who's running around with the wrong kind of kids. And young Bill Lewis looks at me respectfully and wants me to use all my great knowledge—after all, I was his college psychology professor only last year—use all that great store of knowledge to tell him whether to marry little Betsy Carter or just screw her since she's a *shiksa* and his family would have a fit if he married her. That's a simple question, is it not? Surely the statistics on interfaith marriages would make the answer easy for anyone, especially for a professor and doctor. Then there is dear old Ben Fowler, a lush in the making if there ever was one. But Ben is so repentent after every binge. 'Doctor, how can I get myself to stop drinking? I know it's ruining my life. I'm going to lose my family. Doctor-lah, tell me from all your studies of psychology.' Well, Dr. Bugental, what do I say to them, hah?"

"What do you say, Hal?"

"Oh, and I almost forgot Mrs. Palmer, dear Mrs. Palmer. 'Please to give my son some tests and tell him what field he will be a big success in.' Oh, Mrs. Palmer, never use a preposition to end a sentence with. You see, I am a doctor. I know how to speak properly. What's that about your son? Well, he better look out for prepositions too, and propositions also, you Jocasta, you."

"Wow! They really get to you, don't they?"

"Oh do they ever! All those good people. All those good

questions. Like Mr. and Mrs. Green. 'Doctor, why do we fight so much? We really love each other so much. Tell us how to stop hurting each other.' So stop, already! Enough! Enough! I can't do it."

"And you hurt because you can't."

"Hurt, schmurt. They pay their money. What am I supposed to do? Say 'Don't feel bad' and pat their hands, like the old general practitioner did? No, they won't buy it. Their message comes through loud and clear: 'You're a doctor. You've studied these things. You teach at the college. A psychologist! You must know. You *must!* Tell us. Help us. We're giving up things we want and need in order to pay you. Help us. Our lives are being messed up. Help us. Help us!' And so what do I do?"

"What do you do?"

"I say, 'Tell me about it, Mrs. Kanowsky.' I say, 'Now, Bill, let's see, are you the eldest in your family? And what is Betsy's birth order? And was your father orthodox, conservative, or reformed? And how strict was Betsy's Christian upbringing? And did your parents have a stable home life? And did Betsy's? And how long have you known each other? And what degree of intimacy have you shared? I mean do you screw her just on the weekend or every night? But not on *Shabbas!* No, no.' Oh, hell, Jim, I'm acting the fool, I know. But it feels good to pour it out to someone. Now, you be the doctor and fix me all up, will you? I'll just lie here on the couch and cuss quietly to myself while you check any books you doctors use and figure things out for me."

He falls silent, having not really heard me up to this time. I am overwhelmed. "My God, Hal, you really feel the weight of every one of those questions as though it were a ton of rocks right on top of you!"

"You're damned right I do, and I'm sick of it. I'm about through with the whole fucking bit. I'm going to quit. I'm fed up."

"So fed up that you want out, but the only way you can see out is to kill yourself."

"If that's what it takes, okay! I mean it, buddy, in spades. I've had it up to here. You can take the whole thing and shove it right up the world's ass."

"You're not depressed; you're mad as hell."

"Amazing deduction, my dear doctor!"

"And you. . . . "

"No, Jim, I don't want to give you any shit. I'm sorry. I'm just so fed up, so tired, so sad." And abruptly the rage passes, and he sits slumped in his chair.

"Hal, where the hell did you go? You didn't hurt me. I know you, and we know each other. A few fast words aren't going to get to me."

"Yeah, yeah, I know. I'm just sorry to mouth off at you. I hope you don't feel hurt."

"Oh, for Christ's sake, Hal. Who do you think you are— God? You don't crush me with a snappy retort. For that matter, it sounds like you think you're God with those people who come to see you too."

He sits up rather abruptly, looks at me in a strange way, and says with complete calm, "That's right, I do. I do think I'm God."

We sit and stare at each other silently. He means it! He knows it, and I know it. He really means it! A quick shower of half-thoughts hits me: paranoid? hallucinations? delusions? dangerous? But this is Hal. I know Hal. Suppose it were true? Would I believe Jesus himself? Quit wasting time. Need to respond effectively right now. This is an opening. Now maybe we'll really break through. I want to. . . .

And then I shove it all away and read the invisible words inside my eyelids: "If you're not ready, shut up." And I shut up. Look at Hal. He's swamped with feelings himself, or is he? His face is strangely calm. I feel unexpectedly close to him. I've had a few deific fantasies myself. To myself: "There's not enough room for two Gods in this world, stranguh." What the hell's going on with me? Wisecracks at this point? I'm unnerved. Take time, breathe; let the quiet in. We are silent, briefly. Then I hear him sigh.

Hal is talking, almost talking to himself. "I guess I've always thought I was God. Or Jesus. Or something or someone like that. I never believed I would die. Still don't. Really believe I can do anything if I just put my power to it, just really focus in on it. Have done almost everything I really tried to do. Sports, grades, degrees,

marriage, kids. . . . Kids. Kids! Tim sure doesn't think I'm God.
He used to. I think he really did. I overheard him talking to the
other kids one time when he was four, maybe five. 'My dad can fix
it! My dad can fix it!' He was excited about something. I don't
even remember what. 'My dad can fix it,' he shouted. 'My dad can
fix anything!' And some place down inside of me I thought, 'That's
right. I can.' But I can't fix it with Tim today, can I?"

"Tim doesn't think you're God any more."

"No, Tim doesn't think I'm God. That's for sure. I don't
know what I think. When I was little, my mother and father were
in some religious thing in which they believed everybody was God.
You know, we all have powers that we don't use, to heal the sick, to
raise the dead, to move mountains. I don't know even today; maybe
it's so. I'd guess I heard just enough to confirm my own ideas. I
am God! It still feels like that's my secret, like I shouldn't tell you,
or I'll lose it. But it still feels like it's really so. And I don't believe
I'll die—or, at least, not until I choose to."

"It's hard for you to tell even now how much you believe it
and how much you don't."

"Oh, I suppose my educated, adult mind knows that it's all
a lot of crap. But there's another part of me. . . . "

January 22

Hal cancels his next two appointments, leaving word with
my telephone answering service that he is going to be out of town.
Thus, it is a week before I see him again. Since I am uneasy about
this unexpected and unexplained interruption, it is reassuring to see
his big bulk in the waiting room. But not very. His manner is alien,
and the usual surface joviality is missing. He enters with a nod,
takes off his coat, tosses it on a chair, and drops on the couch.

"Sorry to have missed seeing you. Needed to get away. Probably should have stayed longer." Flat, matter-of-fact. I notice the
absence of any subjects for the verbs; significant or picayune? I
decide to play it.

"Who?"

"Who what?"

"Who needed to get away? Who should have stayed longer?"

"I did." No rise to the bait. No response to the implicit message.

"Tell me about it."

"Last time here kind of shook me up. Figured I better think about it. Told my wife I had to go on business. Went to San Diego. Stayed in a motel. Didn't do much real thinking."

"Hard to find your sense of 'I,' of being the one who did those things."

"Yeah, think you're right."

"Who does?" Wanting to needle him, to bring him out of that deadness.

"Sorry I didn't give you more notice. No time, really. Just needed to get alone." No evidence of his even noticing the needle.

"What the hell's therapy for, except to give you a chance to think things through for yourself?"

"Yeah, I know. But I couldn't do it. I'm sorry, Jim. I know you care, but I couldn't do it."

"You had to do it your way, Hal. The point is, did you do it? Where are you now?"

"I don't know. I don't know if I did it; whatever 'it' is. I don't know where I am now. I just don't know."

"Lost."

"Lost. Right, lost."

"And so alone."

"Always been alone. Always will be alone. Don't really belong with people. Can't really be with them."

"What's that mean?" Needling again. Something in this withdrawn, dead mood triggers an attack from me. Feels right for what Hal needs, but I better look into it for what it means for me too.

"How do you do it, Jim?" Sudden burst of feeling; not hearing my question or caring about the needle. "How do you—or anybody—do it? How can you carry all the load? The people who come to see you—like me and the other poor slobs—and your family and all the others. How do you do it?"

My impulse is to say "do what?" but I think I know, and now's not the time for that. Let's risk going more directly, "So many, so heavy, and you're so alone."

"So God damn alone. So God damned alone. I am God damned. I mean just that. I am God damned. Do you know what I mean?" Deadness gone, dreadful urgency. Not panic but anguish.

"You're no God, but God damned, damned by God, huh?"

"Yes, yes. Oh, Christ, I sound like a mad man. Am I mad, Jim? Am I psychotic? Have you thought—of course you have . . . what do you think, am I nuts? I mean, give it to me straight. Have I flipped out? Do I need to be hospitalized? I almost hope you'll say 'yes.' Come on, Jim, level with me!" The last is harsh, commanding.

"You're not God, and I'll level with you in my own way! Just idle back. You're not psychotic, but you're playing with it. You could work yourself up to be hospitalized, but I won't be part of it. I won't help you cop out on being human."

"But I can't do it. It's too much. I don't know how you do it. I don't want to cop out, but I don't know how to carry this load. Really, I don't; can't you understand that?"

"What you're saying is that you can't be responsible for your wife and your son and your daughter and Mrs. Kanowsky and Bill Lewis and the guy with the drinking problem and the couple who fight and all your students and all your friends and everybody else in the whole damn world. You can't do it because you're not God and because you don't know enough and because you can't read enough or take enough courses or whatever. You're just an old ex-jock who tries to get along as best he can but who can't live up to all everybody else expects of him and who sure as hell can't live up to all he expects of himself."

"That's easy for you to say, maybe, but it's not for me."

"What the hell is that supposed to mean?"

"I mean, you never thought you could take care of everything, and so you never set your life and all your relationships up so that people expected you to take care of everything. So you don't have to suddenly face them and yourself with the fact that you can't do a damned thing for them or yourself or anybody else."

"You're still playing God and telling me how special you are and how different I am and have been. Well, let me tell you, buddy, you don't know what's in my life and my relationships."

"You know, that's right! I don't really know, do I? Maybe you're as nutty as I am! *The Christs of Ypsilanti,* eh? How many were there? Three? Six? Maybe you do know what it's like. Do you?"

"Hal, sometime I'll be glad—more than glad—to talk with you about this, but not now. Right now, you stay with your need to take care of everybody and everything, and how you can't do it because you're only human."

"It sounds pretty silly when you say it now. A minute ago, I really could feel it. Now, I don't know. Maybe it's gone. Maybe."

Through the rest of the hour, Hal seems in a quiet place.

January 29–February 7

On Tuesday, Hal is sunk into himself again, although not as extremely. He is either not in touch with deep feelings or is unable to express them. Friday, same story. He is clearly melancholy, preoccupied, but unable to express much. Monday, no change. I'm getting troubled about this prolonged slump. I had hoped we had worked through enough of his unreal expectations of himself so that he would feel relief. Instead, he's mourning the death of his being God and concurrently feeling overwhelmed at the task of being human.

Another week passes with no apparent change. Hal is, if anything, sinking deeper into his gloomy listlessness. His wife calls me, concerned that he is so alienated at home and so overtly miserable. I can tell her nothing, of course, but I do encourage her to stand by Hal, saying that he needs her very much right now.[4]

February 7

Hal is still in his slump, and it's getting to me. I can feel my own anxieties emerging out of some distant place within me. He is staying down too long. He needs to find some other way of being than his old hidden divinity; instead, he's slowly slipping into the relentless waters of nothingness. Most threatening for me is his passivity; if only he would struggle against the slowly rising threat, but there is no struggle in Hal these days. Today he sits on the couch, talking rather superficially about his course at the college, pausing and being silent all too frequently, and punctuating everything with long, unaware sighs. His eyes are vague, not fully in focus, and his body is heavy and sagging.

"I'm thinking of dropping the appointment at the college. For some time it's been getting to be a drag, and I just don't get much kick out of it anymore. Most of the kids don't give a damn about what I'm teaching, or trying to teach, anyway, and. . . . " He drifts off, stares at me.

"What's going on, Hal?" Irritation, sadness, threat—all creeping into me.

"Huh? Oh, I don't know. Let's see, where was I?"

"Where are you now? That's more important."

"Uh, I don't . . . I was just wondering . . . wondering about you. I mean, maybe you have these screwy ideas like I've had. . . . "

"Ideas like . . . ?"

"Like the God-thing, you know. Maybe you've had them too, but you don't seem to have them much now. I mean, I don't get the sense of you trying to be God with me now or. . . . Oh, hell, I don't know, Jim. I can't say it very well. I just was wondering about you, and how you felt about the people you see . . . like me . . . but the others too."

Quick estimate inside of me: Would I help him by sharing how it is in me at times, or would it be playing God for him in some way? Can't calculate that sort of problem. My feeling is to share with him:

"Hal, sometimes I get a kind of image—it's like a kind of dream about you and me and the other people who come into this office. I see us all as people climbing on a mountain. Climbing by night and by day. We don't know quite why we climb it, but somehow we keep doing it. Sometimes it's dark, and we just sort of blunder along, tripping and bruising ourselves. Sometimes we fall, and then. . . . " I'm a little embarrassed to be choking up a bit. "Then, I realize that none of us have any hands or even arms. When one of us falls, it's very hard for him to get back up. But if another one of us comes along and bends down and puts his shoulder against the shoulder of the person who's fallen, then we can push against each other, and both of us can get back on our feet and go on. And those are the scary moments, too, because sometimes the one who's up can lose his own footing as he's bending down and pushing. But those are also the good, the close times. And so we go on climbing, and sometimes the day comes and the fog lifts, and we think we see away off in the distance the city we're trying to reach. But then the fog and the night come back, and we wonder if we just imagined it all the time. But most of us keep climbing, and most of us try to help each other keep going too. . . . "

We sit silently for awhile. I can't tell what my words have meant to Hal. He's staring into the distance. Finally, when the buzzer announces that the next patient has arrived, he rouses himself. "Yeah, yeah." He gets up and puts on his raincoat. "Yeah, Jim. Gotta think about that. Thanks, huh?" And he's gone.

I sit back a minute, feeling my own feelings. It's a corny image, that climbers on the mountain fantasy, or is it? In some way it feels warmly important, at least within me. But it didn't seem to do much for Hal.

February 15

Lately, I find myself becoming more active. Partly it comes from my sense of where Hal is and what he needs, but partly it comes out of my own needs. It is a Tuesday, over three weeks since the session when I challenged Hal's feeling of having to take care of everybody. He's still mourning the end of his own omnipotence. I don't think he has any sense of the rewards of being human, of settling down the deific burden. I want to try to get him back in touch with his own inner experiencing. He's withdrawn from that in recent weeks.

Hal is back in the chair, and he sits sunk into it with a lumpish quality that contrasts with the animal-like grace that usually has been his posture. "I don't feel like I've anything special on my mind to say, Jim." And he sits. He doesn't seem sad or angry or anything else that I can clearly discern. I remember his self-description "waiting," and I feel a tiny shudder in my back.

"Hal, what's it like inside of you right now?"

"Just kind of . . . murky, I guess you'd say. I mean, it's hard for me to know or to describe it to you. I don't seem to have many clear thoughts or feelings. I have a sense that it's 'time out' inside of me right now. I don't know how else to say it."

"Do you have any feelings of wanting, of yearning, of wishing for anything right now?"

"Not that I'm aware of. No, I don't think so. I sometimes. . . " he stops, seems to be considering.

"Sometimes. . . . "

"I don't know what I was going to say. I guess that sometimes I have sort of idle daydreams. . . . No, that doesn't feel like what I mean. Sort of like I'm sorting through old pictures in my mind, and seeing which ones I want to keep and which I'll throw out."

"Like what?"

"Like the other night after June and I went to bed. I don't know just why. . . . Well, yes, maybe I do. We haven't had sex for quite a while now, and I guess my body was complaining, but my feelings just haven't been interested. And June seems not to mind too much and. . . . "

He pauses. I realize how little I know of Hal's on-going life, how little any therapist can know. We know so much about the people we work with, so much more than we know about almost anyone else, but still it is so little. I ought to recall that more often. It would be an antidote to my own deific impulses. Attention back to Hal: he's just sitting there like he's forgotten what he was saying. Feeling of impatience. He scares me when he's that inert, that. . . (Hmmm! I don't want to say it even in my head, eh?) . . . that dead. There. Impatient, want to stir him up. I'm scared, scared of the deadness in him; it's like slowly rising water that may ultimately submerge him, take him away.

"What do you want, Hal? Right now, as you sit here in the office, what can you find a wanting for? I mean inside of yourself; can you locate any feeling of desire, of wishing, of yearning?"

"No, I don't think so."

"You didn't even try, Hal."

"Well." He pauses; his face seems to take form a bit from the inert expression it's worn so much lately. "I don't know, Jim, I just don't seem to have much going on inside these days. Let me try again." He passes his hands over his face, trying to wake it up.

"Let yourself visualize things, Hal."

Hal stirs with a sigh. "Yeah, like I said, the other night I was about to go to sleep when I found myself thinking of one of the girls I see from time to time on campus. A secretary or something, little older than the students, but dresses like one of the kids. You know, no bra, miniskirt, the whole thing kids do now that is so different than when we were that age. This girl, woman, is probably in her mid-twenties, cute, nice figure, and the shortest miniskirts you ever saw. When she bends over, she leaves nothing to the imagination. The kids seem to take it for granted, but an old guy like me. . . . " He lets it drop incomplete.

"What about an old guy like you, Hal?"

"Oh, I look. I'm not so far gone yet that I don't look. I think that's all I want to do, just look. Then the other night, just before I went to sleep, darned if I wasn't having a fantasy about this gal. Guess there's life in the old boy yet."

I feel the relief like a physical thing. Hal's sexy fantasy says exactly that: there's life in him, not just the deadly, rising water. Want to encourage this spark. "What did you fantasize?"

"Getting to know her, finding some excuse to take her away for a weekend, peeling that minidress off of her, going to bed with her, the works." He pauses, a half-smile on his face, more animation than he's shown in a couple of weeks at least. Then the smile fades, the empty look comes back. "But I won't do anything about it. It's just not worth the trouble. I wish June and I had more for each other these days, but we're so far apart. Not just physically; emotionally. She doesn't know where I am, and I don't seem to care enough to try to tell her. She has her own life, all the things she's wound up in, and I've had mine, and we seldom really see each other."

Pausing, he reflects, and his face enlivens from the blankness of a moment ago. "Sometimes I think we should get divorced. I don't give her much, and she doesn't seem to have much for me. The kids are at an age where they could handle a divorce without too much trouble. And then. . . . "

"Then. . . ?"

"Then, I might. . . . Oh, what's the use kidding myself?" The aliveness drains out of him, and he slumps in the chair. I wait, but he doesn't seem about to go on.

"What happened just then? You were thinking about what a divorce might mean, and then you suddenly seemed to go limp."

"Oh, nothing. Nothing, really. I just know damn well I'm just talking, just running off at the mouth. I won't try to make that chick. I won't divorce June. I won't. . . . "

"Won't what?"

"Oh, I don't know. I guess I was going to say 'won't do any of the other things I used to dream I'd do.' "

"Like what?"

"Like get in on some exploring expedition. You didn't know that was my secret ambition, did you? Yeah, I always imagined that some day I'd have enough of a name that I'd be invited—or at least welcomed—on an expedition to some fantastic place, like up the Amazon or to the headwaters of the Nile or some other romantic and exciting place. You know, I always thought I'd see all the world. I mean, when I read about fantastic places—like Timbuktu and Afghanistan and Singapore—in some part of my mind, I kind of thought, 'One day I'll be there; I'll see that.' And now I know I never will. I probably won't see any of those places." He stops and seems to sink deeper into himself.

"I won't do any of it: get a sexy gal in bed, divorce June, go on an expedition, write the greatest psychology book ever, whatever."

"You sound pretty discouraged."

"No, no. It's not discouragement. Just kind of flat. That's just the way it is. No use sweating it. I'm an old jock with big dreams who just doesn't have it. I just dream. I don't do anything; don't do a damn thing."

"Nothing. You don't do anything about your life."

"Yeah, that's right. I just sit on my can and bitch." He is beginning to get angry. This is the opening we need.

"And time passes."

"Damn right it does. Time just goes along, and I'm not having a life. What kind of life have I had? I always used to dream I was going to do so many things; go exploring, have a great romance, write books, make a lot of money, see everything, do everything. . . . All big dreams, but I haven't done anything; nothing, nothing at all."

"How old are you, Hal?" Trying to help him get to the slowly emerging feelings.

"Forty-six! Forty-six, damn you. You know very well. I'm forty-six God damned years old. Forty-six wasted years, trying to be God. Forty-six years of not having my own life. I'm still twenty-one or maybe even younger. I'm not ready to be forty-six! I'm not ready to be middle-aged! I'm not ready to be old. Damn! Damn! Damn! Damn!"

He is furious, but he is also hurting terribly, I know. He is pent up, beginning to be restless, rousing from his torpor, seeking an avenue of release.

"Hal, you're full of feeling and. . . . "

"Damn!" He shouts, cutting me off. "I just want to scream and cuss and. . . . "

"Go ahead."

"Aaaghh." He makes a strangled cry in his throat.

"You're holding it in."

He tries again to scream, but it is an abortive sound. "You're holding yourself in, just as you always have, Hal."

"Aieee!" It is more a wail than a scream, but it comes out with surprising strength. "Aw hell, this is silly, Jim."

"Again!" Urgently. "No, it's not silly. Stay with your feeling."

But this time, Hal is self-conscious, and the sound is strangled again.

"You're choking yourself off, Hal. Just as you have for forty-six years. You're choking off your life."

"Shit! Sheeeeeeit!" He suddenly bellows so that, although I thought I was expecting it, I am startled. Now he begins screeching at the top of his lungs, and the sounds become more open and full throated with each one. He pounds on the arms of the chair with both fists in time to the wild screams that burst out of his throat. They are ear-splitting and terrifying sounds. Gradually they seem to be less constricted and tearing, yet even so my own throat is aching sympathetically. I find I am leaning toward him with each cry, feeling the sounds as though they were coming out of my own guts as well. Hal is screaming for me too, I realize, as I hear myself make sort of a half screech with him. I do it again, and it feels good and terrible at the same time.

I don't want to be in my fifties. I don't want to have my children grown and to have had so little real experience of them. I scream with Hal, and he looks at me, and the tears well up in his eyes. I don't want to have wasted so many years in hiding my own self, my own real feelings in order to try to be the way I thought I was supposed to be. And Hal and I scream. My throat hurts, and some part of me is glad. And we scream. It is too late, and we scream. It isn't too late, and we scream. It is too late for so much, and we scream, and we scream, and we scream.

Gradually we stop our cries, and both of us are weeping. And we sit drained and strangely at peace. Each of us is within himself, and yet each is with the other. After a long time, Hal whispers, "You too, Jim?"

"Yes, oh yes." And we both weep anew.[5]

September 10

These were the birth cries of a new-born forty-six-year-old mortal. Hal now enters into a period in which he rather rapidly works out his new perspectives on himself and his life. He and June separate for nearly six months, but eventually they decide to try it together again with the help of a marriage counseling program. Hal decides to reduce his activities and concentrate on his psychotherapy practice, where he is dealing increasingly with the sorts of subjective things he has learned to value in his own experience. Finally, the day that we both know is coming arrives.

"Well, Jim, I'm going to miss coming here and giving you a hard time."

"I'm going to miss you, Hal."

"Yeah; seriously, it's been very, very good. Funny, in a way it's hard to say what we accomplished. Had a fight with Tim only last Wednesday. Felt good and sick of the whole practice last Friday. Had a sexy fantasy about a new patient yesterday. Feel scared of endings and of dying right now. Hell, maybe we ought to start all over."

"My God! Hal, I didn't know you had deteriorated so. Lie down at once. And your fee will be double."

"Aw, Jim, it has been good." He stands and comes over to

me and gives me a hug that is all warm affection and awesome in
its power.

In its Greek origins, the word *psychotherapy* means the
process of nursing or curing the soul. In everyday usage, psychotherapy tends to be linked to the other therapies, especially those we
associate with medical treatment of the body. Yet the psychotherapy
that I have been describing in this book has little in common with
the medicine of malaria, broken arms, virus infections, and heart
surgery. It is in almost direct contrast with procedures in which
patients tell the *doctor* their *symptoms* and the doctor then makes
his own examination (which the patient understands little or not at
all), and in which the doctor writes a prescription in Latin, and
the patient has it filled and follows instructions with no thought
except to be "patient" and wait for the healing to occur.

Yet this seductive picture entices both patient and therapist.
Often, in a very real way, both want the therapist to be a "real
doctor" or, even better, to play God. Hal was not the only one who
had this idea. Many patients want the therapist to accept this role
and are ever ready to help him get into the part. They want someone to take over the painful decisions, someone to rebel against,
someone to provide dependable answers, someone to guarantee outcomes, someone to be more than simply a human companion. (And
at the same time, of course, they do not want someone to do these
things—just as the therapist does not want to play God, even as he
finds himself tempted to.)

It is very easy for the therapist to slip into the God role in
the consulting room drama, and there are many inducements for him
to do so. His authority on the scene is rarely disputed, his statements
are often treated as inspired pronouncements, and his approval and
disapproval manifestly and profoundly matter to those who are frequently devoted followers. As much as the therapist may remind
himself of his ever-present limitations, he often yields more than he
would like to the subtle, even unconscious, suggestion that indeed he
has more than usual perception and power and that he can intervene benignly in his patients' lives.

As expert as I get at coping with the invitations to take
unwarranted responsibility for my patients' decisions, I still find my-

self tempted to intervene in ways that seem so harmless, so sure to help. "If only I set it up for Betty and Dick to get together; they're both so lonely. . . . If only Greg could be helped to get up the gumption to leave that terrible wife and find someone who could really appreciate all of his dammed-up warmth and tenderness. . . . If only Ellen would get a better lawyer to represent her interests; perhaps just a word would bring her to think of doing so. . . . If only Ben could be given that minute shove he needs to quit his job in that deadening organization; soon he'll be captured by the benefits program and won't be able to afford to break loose."

There are usually several occasions with every patient—probably more—when I find myself so tempted. And even though I try to resist the temptation, I also yield to it; I do intervene. I encourage Ben to leave his job and Greg his wife. I suggest to Ellen that perhaps she is overly trusting of her attorney, or I arrange to introduce Betty and Dick. And often there are benefits. Ben is grateful that I think well enough of him to encourage him to find a more rewarding job. And Greg's new strength in threatening to leave his wife has opened up a new phase in their relations, the result of which may be a better future for both of them. Yet, there are often untoward results. Ellen has a fight with her attorney before she is ready to face such conflicts and now feels more alone than ever. Dick is shy, and he worries too much about what I expect of him with Betty; thus, he experiences another failure in relation, and our work together is made more complex. Betty feels she has let me down by not liking Dick.

Increasingly I feel that when I intervene, I am demonstrating a failure of confidence in myself, my patient, or the therapeutic process itself. If I can keep faith and help the patient to claim his own wisdom and autonomy, then I see how much more sure are the patient's gains. The important question is why Ben cannot see for himself how stultifying his job is. That's the work of therapy, to aid him in taking a better and more responsible look at his own way of being alive so that he will not accept such waste of himself. What is it that keeps Betty from developing her potential so that she doesn't have to be alone? If I try to supply companions for her, I'm supporting her incapacity rather than helping her growth. Each time I try to intervene to aid a patient in a particular life situation, I have failed him and myself in some measure.

When I stick to the main task, to what is going on right at the moment when a patient and I are together—such as when I help Greg to deal with those attitudes of his that keep him in a vicious, destructive relation with his wife—then I help him much more. The release of his potential not only affects our work positively but it has important benefits for him on his job, with his children, and in his relations with others.

Yet I never fully overcome that temptation to play God. I am, and need to be, guilty about that—guilty in the existential sense of recognizing that I am not keeping faith with human potential, my own and my patient's. Still too much of that guilt can be a distortion too. I am not God that I can perfectly avoid playing God.

It looks to me as though only God never plays God.

If Hal were running for God, he might well get my vote *now*. When he was so heavily under the influence of his unconscious need to believe that he was divine, he was out of touch with his inner sense. Thus he could not know himself well or hear others accurately. The only way Hal could continue to hope to comprehend and deal effectively with everything he encountered was by radically shrinking his world. Thus he focused on the overt, on behavior, on the explicit. He denied the realm of the subjective; he hid from his human limitedness. He shrank his world to apparently manageable size, but he lost his ability to guide his own emotions and his relations with others.

Hal, like many of us, tended to see not-knowing as failure, as something lacking, as the antithesis of knowing. As he came to accept his limitedness, Hal could recognize that not-knowing is, in fact, a part of the experience of knowing. Only the unaware or the divine (strange parallel!) can fail to recognize the limits of their knowing. We who are finite and human recognize that we cannot know all and that we must take into account what is still speculative or subject to forces beyond our grasp. As we have come to accumulate more and more knowledge, we have also accumulated awareness of more and more areas in which we are ignorant.

Hal still is eager to learn, but he has dropped the terrible load of trying to know *enough* before acting. Where we truly know enough, we can turn the matter over to machines. As Jennifer also discovered, human beings are essential to decisions that must be made without knowing enough—in other words, most of the truly significant decisions of life.

Hal needed to deny his limitedness. Limits meant for him death and incompleteness. He tried valiantly to learn all about his field. He tried to be prepared to help all who consulted him. He tried to drive himself to do all that was open to him. He was amazingly successful in all of these things, but he was dying inside from being driven to do more than a man can do. He was beside himself with his rage at his son who so clearly demonstrated that he no longer saw Hal as all-knowing and all-competent.

Hal's opening his inward sense and accepting his limitedness relieved him of an impossible load of responsibility and guilt. He let himself become human and fallible and needing. He let himself cry out in anguish for the loss that his denial had brought about. And then Hal began to live his own life and experiment with changes in his way of being. He had learned that a god is locked into a static way of being by the very fact of his omnipotence and all-knowingness.

Hal's struggle for his life confirms some of the generalizations already made in this book, and it throws light on some other important facets of being alive:

If I am to be fully alive, I must accept my limitedness as well as my freedom.[6] *If I attempt to know and do everything, I am apt to lose track of that which I can genuinely master. I cannot know everything, do everything, live forever. I* can *know much more than I presently know, do much more than I now do, and live much more fully and keenly than I now experience.*

I am only able to have my life truly if I am innerly aware of my subjective being. *This is a sense dimension more vital to being fully alive than any of the external modes of awareness.*[7] *Too many of us—especially in our middle-class Western culture—have lost our sense of living in the center of ourselves. Having access to so little of our inner experiencing, we are as alienated from ourselves as from a totally separate person. We have largely lost direct awareness of our own feelings, wantings, needings, intentions.*

When I am preoccupied with how to get myself to do or not do something, then I am surely out of my own center; I am treating myself like an objective machine, and then I am apt to be frustrated and ineffectual in my own life. When I am in my own being, there is no meaning to the question of how to—of how to discover what I feel, understand why I am reacting as I do, and so on. I am the feeling, the acting, the intending. How to means manipulating what is external to me. To the extent that I truly have my inner vision, my intention is my process; in other words, what I want is apparent and I don't need some "procedure" to discover it.[8]

Some years after Hal left therapy, I had a time of great turmoil and pain in my own life. I went back into psychotherapy myself, and it helped me to survive some days and nights when I was so torn and uprooted within myself that I doubted I could hold out. Although this chapter is not the place for that story, I do want to record that my therapist suggested I go into a psychotherapy group as a patient; she recommended a group of which Hal was the leader.

And so our roles were reversed. I felt strangeness in this reversal only for a brief time. Very soon I came to know that strong sensitive man, his big body sprawled comfortably in a chair or lying on the floor, his warm voice giving encouragement or insistently prodding. I came to know Hal in new ways, and yet they were not new. He was still the big man, but now his bigness had burst out of its former confining blindness, now he was at home in the subjective as well as the objective realm. He no longer mastered everything, but he could really hang in with those who—like myself—needed to draw on his strength.

I recall especially a marathon weekend in which our therapy group met with Hal and his cotherapist for many hours in a place some distance from our homes. Late one night, I came to such a monumental block of guilt and fear within myself that I simply could not get through it. For several hours the group worked with me—supporting, badgering, prompting, loving—and still I couldn't break through. Finally everyone except Hal left to go to bed, and for three or four hours into the early morning, Hal stayed quietly but determindedly with me while I struggled with my demon and finally won through to tears and rage and relief. And as I wept and drained the awful abscess of my conflicted, self-blaming, hurt-filled heart, Hal's big arm was steady around my shoulders.

I only see Hal on rare occasions now. We live in different cities, and neither of us is into "going-to-meetings" any longer. One time when we did meet, Hal asked if I'd read a certain piece that he'd published recently. Embarrassedly, I mumbled something about "thumbing it quickly," trying all the while to recall more about it. I had indeed seen the article; yet I could not for the life of me remember whether I'd read it or, if I had, what it was about. Then I quit pretending and told all this to Hal. He smiled with a kind of warmth and tenderness that has become more and more a part of him in recent years. "I'd like it if you would look at it, Jim. It tells about our experience together."

And so, back home, I read it immediately. And what I read was such a humble, honest, and insightful statement that I knew my own good luck to have shared journeys with this big man. No longer seeking to be God, Hal was clearly in touch with the most human roots of his own life.

7

KATE

Isolation and Need

The external eye sees objects and substance; it tells us of the world of things. Our internal vision is of processes, of flowingness. We are surprised when the building that has always been at the corner of University and High is torn down. Something is missing in the familiar objective world. In the same way, we are surprised when a part of our identity that has been familiar ("I am a young man") gives way to a new one ("I am middle aged now"). We expect ourselves to be the same, even in realms (such as age) in which we logically know very well we are changing.[1]

We even expect our emotions to be constant. "A few minutes ago I was angry and yelled at you; now I feel relieved and even rather warm toward you. What is it with me that makes me so changeable? Only superficial feelings would alter so quickly." Thus runs familiar reasoning, and it is dead wrong. Feelings flow and evolve. Expressing them aids that movement. When we do not recognize this simple truth, we feel foolish and vulnerable when we are, in fact, expressing our health. "Since I was angry a minute ago, I'd better keep on being angry or you'll think I didn't mean it, or you'll get back at me now that I'm not armed with my fury. I must think up something to keep this fight going in me and with you." So the relationship suffers, and bitterness is prolonged.

When I trust my inward vision, I know my feelings and I experience their flow, and I don't have to strive for a consistency that is more valid for objects than it is for persons.

Kate feared the endless changes of inner life. They had caused her much pain in her childhood and still seemed threatening. She tried to find a way in life that would exempt her from the hazards and uncertainties of being. For a time it seemed she succeeded, but the cost to her vitality in living was exorbitant. Even then, she probably would have stayed with her rigid, protective pattern of life had not it begun to disrupt her professional career as well.

That's the joker in the deck. Each of us, like Kate, dickers for promises of safety and fulfillment with a minimum of the threats that were most powerful in our early years. The deal we work out with fate usually involves trading off some of our aliveness, some of our full awareness of our inner sense, some of our potentiality in exchange for apparent protection. This is the bargain with the devil— the selling of our souls; and as with such bargains in legend, it ends up taking far more than it gives.[2]

One early spring, on a Saturday morning when she was eleven years old, Kitty woke up later than usual with an odd mixture of sensations. In some ways she felt relaxed, which was nice because she'd been so tense and irritable lately. But in other ways, she felt a vague uneasiness that she couldn't define at first. Then, with a rush, she knew its cause, and the nice, relaxed feeling was gone. There was a wetness between her legs, and when she investigated it was clearly blood. Kitty lay very still, hardly daring to breathe. She was frightened, vaguely guilty, and searching frantically for memories that would only half form. After a very long time, she heard footsteps in the hall, and she whispered, "Mother! Mother!" She was afraid it was her father or her brother, and she knew she couldn't talk to them right now. Whoever it was didn't hear her anyway, and she lay there so rigidly motionless that her arms and legs ached.

After another long time, Kitty heard her father working outside in his garden and guessed that her brother also must have left the house. She mustered her courage and got gingerly out of bed and put on her robe. Walking stiffly, she made her way to the kitchen and found her mother doing the dishes. With some apprehension, she told her mother what she had discovered. Then a wonderful thing happened: Mother first seemed startled, then she brushed Kitty's cheek with her hand while tears came into her eyes. She led Kitty into the bathroom and gave her a belt and a pad and showed her how to put them on and then told Kitty to get back in bed.

Kitty did as she was told with a sense of wonder. Mother seldom cried except when she was fighting with Daddy, and this was a very different type of crying, Kitty could tell. Soon Mother came with some orange juice, an egg, and toast, and Kitty tasted the ambivalent luxury of breakfast in bed. Mother said that everything would be all right and that Kitty might stay in bed today. Moreover, Mother told Kitty to pick out a game she would like to play and that after a bit she, Mother, would come and play it with her. This was truly a miracle for, though Kitty liked games very much, Mother never could find time or interest for them. Kitty hastened to get out the *Monopoly* set and to fix everything up in the most cozy way she could conceive. Then with everything in readiness, she waited. She decided against looking at her book so that when Mother came there would be nothing to cause her to delay the game.

It was quite a while before Mother did come, and several times Kitty grew restless and started to play with the *Monopoly* cards. But as soon as she heard footsteps, she hastily shuffled the cards and had everything ready again when Mother put her head in the door to say she had to go across the street to Mrs. Gantly's for a few minutes first. Kitty couldn't be sure, but it looked as though Mother had been crying some more.

Quite some time passed now, and Kitty grew first restless and then frightened. She tried to read her book, but somehow she couldn't follow what it said very well. She wondered about the bleeding, and though earlier she'd felt very comforted by how Mother had reacted, now she began to worry that maybe something was really wrong with her and that that was why Mother was crying and acting so strangely.

Finally, when she thought she couldn't breathe she was getting so scared, Kitty went to the phone and called Mrs. Gantly. After a few minutes Mother came on the line, but her voice was funny. She said she'd be home in just a few minutes and for Kitty to get everything all ready for their game. Somehow Kitty didn't ask the questions she'd planned. Instead she went back to her room and fixed everything up and again waited. Once again, she waited a long time. She cried a bit now and thought of calling Daddy, whom she could still hear in the garden. However, she just couldn't imagine telling him about the blood. She must have dozed a bit for it was early afternoon when she next looked at the clock, and she was getting kind of hungry. But when she took her breakfast dishes out to the kitchen, she didn't want to eat after all. Instead, she called Mrs. Gantly's again.

Although she really didn't want to know it, this time Kitty knew that Mother's voice sounded funny because she had been drinking. She remembered another time when Mother had gotten drunk, and Daddy had yelled at her and hit her. Kitty didn't really try to keep back her tears this time. She cried into the telephone and begged Mother to come home. Mother insisted she was coming right away, but when Kitty got back in bed she didn't do more than half try to fix up the *Monopoly* set. After a bit, she heard a noise that might have been the front door, so she hurriedly fixed the game and turned on the light, because it was getting kind of dim. But the noise must have just been the paperboy or something because nobody came.

And nobody did come the rest of the day, although Kitty called once more with tears and pleading and protestations of love for Mother.

When Mother finally did come home and Daddy saw her condition, they had an awful yelling fight. Then when Mother had gone to bed, Daddy looked in a minute to ask Kitty is she was all right or needed anything. She hardly looked at him, and he couldn't see her because she had put the light out. Her voice was even and calm, though, when she told him she didn't need anything.

That was twenty-five years ago. To the best of her ability, Kitty has never let herself need anything from anyone again until the day she walks into my office.

February 6

When Dr. Kate Margate first comes to see me, she looks like a Hollywood stereotype of a prim governess. Actually she is a physiologist. She wears no makeup, a nondescript but neat tweed suit, and the kind of shoes that have become notorious as "sensible." Her face is composed, intelligent, and completely unreachable. By that I mean she smiles or frowns appropriately to what is being said but without any of the small changes of expression that usually animate a face in interaction. She responds to the content of what I say in a restrained way but not at all to me as a person in conversation with her.

She is, she says candidly, somewhat irritated at having to seek psychological help, but she realizes she has not been working as well lately as she did in earlier years. In view of her responsibilities to her employers, she feels she should see if something can be done to help her become more efficient again. This is Dr. Margate, once—but not for many years—Kitty.

Dr. Margate gradually unfolds a story of a life devoted to the intellect. She made an exceptional scholastic record and, on finishing her doctorate, joined the research staff of a large pharmaceutical corporation, where she now holds a responsible position. She married a colleague, but the marriage was short and its ending cold and abrupt. She now has a number of acquaintances with whom she relates in terms of shared activities, but she has no one with whom she is intimate and certainly no one toward whom she will let herself feel any need or dependency. Her independence has a defiant quality: "I *will not* need you or anyone," is its clear message. Of course, she is largely unaware of any inward sense.

As her story comes out (it is many months before she remembers that Saturday I just described), she becomes more caught up in telling it. This involvement leads to the first of a series of frightening episodes.

June 10

Kate comes in late this morning. This, in itself, is unusual. She is always on time, always. Her face is tight in a way it hasn't been for a month or more. She does not use the couch, has never used it to this point. She sits rather stiffly in the big patient's chair, her body resisting the chair's invitation to relax. I greeted her casually in the waiting room a minute ago, but she did not reply. Now she says nothing as she sits stonily before me.

"You look very forbidding, Kate."

She frowns slightly but says nothing. I wait. For several minutes we are silent together, then she stirs a little, tightens her hold on the purse in her lap, and speaks in a flat voice.

"I have nothing to say."

"I see." Again silence.

"I've told you about my life. What more do you want to know?"

"What you're experiencing right now."

"I told you, nothing."

"I can't believe that, Kate. You're shouting at me with your facial expression, your tightly held body, and your whole manner— shouting that something very powerful is going on in you."

"I don't know it, if that is so. You seem to read all manner of things in what I do without my knowing it. Suppose you tell me what's going on."

"I don't know, but it feels like you're very angry or very frightened."

"If I have nothing to say," ignoring my reply, "I suppose there's no point in my being here." Abruptly she seems to be preparing to leave; although she hasn't actually changed her posture.

"I have the feeling, Kate, that you'd like to have some good reason to walk out right now."

"I don't see any reason to stay. I have nothing more to tell you, and you either can't or won't do anything to help me." She seems, if anything, to be holding herself even more tightly.

"I think you'd like to anger me. Then you could tell yourself you left because of my anger." I feel the tiny prickles on my cheeks and the tightness in my chest that signal that Kate's darts are getting to me.

"I really don't have any desire to anger you, Dr. Bugental." She has never called me "Jim," as most of my patients do. Now, as she says my name, there is a strong feeling of being held at arm's length. "I simply want to know whether there is anything you can do to help me."

"I'd like to help you, if I can, Kate, but right now I feel that you are all set to ward off anything I might say or do."

"I will listen carefully to any suggestions you may care to make. I can't do more than that." Her voice is even; her enunciation precise.

"I think you can do a great deal more than that, Kate, but it is clear that right now you can't let yourself be aware of any such possibilities. Let me make one suggestion anyway. You're in the grip of some kind of strong feeling right now. When did it begin?"

"I don't know what you mean. I don't really experience this strong feeling you seem to think I have. Do you think you could be mistaken?" The irony in her voice is barely covered by a veil of polite detachment.

"Ouch!" I grin but get no response. "Yes, Kate." My voice is tender for I can feel her fright intensely now. "Yes, I could be wrong. I have been many times. But right now, I don't think I'm wrong in thinking you're frightened and angry. But," I hasten to add before she can protest, "I do believe now that you really are not experiencing those or any other feelings here as we talk."

"I feel like granite or ice inside, nothing else." She seems to have become even tighter in response to the tenderness in my voice.

"Yes, I believe you, Kate." I try to keep my voice deliberate again. It is clear now that sympathy from me only makes her pull away all the more. "Will you try to think, though, when did the granite-like feeling begin?"

"I'm afraid I don't really know. I often feel this way. Why does it matter?"

"You haven't been feeling this way as much lately, Kate." Need to get her started talking. "Kate, tell me what you've been doing this morning before you came here."

"I really don't see the point of doing so. I had a very ordinary morning." She pauses. "I woke, breakfasted, took care of some correspondence, and came here. There was nothing out of the ordinary about the morning."

"How did you feel when you woke up?"

"Oh, what does it. . . . Well, actually, now that I think of it, I felt rather well. Let's not waste any more time, though; can you be of any help to me, Dr. Bugental?" The taunting edge has diminished ever so slightly.

"Wait, Kate. You felt rather well when you woke up. What about at breakfast?"

"I don't remember. I don't make records of my feelings you know. Perhaps I should. Do you think. . . . "

"What were you thinking about at breakfast, Kate? Come on, work with me." I feel encouraged, want to win her back to cooperating. "You know you do want to feel better and do a better job at your work. Try to remember, what were you thinking about at breakfast?"

"Oh, I can't. . . . Well, I started to read the paper, and then. . . . " She pauses, and a brief look of recognition flashes across her face.

"Yes, Kate?" Softly, but insistently. Excitement beginning in me.

"I thought about coming here today and about my sister's saying that Mother may need an operation and. . . . " She trails off. Her eyes look pained.

"Your mother is ill?" The tempo has slowed, but maybe something about her mother or sister is setting up the tension in her.

"Yes, Nellie says it's her back. I think she had a fall last year. Yes, she did, that's right."

I've taken the wrong track. Kate's tone is altogether too matter-of-fact to go with that look of a minute ago. I hope I haven't lost the thread. "And Kate, what did you think when you thought about coming here this morning? At breakfast, I mean."

"I thought of some other things about my childhood that I might tell you. I. . . . " Abruptly she stops. Once again I feel anticipation.

"Kate, what is it? Somehow I don't think it's the things you thought about to tell, not in themselves. Can you let yourself know now?"

"Well, really, it's very simple." Her tone is icy again. Her hands grip her purse so tightly that her fingers whiten. "I recognized that I was having certain feelings that would get in the way of our work. 'Transference,' I think you people call them." Of course! I should have known; the warming of her granite self is terrifying her. Her inner awareness is beginning to open. "I have taken care of them, however, so there is no problem. I do wish you would finally have the courtesy to answer the question I've posed to you several times: Can you help me?"

"And what were those feelings, Kate?"

"I told you they have been taken care of." Coldly, impassively.

"What were they, Kate?" Insistently, quietly, hopefully.

"Well, I realized I was looking forward to coming here and to telling you more about my life. Of course, that is not the point of our work. I am not here to get some cheap gratification from a listener paid to hear my story." The thrust calculated to push me away is too obvious.

"It frightens you that you are involved in letting me know about you." I try to be gentle. I don't want to frighten her by focusing on the connection to me yet. I must remember that in a quarter of a century she has scarcely risked any bonds at all with other people.

"It is not only unnecessary but quite inappropriate, and as I told you. . . . "

"It is quite appropriate and completely necessary to our work that you let your life matter to you!" Suddenly, sharply. It is essential to break through her rejection of her feelings at least to some extent; otherwise the hour will end, and soon she'll quit therapy as she finds the involvement with the process (and me) coming up again and again.

Kate's face is fluid as she assimilates the sharpness of my response, struggles with an answering anger, and tries once again to put her granite mask back in place. Hesitantly, "I can't see how. . . . That is, I hadn't thought of these feelings as concern for my life, as you put it."

"Kate, I imagine there are all sorts of elements in them. For our work right now, however, the truly important part is that you are beginning to get in touch with your own motivation for your life and its activities."

She considers this. I question myself. Am I misleading her by directing her attention away from the relation to me? That's what's frightening to her. That's what we'll have to deal with sooner or later. But she can't handle that yet, and we'll never get any farther if she stops her efforts now. These feelings are essential to our work and to her hope of a revived living. She must be helped to see beyond the immediate and frightening link to me, to whom she talks, to the longer-term significance. I am using the word *motivation* quite deliberately because it will tie in with her conscious concern about her will to work, and it may lead to more inward tolerance.

"Very well. I suppose that is so. However, I will try to keep my feelings from unnecessarily intruding into our work." Pause. "Now about those other childhood events that I thought of to tell you. . . . " She's beginning to suppress her emotions again. I must try to help her keep open to them.

"Wait, Kate. Look at the matter this way." Slowly, Jim, keep it as impersonal and academic as possible while staying in touch with her emotionally to the extent that she can handle. "It's no good for us to try to recover the emotional upsets that have occurred in your life and that have affected how you live and work if, at the same time, you control them prematurely. It will defeat our efforts completely."

This is the crucial point. Can I give her enough understanding to get her to work with me for emotional exploration? She does not want to agree to that, for she senses it will carry her out of her isolation. That possibility is terrifying to her, but it is essential.

"I do not understand what you are saying. I believe you persistently try to confuse me." Stiffly, distantly; but tears are near, even though the anger is closest to the surface.

"You're angry, Kate. And, Kate, I'd guess you're angry at least in part because you are beginning to understand, and you don't like what you're beginning to recognize."

"You do seem to insist on being very mysterious and in making me guess your meanings. Is that necessary for our work, or is it a personal idiosyncrasy of yours?"

"Kate, maybe my way of speaking expresses my personal needs; probably it does. But that's beside the point now. It is more important for you to face your inner awareness as much as you can right now." Damn it! I'm being drawn into all sorts of side issues. It's getting too talky; she'll lose the point.

"Well, that may be, but I don't know just what it is you

think I'm understanding." She is very far away now; too many wordy ideas, no matter how necessary.

"And, Kate, you're out of touch with it now, partly because you needed to bury it under your protests and your questions about my style." How to help her see that without inflicting guilt.

"Do my questions offend you or seem inappropriate?" Damn again! She's determined to pull farther away. Can I get her back?

"No, Kate, you're not hearing me."

"It seems to me that I hear you very well but that you seem determined to talk to me in vague terms."

"Kate, we're into a circular argument now. Let me try to help us get clearer. What I'm trying to help you bring to awareness within yourself is not something that can be reduced to a set of explicit meanings and words. Therefore, I. . . . "

"Do you mean you're trying to engage in some sort of tele-pathic communication with me?" Oh wow! She's really going to an extreme to hold off understanding me.

"Oh, Kate, no." I am confounded and at once amused and chagrined. "Really, I feel like I lose a yard for every foot I gain in trying to help you see what's going on." Oh-oh, I've been stung. I can hear my anger coming out. Remember this woman is fighting off a terror that she thinks can literally destroy her.

"I don't know what you're talking about." There is a hint of something else in Kate's tone. She sits overtly composed and dis-tant, as I inwardly squirm, feel like a ham-handed bungler, and wonder what happened to all my excellent therapeutic technique for disclosing the resistances. How entrenched against the subjective she is!

"Kate." I say with my most reasonable and composed voice (how she has me playing her game!). "Kate, let's see if we can find out where we are now. Would you try to tell me what feelings you had just now as you informed me that you didn't know what I was talking about?"

"Well, I was genuinely puzzled at your apparent distress and wondering why you felt it necessary to assign responsibility for it to me."

Carefully, now, I'm not playing with an amateur, I remind

myself. "I think those were probably your topmost feelings, Kate. I think I sensed something else, some other feeling in reaction to my confusion and chagrin. Go slowly, Kate, can you catch anything like that?" Will she respond? Can we find our way back?

"No. I don't think I was aware of any such feelings on your part. Does it really matter?" She's too frightened. She can't let through more awareness—especially of me.

"Yes, it does matter, Kate." I say it in a subdued voice and realize with renewed chagrin that in some way I am trying to make her feel guilt for having overcome my efforts. I shift in my chair and seek a fresh and more useful perspective. "Just now, Kate, I am suddenly aware that I'm feeling licked in trying to get through to you today and that by my tone I was trying to make you feel guilty. I don't approve of doing things that way, but there it was. That's the kind of awareness we need to share with each other, because in that way. . . . "

"I'm sure that if I've done anything to upset you it was quite unintentional, Dr. Bugental; however, I can't really make that my concern, now can I?" She is almost regal and certainly quite stilted and determinedly detached as she brushes off my attempt to flank her guard. With relief I note that we are actually several minutes overtime.

"Well, Kate, we weren't able to get into deeper communication today. Let's try again on Thursday. Okay?" I smile, I'm afraid a little wanly, and stand.

Kate rises promptly, businesslike, picks up her jacket and purse, goes to the door, and then turns. "I hope on Thursday you will answer my question, Dr. Bugental. I really need to have your judgment as to whether you can help me."

I sink back in my chair, knee deep in the invisible debris of of words, intentions, observations, half-phrased ideas, and interventions not quite carried into effect. I need a drink or a brisk walk or ten minutes at a defenseless punching bag.

And so Kate's fear wins a round. In the long run, however, Kate's courage and her will to life overcome that massive dread. In the above session, much is happening: She is terrified by the dawning recognition that she is looking forward to our interviews, that she is thinking of things to say, not just to provide missing pieces of a puzzle, but as a participant in our joint endeavor. Behind that is her growing trust in relating to me, a threat-filled recognition just coming onto the horizon of her awareness. Even further back of that, quite out of any possibility of being tolerated at this point, is her need for me, the person, and for my caring. Were this broached now, Kate would probably deny it out-of-hand and quickly break off the relation to me in a rage. Her inner wanting—especially of relation—is sheer threat to her.

There is no sudden, dramatic breakthrough in which Kate comes to accept her emotionality with less anxiety. Dramatic breakthroughs certainly occur in psychotherapy, but they are not the mainstay of the process. Only in the movies or on TV does a single insight unsnarl a lifetime's confusions. The day after day after day business of therapy is repetitious, low key—would even be boring for an uninvolved observer. Even for the two participants, it often has a wearying quality of sameness. Yet, slowly, the gains accumulate. And so it is with Kate. Together we persevere, through deadness, through seeming lack of significance or progress, through recoveries of lost ground, through the endless detail of life in process.

My role is chiefly to insist that Kate's emotional responses to our work are absolutely essential, to help her recognize her fear of those responses and her need to try to push them away, to provide reassurance that having emotions is not the same as being totally dominated by them, and to disclose my own emotions by way of example. In time, Kate begins to risk timid and very minimal disclosures of her own feelings about events that she relates. She seldom admits to any feelings about me or what transpires in the office, clinging to the fiction that we are two dispassionate scientists at work on an intellectual task; yet cautiously she is opening up her inner awareness.

Kate herself characterized her posture in life when she spoke of feeling like granite inside. Kate Margate had attempted to deny her humanness, to become a thing sculpted out of cold, unchanging stone rather than a creature of soft, vulnerable, changing flesh. She feared to know her changefulness and took drastic steps to negate it. Kate especially needed to avoid any emotional entanglement with other people, for she accurately sensed that would lead to change. The most powerful influence that can move a person is a caring relation with another person.

November 19

As she is working her way out of her dread of emotions and toward risking some degree of relation with others, Kate has an experience that makes a marked impression on her and that changes our relation significantly.

Kate is a forbidding woman at this time. She still comes to therapy reluctantly, treats it as bitter medicine to be taken resolutely but detachedly, and seeks to be finished with the whole unpleasant business as quickly as possible. She is formal to the point of being a near parody of herself. She has worked with me almost a year and has yet to call me "Jim," preferring the careful "Dr. Bugental."

Today she is talking about having visited a children's ward at a hospital as a part of her work. While there, and to her own surprise, she found herself drawn into a conversation with a severely crippled but extremely bright child. Later in my office she tells me about this talk.

"You must understand that I generally do not like children, and I suppose I might as well admit that I'm usually uncomfortable around them. When this little girl came into the office in her wheelchair, my first thought was one of annoyance. I had much to do, and I didn't want to be interrupted. Oh, I suppose I sound like a witch in a Walt Disney story, but I really don't think children are all that delightful and interesting. Generally their minds are undeveloped; they are only interested in their own worlds; and they are often inconsiderate and messy. I don't usually go on like this, but you must understand this about me to realize what an unusual experience this was."

"Kate, you sound as though you are giving a speech about some strange creature you had dissected, rather than talking about your own experience."

"You are always telling me things like that, and I suppose that is what you think you should do, but I can't see what help it is supposed to be to me. Anyway, I don't want to get distracted now.

I was telling you about this child, and. . . . " Coolly, sailing on unruffled.

"I don't want to hear about the child. I want to hear about your experience," I cut in. I'm challenged; come on, Bugental, face it.

"Yes, yes, of course. I'm telling you about my experience as best I can under the circumstances. And now will you listen to me, please?" Kate's acerbic manner is not unusual for her, but today it seems to have some additional edge.

"Go on, Kate." Conceding. I am challenged, I know, and tempted to press the point, but as far as I can tell, to do so would be more for my need than for hers.

"Well, this child—her name was Tanya, a ridiculous name for a nine-year-old—somehow engaged me in conversation. And do you know, I was really quite enchanted! I found her simply charming and very intelligent. In no time at all I was explaining to her about our research program—imagine explaining that to a nine-year-old! But I do think she understood! She seemed far beyond her years, but then that's not altogether so. . . . " She pauses, musing. I sense a change in her mood. She seems momentarily, incredibly, vulnerable.

"She seemed older in some ways, but then in others. . . . " I let my voice trail off, open-ended.

"Yes, in other ways. . . . " Still engrossed in the feeling within her. "In other ways, she seemed even younger than her nine years. I mean, perhaps it was because she was so crippled and so helpless. Some way I could feel her helplessness physically, I guess. And it made me feel. . . . " Suddenly she breaks off, and I realize with a start that she is close to tears. Kate has only cried once or perhaps twice before, and then there had been more bitterness than sorrow in her emotion. This is clearly a different Kate.

"She made you feel. . . . " Softly, ever so softly.

"Oh, I don't know." The tears are near, but anger is threatening to replace them. Oh, delicately now.

"It would be easier for you to be angry now than to let your true feeling through, Kate." Voice even, no challenge.

"I felt motherly! There, I said it. Are you satisfied?" She

pulls her head erect and stares defiantly at me. Looking into her hot, hurting eyes, my own steady, seeing, not pulling away, not commenting.

"You still want to use anger to get away from your tender feelings." This time she's working with me.

"Oh, what's the use of them anyway!" But she softens a bit, and the tears well out of the corners of her eyes. "A lot of good it will do me now to weep about children! I'm too old. Too old, and you know it. So why take on about it?" The anger is thin; the pain shows through starkly.

"You're trying to tell yourself you are too old to have any children of your own, so why feel the grief, is that it?" No lead now. She's with herself.

"Yes, yes." The tears are coming faster now, and the anger is weakening. "Oh, it just isn't any use doing this."

"Kate, you're doing the very thing you need to do. Quit getting in your own way." Firmly but warmly. I feel like comforting her but know that she can be frightened into total retreat by too much tenderness. There is a surge of feeling rising in me.

"I had the ridiculous thought that perhaps I could adopt that child! Oh, it makes me so mad to carry on this way!" Now she is sobbing.

"It's so hard for you to just be with your own emotions and not try to order them to be unemotional and reasonable." Insistently, but with understanding.

"Yes, yes. Oh dear!" She stops talking and gives herself up to her crying. I sit silently as the sobs shake her. She cries for several minutes, and then when she looks up, shyly, the anger is gone from her manner. In a wondering voice she says, "It feels like I had a child or children, and they are dead." My eyes are hot, filling.

"Yes, Kate, the children you would have had are dead. Just as surely as though you had had them and then lost them. And you are doing what you need to do—grieving for them." This triggers a whole new wave of sobbing, and she seems so hurting that my own hot tears can no longer be restrained. I reach for a Kleenex from the box she is using, and she suddenly looks up to see my weeping. This renews her crying all the more. She has been sitting on the edge of the couch, and now I move over and sit beside her.

She leans against me, an incredible thing for stiff, formal Kate, and I put my arm around her. Then she collapses against me, crying bitterly, and my tears stream down my cheeks as well.

As Kate said of herself, she felt "like granite," solid, unyielding, and unchanging. Not only had she tried to find security in being stone-like, but she has come to an inner conviction about herself that functions as a self-fulfilling prophecy: "I am a particular way, and I can be no other way, and I cannot change from being this way." This so subtly pervades her thinking that, in itself, it is a major resistance to the therapeutic work. Thus, she comes to therapy supposedly to change but actually with the intention of being unchanging. She wants to have her ability to work effectively repaired without herself being altered in any way, very much as she might take her shoes to be half-soled and heeled without any expectation that she would be affected.

Kate has so little inward vision that she relies chiefly on "rational" thinking and very little on subjective awareness in looking at her life. Thus, though she feels lonely, depressed, and fearful of closeness, she has convinced herself that that is just the way she is; she has not thought of seeking to change these ways of being. She literally cannot imagine feeling otherwise. When, after the incident of weeping with me, she breaks through and experiences a period of insight and relative emotional freeing, she is, of course, delighted. Underneath, however, it soon becomes evident that the same conviction of unchangingness is still functioning. She is now sure that she has overcome her difficulties and that this new subjective state will last. This conviction concerns me seriously because it demonstrates that her underlying self-image is still unaffected, and because I know how dangerous her reaction may be when the next change in her feelings takes her back to unhappy emotions. I know such a swing will surely come sooner or later, probably sooner.

February 7

"I woke up this morning with such a good feeling." Kate smiles with an odd little twist to her mouth. She seems childlike in her pleasure. "It's been years since waking up was a good feeling. I can't really say how it happened, but I just know that I felt so much more ready for the day. I haven't looked at my mail in months really, and now I'm curious to see what's in it. I've collected a whole box of mail, you know, and it's like I'm going to open up those envelopes and find interesting things and hear from people I've forgotten about all these months."

"Um hum." I'm trying to get a better sense of her deeper feelings. In some way, she seems to be skating on the surface, and I feel troubled as I listen to her. At times, it seems that the secret of a psychotherapist's task is to be perverse. When the patient is unhappy, the therapist suggests that there is another possibility; when the patient says he is happy, the therapist sniffs around for the hidden unhappiness; when the patient talks about other people, the therapist urges focusing on one's self; and when the patient is dealing with the past, the insatiable therapist asks that attention be directed to the present.

"I have so many plans, so many things I want to do. All of a sudden, I find my work interesting again. I've gotten a new assignment on some of the amino acids, and I really think I'm going to like working at it. Imagine that! I'm going to like working at it!" She smiles with delight at her own feelings.

"Kate." My voice is very gentle, for I really hate to puncture her balloon of delight. "Kate, it sounds as though you're all through with the bad feelings."

She is silent, but the smile drains rapidly from her face. I wait. She seems to be holding quite still emotionally. I have the impression that she is avoiding any movement of thought, of feeling, or even of body. "What's going on, Kate?"

"Nothing, nothing at all." She tries a smile, but it isn't the same. "I was just thinking about what you said."

"Uh-huh. What are you thinking?"

"Oh, I suppose I'll have some times that aren't as good as right now, but. . . . "

"But?" She knows, but she doesn't want to know.

"Well, I really don't see why I need to. And besides I don't want to think about it now. I'm feeling better at last, and I'm going to stay that way. Or at least I want to as much as possible. So why are you trying to worry me?" Her tone isn't as sure as her words. She is clearly trying to persuade herself as well as me.

"It seems hard for you to think of yourself as flowing."

"We have worked some things out," protesting, "and now they are taken care of, so why should I go back to the bad feelings? Don't you think we got rid of some of the problem when I told you about that time my mother got drunk?"

"No."

"No? Well, what's the use of what we're doing if you say 'no' like that?" Annoyed, ready to obscure the issue in a fight with me.

"It makes you mad when I don't see you as some kind of machine where we can remove the defective parts and put in better ones and then let you run more happily."

"Oh, I don't know what you mean. You're just trying to confuse me."

"Kate, you still see yourself in terms of a machine and you think that how you feel is a product of how the parts are working; you expect that the way you feel today is going to be the way you will feel from now on."

"Well, why not? Isn't that what psychotherapy is all about? Don't I come here to find out what has upset my emotions, then to correct that, so that I can feel better?"

"Phrased that way, the answer is, of course, 'yes,' but that's misleading. Think of it this way, Kate: Can you imagine yourself as a river, rather than as a machine?"

"A river?"[3]

I'm not much of a believer in lectures, but sometimes they help the patient sense what we're doing or where we are in the process of doing it. Besides, Kate has a way of being so plausible that I'm continually drawn into explanations. Maybe it's okay, but I have a secret guilty feeling that a really good therapist wouldn't talk as much as I do. Still, this seems like a good time to try to give Kate a different idea of what she may expect and perhaps to provide a basis for future reference when she has the inevitable slumps in feelings. "Yes, a river. A river is never the same. It is always flowing, moving on. The water in the river at any given point today is not the same water that is there tomorrow. Moreover, the river is sometimes in sun and sometimes in shadow; sometimes in the city and sometimes in the forest. The very essence of the river is that it is changing, flowing."

"That's all very poetic, I'm sure, but I can't see what it has to do with my feeling good." She's not yet ready to meet me on the more emotional, implicit level.

"You're a river, Kate, and right now you're flowing happily in the sun. On other days, you will be in shadow and in rain. But there will be still other sunshiny days after that and so on. It will never be just one way."

"I don't like that. I don't like that at all. Why can't I do whatever needs to be done so that I can get past the misery and have a little happiness that I can count on?"

"We'd all like that, Kate. I sure would, for one. But it just doesn't work out that way, as far as I know."

Once again we work together in our separate ways. Continually, Kate is afraid of risking the involvement that is intrinsic to our efforts. She is terrorized to let go of the seeming security of believing that each new experience is the way she will be from now on. She is like a mountaineer who makes his way along a precipitous ridge, hoping that each broadening of the path is the one where he can finally set down his pack and rest but who repeatedly finds that the security is too little and the space too skimpy, and that he must continue. Kate is frightened, close to panic, wanting to give up the whole terrifying enterprise; but Kate is also persisting, trying to do the dreaded things, facing up to her lifelong fears. And gradually Kate is winning through to a plateau with more space and less imminent disaster. Then, from the quarter from which she has learned to expect only support, she is hit by the blast of unexpected change. That is, just as Kate is beginning to find a new perspective and better feelings about her life, I bring her whole effort to the brink of disaster.

October 21

On a bright fall day trailing memories of the summer's heat, Kate comes in wearing a more colorful dress than I have seen her wear before. She has had her hair fixed too, and altogether she is quite a contrast to the gray, prim woman who first entered my office more than a year and a half ago. There is a lift to her chin and a tempo to her speech that speak of her growing satisfaction and her emerging hope for herself. Her face shows so much less of the granite-like tension these days. Her step no longer mechanically moves her from place to place.

Yet I watch Kate come in and get settled on the couch with apprehension. I have been dreading this day for six weeks or more, and now it is here. I have accepted an invitation to serve as a consultant to a research program in another city and will be away for at least a year. Although it is nearly six months before I must leave, it is too soon for Kate's state of progress. I have arranged for a valued colleague to begin seeing Kate now in the hope that concurrent sessions will ease her transfer to him, but that is a poor response to meet the trust that she is beginning to give me. I feel guilty and conflicted and that I should not have accepted the appointment; then I insist to myself that I must balance respect for my patients' needs with response to my own.

I have tried to prepare for today by suggesting to Kate that she enter a therapy group so that her relationships might be broader, and I encouraged her to attend a professional meeting that took her away from her regular sessions with me. These and other steps I've taken may have helped, but they seem feeble to me now as I look at her newly open face. Tragedy is so ever-ready as an understudy to replace joy; it hovers in the wings, hoping for the mischance that will call it on stage. Kate, for whom I have come to care so genuinely, seems so defenseless, so trusting, so open to hurt. My resolution fails. I can't tell her. I can't do it. I'll have to withdraw from the appointment. Maybe next year. But I know next year it will be Ellen or Ben, who are only now beginning to risk trusting me at all. There never will be a time when there will be no Kate or Ellen or Ben, not as long as this sort of intensive relationship is fundamental to the work we do. Briefly I feel trapped, resentful. But I am grateful too. I feel enriched daily, and that is no pious affirmation but genuine truth.

"I've been thinking about what Larry said in the group last week." Her voice communicates a reflective quiet so in contrast with the impersonal precision with which she dispatched her words for so long. Every such contrast troubles me today. "He thought we were being too nice to each other, you remember, and that we ought to be more honest. That may be so, according to the group dynamics people, but I don't especially relish the idea of the kinds of brutal things I hear about in some of these groups."

I must tell Kate early today. She needs time to react and I want to have a chance to help her get at her feelings. I should interrupt her, but she's already begun on a useful topic. Maybe I could tell her next time. No, I purposely chose today, a Monday, because we'd have three more interviews this week without the long weekend intervening. I'll have to wait until next week. No good; that would just be delaying.

"Kate." Abruptly, in the middle of her sentence. "Kate, I'm sorry to interrupt you, but I have something I need to talk with you about. It is important, and I want to have plenty of time for us to think it over together."

She turns on one elbow, looking up at me, troubled, questioning.

"In brief, it's this, Kate: I'm going to be away for a year starting next April. I've accepted a research consultant position up north and. . . . " Her face is unchanging; perhaps the eyes are set a little too fixedly, but I can't tell. My words won't flow easily. I'm scared, guilty. "Well, I've talked to Dr. Lasko, and during the six months before I leave, he will work with us from time to time so that when you feel ready you can continue with him. And besides. . . . "

"When I feel ready? I'm afraid I don't understand." Her tone has some of the old formality, distance. Somehow it's a relief though to hear her speak, to deal with a detail.

"Well, I mean we can arrange for you to transfer more to him whenever you like in the next six months." I'm fumbling; don't like the flavor of what I said.

"I see." Quiet, unemotional, controlled. I think she's frightened.

"And besides, I'll be coming back down here from time to time so that we can keep in contact in any way that seems useful." I still feel wooden, self-conscious. The tone is saying that it is all mechanical, impersonal; that's what's wrong. Quick relief at identifying the problem, that's something I can deal with.

"Yes, I'm sure we can do that." She's withdrawn, impersonally meeting my impersonality, escalating the detachment.

"Kate, I feel a lot of feelings right now. I feel troubled to be leaving at all. I feel guilty for hurting you. I feel awkward in trying to express my concern and my wanting to do everything possible to make this a positive experience for you."

"Of course, I understand. It's really quite all right. I certainly understand your wish to advance your own career, and I'm sure Dr. Lasko will be very helpful should I need to continue in therapy next spring."

All so smooth. It's too smooth, but there are no obvious places to take hold of it. "Kate, I think this has more impact for you than you're letting yourself know. I appreciate your reassurance, but I'd like to help you get in touch with your deeper feelings about my going away." I'd guess she's clamping on controls to head off panic.

"Yes, well, it does come as a surprise. I hadn't really thought about the possibility before. But really, I don't think you need trouble yourself so much. Six months is a long time, and I'm sure whatever needs doing can be done in that time. Don't you agree?" Pleasant, distant, formal. Too pleasant, too formal; she's turning herself off.

"No, I'm not sure I do, Kate. Your being so agreeable and so distant right now really feels bad to me. Lately we've been able to talk with each other in a much more straight way than this. I think, I'm guessing, that you're hurt and probably angry. Can you find any feelings like that?"

"No, I don't think so. I just am aware of needing some time to think over what you've told me and feeling a bit of annoyance that you always seem to make things into Greek dramas. Really, I don't feel that distressed." Evenly, reasonably. Have I underrated her progress? True, she's pulled back a bit, but isn't that appropriate? Do I need her to be so attached to me that my leaving would be a major trauma? Or do I want to believe she's handling it well because it's too heavy to fight through her wall again?

"Well, Kate, we have plenty of time yet today. Why don't you do that, think over what I told you, and do it out loud so that I can listen in and be of any help I can be?"

But there is little need for me to do anything. The hour goes quietly; Kate talks in even tones, keeps a careful distance emotionally. I try—do I really try?—to penetrate the polite wall, to get back the closer working relation. She is pleasant, detached, and quite unwilling to remember any other way of relating. I think: She needs time, just as she said; it is normal, even healthy, to get a bit of space when something unexpected comes. She's handling it very well, all things considered. But then I think: She is walling off; we're losing the ground it took us months to win; she'll retreat so far that she won't ever risk coming out again. I feel hopeful, troubled, expectant, depressed. Her brightly colored dress seems mocking and sad. Her face, although not apparently troubled, certainly no longer accords with her dress.

October 22

The next day is Tuesday, and Kate's appointment is at ten in the morning. She doesn't come. No word; nothing. I sit waiting, try to read, find myself restless, worried, angry, guilty. Usually I don't go after patients when they withdraw—partly on principle (it's better that the patient feel his own need is primary), partly because of pride, partly out of respect for the person's autonomy— but this time? I call Kate's apartment. No answer. I call her work. She is there, comes promptly to the phone, is businesslike in tone. She forgot, got engrossed in her work. No, she doesn't think it has any particular meaning. No, she doesn't want another time today. No, she doesn't want a special time tomorrow (Wednesday we do not usually have appointments). Thursday's regular time will be quite convenient. She's sorry to have troubled me. Thanks for my call. Careful, polite, out of reach.

October 24

Thursday is very different. I can feel the vibrations of her anger when I open the waiting room door. She does not respond to my greeting, does not look at me, marches into the office, takes the straight chair by the desk, stares me directly in the face.

"I have been thinking about your plan to leave and the unilateral way you announced it to me, and I have concluded that you are high-handed, irresponsible, and completely deceptive." Tough, hard, letting me have it right between the eyes.

I feel the impact. This woman isn't playing. She's mad, and she's determined to let me know it. I want to protest, to explain; but back of that I feel a kind of pride in her. She's not going to take it lying down. This is a gutsy thing to do. And I feel some relief. "Tell me about how you see me, Kate." Quietly, wanting to be very straight now.

"I want to ask you if you think that you have the right for some reason to invite people to begin work with you, to encourage them to put their trust in you, to insist that they regard this psychotherapy as the most important event in their lives, and then to announce, 'Well, I feel like going away for awhile now. Somebody else will take care of you.' What gives you the right to treat people that way?" Her eyes are fierce, her voice tight, controlled, and forced through jaws that do not open very wide.

"Kate, I really feel your anger with me. You are just furious, and it's coming over like a solid force." Ugh! What a stupid shallow response to her! I want her to know that I still value her, that I think she's great right now; and I don't want to be patronizing or to pull back from her in any way. Yet my answer is stilted, and it's not really an answer. The force of her feelings joins with my own self-blame, and I'm on the defensive and talking in a forced, self-conscious, clumsy way.

"Dr. Bugental, I asked you a question. I would like your answer, please."

"You're right, Kate, I didn't answer you. I think the strength of your anger hits me right where I feel regret and guilt so that I. . . . "

"Are you going to answer my question, Dr. Bugental?" Coldly, intently. The question is unimportant; asserting her identity against me is everything. She will not accept "therapeutic" responses. Yet I'm reluctant to confront her fully, to give her the only real answer.

"Kate, I have wrestled with that question for a month or more now. I don't know for sure whether I have that right. I try to tell you and the other people I see that they must know and respect their own needs while trying to be responsible in relation to the people around them, and. . . . "

"And you have decided it is responsible to go away because it suits your convenience now, I gather." She is slightly less intense, but her manner shows no relaxation of the vigilance with which she eyes me. I feel like she has me pinned at the point of her sword and at any sudden move she will run me through.

"I've tried, Kate. Tried to think about the needs of each of the people I see, and tried to think about my own needs. How well I've done, I really don't know. I do know that you feel shocked and furious with me."

Oh, bah! I still sound so stiff and tight. I am tight, tight with worry and guilt and ambivalence. I'd really like to keep Kate's feeling for me, but even more importantly I'd like to help her hold on to the gains she—we—worked so damned hard to make. It could all be shattered now. Hell, I wasn't trained to be this personally involved with patients. I shouldn't let my own feelings get in the act and be so needful myself. But I am. And I'm dodging with Kate. Have to. I don't want to have to point out the difference between her needs and mine; it will sound too rejecting.

Kate has been silent, watching me intently. "Yes, I am shocked and, I suppose, angry with you. I had thought you might be more responsible than it now appears you are."

"Kate, you're mad as hell, really pissed off at me, and I can't say that I blame you a damn bit. That's the way it is, isn't it?"

"How is it, Dr. Bugental, that last year when I wanted to go to a meeting that would have taken me away from therapy for a month, you objected and insisted that it was more important to me to be here? How is that? Was it more important to me? Or was it more important to your bank account?" Coldly, ready to destroy any response, well prepared to fire round after round. She's unconsciously pressing toward the answer I'm reluctant to give.

"I really believed that it was the best advice I could give you."

"How is it that I could not be away a month and you can

go for a year?" That's it; she's laid it bare; there's no honest alternative.

"Because, Kate, your therapy is the most important thing in your life, but it is not the most important thing in mine." There, the core of it, so stark, so bitter, so true. I half-wish the words back, to say them in some other way. Although I feel strangely good to have said it so straight, I am also frightened; did I need to strike back?

Kate sits quite still, looks at me very intently, considers, then nods. "Of course, that is so. I have been quite silly, haven't I?" She gathers her purse close to her, rises abruptly, and starts toward the door.

"Kate, where are you going?" I am on my feet.

"Don't trouble yourself." She has the door open.

"Kate, come back!"

No answer. She is into the hall, heading for the outside door.

"Kate, I'm going to keep your time tomorrow for you."

"No." She pauses, half turns. "No, that won't be necessary. I will call Dr. Lasko or someone else if I need to discuss anything with anybody."

"No, Kate, I won't stop this way. I'll keep your time tomorrow for you, and I hope you'll come."

"Suit yourself." She is gone.

October 25

On Friday, she does not appear. I debate all over again whether to call her. If it seems I am pursuing her, will she have to fight me? Will she be unable to call on me if she really needs to? If I don't try to reach her, will she think I have crossed her off, will she feel confirmed in seeing me as uninvolved and uncaring? Back and forth; yes and no. No resolution. Her time passes. I see two more patients, but my mind keeps going to Kate. I call her apartment; no answer. I call her office at the laboratory. Dr. Margate called to say that she would not be in today; any message? No.

During dinner Friday evening, the phone rings. My telephone exchange has a Mrs. Cudahay on the line who is anxious to speak to me about Dr. Kate Margate. Chill down my back; tighten grip on phone. Of course, put her on.

"Dr. Bugental? I'm a neighbor of Dr. Kate Margate. I hope you won't mind my calling, but I thought I ought to let you know, or somebody. I didn't know who to call. She gave me your name last month when I was feeling nervous, and so I thought. . . . I mean, Dr. Margate doesn't seem to have many friends; at least I haven't seen many people going into her apartment. She lives in the next apartment to ours. Not that I watch who goes in and out of her apartment, of course. She can do anything she wants. You know what I mean; I'm not one of those nosy neighbors. But I did think I ought to tell you or someone; so I hope you'll forgive me for troubling you. You see, we've lived next door to Dr. Margate for three years and. . . . "

Impatient, but know she's trying to be kind, to do something; so few people risk getting involved. Don't blast her just because I'm anxious. "That's all right, Mrs. Cudahay. What is it you wanted to tell me?"

"Well, it's nothing really. At least, I don't think it is, but it just isn't like Dr. Margate to go off and leave her apartment door wide open, and she's been gone over an hour now. Do you think she's all right? She stopped at our apartment to give me a package from the May Company that had been left with her. I mean the package was for me. And she just looked awful. So I said, 'Are you all right?' and she said she was, but she sure didn't look it. Her eyes looked like she'd been crying, and her clothes were kind of all mussed up. I asked her to come in, but she said no she had to go out and then she just walked out, didn't even go back and shut her door, just walked out. And I don't know whether to shut it or not or whether she has her key. I don't think she had her purse with her. So if I shut it, she won't be able to get back in, but I don't like to leave it open that way. I mean, just anybody could walk in. I've been keeping my door open so I could try to watch that nobody goes in her apartment; though I don't know what I'd do if they did. I mean, I'm all alone here. Do you think I should close the door? But I'm almost sure she didn't have her purse and then she wouldn't be able to get back in. . . . "

"Mrs. Cudahay," I cut in. "It's very good of you to be so concerned. Is there a manager in the building who could let Dr. Margate in if she came back without her key?"

"Well, there's supposed to be, but lately nobody's there much. So I don't know whether there's anybody there or not. I just don't like leaving her door like that though. Why only last week there was a robbery over on Allen Street. They just went in and cleaned out the whole apartment of an elderly couple while they were out to the grocery. So I keep worrying that. . . . "

"Would it be too much trouble, Mrs. Cudahay, to check whether the building manager is in this evening and would be there to let Dr. Margate in if she didn't have her key when she came back?"

"Oh, no, not at all. That's a good idea. Hold the line—I'll be right back. It may take a minute, because if Mrs. Hennessey is there she's such a talker that it's hard to get away from her. But," laugh, "I guess I'm that way too, huh? My husband's always saying that when Betty and I get together it would take thunder and lightning to make us stop talking. Well, I'll go see if anybody's there. I'll be right back."

I manage several bites of cooling supper while waiting for her return; meantime, my mind is busy: Where is Kate? Was it a simple oversight that she left her door open? Is she suicidal? Possibly, but probably not. I don't like the thought of her wandering around, not taking notice of where she is, what she's doing. What could I have done? What can I do? What about that damned apartment door? Should I tell Mrs. Cudahay to close it? If Kate comes back in a low state, will she think to ask the manager for the key? I can't be her nurse, yet I can't ignore her need. I helped to put her into whatever she's in. I had to consider my own needs too, but I could have handled it better. The food is hard to swallow. Should I try to find Kate? What's the matter with me that I'm so involved? Would Kate be apt to get drunk? I don't know; doubt it, because drinking is linked with her mother. But maybe that would make it more likely. I don't know anything about her or about people. She's right to be mad at me. Oh, this is ridiculous.

"Doctor? I talked to Mrs. Hennessey, and she'll be in all evening. So I shut the door to Dr. Margate's apartment. Believe me that's a relief to me. Doctor, do you think she's all right?" A lot of genuine concern mixed in with the need to be involved and to know.

"Well, I can't really say much right now, Mrs. Cudahay, but I'm sure that Dr. Margate will appreciate your concern for her and your keeping an eye on her apartment. That's very thoughtful of you." Want to express appreciation but not get caught in another long monologue or in fending off questions about Kate.

"Oh, it was nothing, really. I just like to be a good neighbor, you know. Doctor, what could I do to help her—Dr. Margate, I mean? What do you think would be good for me to do? Do you think I ought to have her come over for dinner or something? She's not a great one for socializing, if you know what I mean, but she's really very nice. And she's so smart, being a doctor and all. . . . "

"Mrs. Cudahay, I think you're being a very good neighbor. Now, I wonder if you'd excuse me? I'm right in the middle of dinner, and. . . . "

"Oh, my goodness, yes, of course. I'm sorry. I didn't know."

"That's really all right. Thank you for your concern. Good night." Relief; hope I didn't sound too abrupt. Dinner cold; no appetite to make it worth heating up. Where is Kate?

October 26–27

No news Saturday. Sunday evening, the telephone exchange has Dr. Margate on the line. Put her through!

"Kate?"

"Dr. Bugental, this is Kate Margate. I hope I didn't inconvenience you by not coming for my appointment Friday?"

"No, no, Kate. Are you okay?"

"I'm sorry not to have come on Friday. Have you filled my Monday time with someone else?"

"No, Kate, I've held it for you. Kate, tell me how you are."

"Then I'll come in at ten o'clock tomorrow morning. Thank you."

She's hung up!

October 28

She is rather pale, sitting hunched in the waiting room. Coming into the office, the old gray clothes, her manner careful but not exaggeratedly stiff. She sits on the straight chair; not "in," but "on." Eyes downcast, both hands on her purse, lips closed. I wait.

Have I done this to this woman? No, it is her own emotional distress. I should have foreseen better. There is no way to foresee better really. That's the myth of omniscience. I did the best I could. It wasn't good enough. Could anything be? Something needed to be.

"Kate, can you tell me how you are this morning?" Easy, kindly, concernedly; don't push the tenderness; she can't handle that now.

No movement of head, eyes still down. Lips move. "I'd rather not talk right now."

"All right, Kate, let's just sit here together for a bit. When you can, though, I'd like to know something of what's going on in you." Sit back. Seek a comfortable posture; none lasts more than a few minutes. Kate, on the other hand, is unmoving . . . carved of granite, again.

And so the whole hour goes. She barely moves, says nothing. Gradually I settle down, deal with my own contending feelings. There is a kind of companionship, a kind of shared pain, even a shared separateness. At the end of the time, actually past the end, for I'm reluctant to let her leave knowing no more than I do, I say softly, "Our usual time tomorrow, Kate."

She rises, goes out; no words, no acknowledgment.

October 29

Tuesday is the same as Monday. To my early question as to how she is feeling, she answers only that she doesn't want to talk today. Again, we sit in silence through the hour. I decide against offering her a special Wednesday appointment, feeling she would experience it as crowding her. I mention our Thursday appointment time, and she leaves.

October 31

Thursday she is looking at me. Slowly, carefully, she marshalls herself. "I realize I am overreacting to your decision. I have found it hard to deal with things. I mostly just walk. Every day.

Sometimes I just wander. Sometimes I walk down to the ocean and back. I haven't been taking care of things at the office. I just walk."

The walk to the ocean is, I estimate quickly, at least 10 miles each way, probably more. She is drugging herself with fatigue. "Kate, can you talk about what's happening in you? Let's see if we can't help make things a little less painful."

"I think I am just very sad. I know it's out of proportion. You've certainly tried to be fair, and you've done a great deal to help me. I'm sorry not to be able to deal with things better."

"You're very sad, Kate. I feel sad too. But together I think we can make it different." Earnestly, hoping to reach her, wanting her to know I haven't withdrawn, not wanting to frighten her.

"I don't know how much I can tell you. I know you want to help, but much of the time I don't know it or believe it. I want you to help me, and eughh! There, just like that, I hate you! I said I want you to help me, and now I hate you and I want to scream things at you, horrible things. Don't come near me." She is fighting a miserable battle within herself right now. I can see how much she wants to be helped and yet how strong her impulse is to attack me or to leave.

"I won't come toward you, Kate, but I won't go away either." Quietly, firmly, without pressure.

We sit silently for several minutes, but it seems to me I can hear silent screams from Kate as her inner struggle goes on. I feel such sympathy for her, but I know how important it is for me not to crowd her in any way right now.

Finally she speaks, and her voice is colder and more controlled. "I think it is all right now. I don't hate you now." There is some kind of a spasm within her. "But I hate myself. When I feel like this at home, I really frighten myself. Last night, yesterday, sometime, I was looking in the mirror to comb my hair, and suddenly I realized I was just standing there looking at myself and hating myself. I wanted to smash the mirror and then use the pieces to cut myself, my face and . . . and other parts of me. Just slash and tear myself. I got so frightened; I just went out and started walking right that moment."

She stops talking and sits sunk within herself. I am busy with my own thoughts. She really could do it. She could kill or mutilate herself. People really do those things. Should I let her leave? Am I being irresponsible by not hospitalizing her? I should see that she is protected against herself. Also, she's in real danger walking the streets in this condition. She could walk in front of a car or truck and never know it or perhaps intend unconsciously to do it.

Kate looks up as though sensing my thoughts. "I don't think I'll do it." Her voice is low, from deep within her, only partly a communication to me; the rest is simply saying out loud her inner thoughts. "I don't think so. Some part of me wants to live. Sometimes I hate that part, too. I don't want to want anything. Nothing! I *will not* want anything or anybody!"

Once again she falls silent, but it is enough for me. I'm going to back Kate's bet on her own life. To take the choice from her, to put her in the hospital might save her physical life, but it would very likely end lastingly her struggle to have a more vital life. But the minute I decide, I feel scared and want to back down.

For the rest of the hour, we sit mostly in silence. Occasionally Kate provides a scrap of information about how she lives these days—the endless walking, the brief visits to her office only to leave almost immediately, the irregular bits of food half eaten, the drugged sleeping. She cannot tell me much of her inner feelings and thoughts right now. Clearly, she feels she must keep them shut off. Nor do I press her on this resistance to self-exploration. She must resist right now to hold herself together. I know, as Kate does not, that if only she can hold on, the same inexorable changefulness that she so deplores will help her come through.

November 1

Friday Kate calls from her laboratory. She is at work. There is so much to catch up on. She just cannot come in. She thinks yesterday's visit helped. She will see me Monday. Relief, doubt, hope, apprehension.

November 4

On Monday she does not come, but she does telephone to say that she is far out toward Santa Monica and doesn't feel she can make it to the office before her time is over. She refuses a later appointment time, says she will be in tomorrow.

Later Monday, Dr. Taylor, Kate's physician, calls. He's concerned because a pharmacy has just called him to ask approval to refill Kate's sleeping pill prescription. It was filled only last month. I tell him Kate's in a bad place, and he wonders whether he was right to okay the refill. We agree that for the moment it's best to go along with Kate, especially since he authorized only a small number of pills.

November 5

Tuesday and Kate doesn't come again. Midway in her usual time, she calls and apologizes for missing the appointment. She took sleeping pills in the middle of the night and has only now awakened. She is groggy, probably needs to sleep more, she says. She does not want a later appointment or one on Wednesday. She wants to try to catch up on her work at the laboratory. She will see me Thursday.

It's hard for me to assess how she is on the phone. She is still very formal, distant, but she is making the effort to keep me in touch. I feel tense, irritable, worried, sad.

November 7

Thursday Kate is fifteen minutes late. She is shocking to see. Her clothes are carelessly arranged and ill-matching. She has not made up her face nor fixed her hair. She has been walking again, she tells me. She worked Tuesday and thought everything was going to be okay. Wednesday she left work after less than an hour and began walking. As on so many nights, she only went back to her apartment when she was too dazed with fatigue to keep on her feet any longer. She had a can of soup and fell into bed. But she only slept an hour. She cannot stand being awake at night, and so she takes too many pills to ensure that she will sleep through till morning.

"Kate, I'm concerned about the pills. You take too many."

"I have to sleep. I must have them."

"Yes, Kate, I know you want the sleep, the shutting out of awareness, but. . . . "

"I have to have them. I simply have to have them."

"Can you ration yourself better, Kate? Being as tired as you are from your walking, you could easily take too many by mistake."

"I've got to have them. I'll get them some way."

"Kate, you don't have to threaten. I'm trusting you. But I'm concerned, and Dr. Taylor called when you got the refill the other day, and he's concerned too."

"I'm not going to kill myself. I have thought of that many times, but I am not going to do it."

"I believe you, Kate, but I'm worried about a mistake."

"I've got to have them."

But she never takes an overdose. Something within her is fighting for her life.

And so it goes. For nearly two months, Kate lives in hell, on the brink of disaster. When the sleeping pill prescription runs out again, Dr. Taylor calls and feels strongly that Kate should be hospitalized. It is tempting, but it would be a failure of trust. To take responsibility for Kate's life now would very likely end her chances for truly having her own life. Too many Kates learn that they can let go of choice and have kindly helpers take over. Then they never really have their lives; instead, they (and others) label themselves "sick" or "emotionally disturbed," or they put themselves in some other category which is hard if not impossible to ever break out of.[4]

With my encouragement and his own courage, Dr. Taylor gives Kate another small refill. This one lasts a bit longer. One more is required, but this time Dr. Taylor is more hopeful (or resigned to my madness?).

November 17

Finally it is over. A day comes when Kate arrives for her interview and her wall is lower than it has been for many weeks. She is not as open, as content as she was before I told her about my plan to leave, but she is back within herself. She knows it too.

"I think I'll be all right now. Somehow it's as though I've had a bad fever and been delirious, and now the fever's gone. I still feel weak, but I know that I'll get stronger."

"Yes, Kate." Warmly, feeling emotionally full myself. "Yes, I can sense that the fever has broken too. It's good to see you again."

"Oh," a quick intake of breath, "go slow please. I am so afraid of my feelings still. When you are warm toward me, I want to run away or lash out at you. But you know that isn't all, don't you?"

"Yes, I do know that, Kate."

"Sometimes I didn't think I'd ever be here like this again. Sometimes I wanted to come here and kill you. I mean, really kill you. I even thought how I would do it."

"There've been times you just wanted to destroy me."

"And other times, I wanted to run in here and throw myself in your arms and say take care of me and forgive me for being so much trouble."

"It must have been very lonely for you these weeks, Kate." It is a sudden recognition for me how terribly alone she must have felt. My words reach straight to her feelings. She drops her head, the tears stream down her cheeks. She does not sob, but cries quietly and steadily. I lean toward her but keep from crowding her. She cries in this way for several minutes, then shyly her hand comes groping out toward me. I take it eagerly and hold it as she continues to cry. My own eyes swim in empathy with her and in relief that the trial seems over.

"Do you know what helped a lot?" She looks up at me with her face dripping but with an excruciatingly sweet expression of appreciation and shyness.

"Two things I believed—still believe—you felt about me. I said them over to myself again and again. First, I believe you took me very seriously. You really knew what I was struggling with and let me struggle with it. And second, you trusted me. Dr. Taylor said you didn't let them put me in a hospital and that you told him to give me the pills. Sometimes I hated you for one or both of those, but mostly I . . . mostly I . . . mostly I loved you for them."

"Yes, Kate." I say it softly, feeling so given to, so valued.

This crisis climaxes Kate's and my work together. We still have over three months in which to consolidate the gains she is making. In the long perspective, she seems to have grown markedly from her journey into hell, for that is certainly where she has been. She has emerged with more readiness to risk relationship and more acceptance of her own flowingness, more trust in her inner awareness. Although she certainly has further peaks and valleys of emotionality, she never again seems quite as granite-like in her belief that she had arrived at some ultimate state.

February 10

On a number of subsequent occasions, we go back to the river image. One of these times occurs when Kate has progressed considerably toward recognizing that she is always in process, but she is also protesting against it, as she is inclined to do from time to time.

"Why can't I ever count on how I'll feel from one day to the next? Oh, I know all about your river business, but I do wish I could freeze some of that river for at least a little while. Yes, that's it: Why can't I at least be a river of ice cubes and not constantly feel everything changing all the time?" She pauses, delighted with her own image; then she goes on. "But I suppose that would be pretty cold, wouldn't it? And I can't say I like the thought of all those ice cubes clinking and bumbling along on their way to the sea. Oh, darn, it looks like I'm stuck with flowing!"

March 21

On another occasion, in the therapy group, Kate participates in a discussion that centers around this experience of continual change. With what I am afraid is wearying predictability, I advance the contrast between the images of one's self as a machine and as a flowing river. Shortly thereafter, the scheduled part of the meeting ends. The group is accustomed to meeting without me after the end of the scheduled time, so I start to leave. At this point, Kate suddenly gestures toward me and says, "There goes Old Man River!"

Then she turns to the group, and with elaborate conductor's motions,
She leads them in the immortal words to which I make my exit:

> *He don't say nothing*
> *He must know something*
> *He's Old Man River and*
> *He just keeps flowing along.*

Within each of us is a flame that seeks to grow. The hunger
for life is always drawing us on. As much as we may have learned to
cramp, deform, and shrink our being, there is always that within
us which seeks greater horizons, room enough to stretch and grow,
and grow again. We fear the costs of that growing; we are terrified
by the open spaces that our cleared sight at times reveals all around
us; we want to shut our eyes to our further potential.

Change, endless change. The flame images dance and form
and reform and change yet again. We dread the fire, but we are of
it. We cannot resist it; we can only go with it. When finally we
yield to it, we may experience its blessing, its release.

To be fully alive is to be committed to continually evolving,
to endlessly changing. To be fully alive is to find our identity in this
flowing process, knowing that the flames will surely consume any
stable structures we may try to erect.

Wanting and needing are the fuel of the fire of life. We can
no more desist from wanting than the fire can burn without fuel.
We must know our wants and needs as fully as possible if we are to
live as fully as possible.

We are of the flame, and its dance is the dance of our lives.

Kate sought to deny her inexorable changefulness. Seeking
to become a woman of granite who would need nothing and no one,
she discovered she was dying in the one area where she let herself
make any real investment—her professional work. She feared to
change, to need, to relate. She rightly sensed the vulnerability that
is intrinsic to being changing, needful, and in relation to others, but
she wrongly thought she could avoid or deny that vulnerability.

Kate is like an astronaut who ventured far out to a planet in
another solar system and found it unsuited to human life. She tried
to create a way of being in which she would not need or want close

relations with others, in which she would be an efficient professional machine, and in which she and her world would be unchanging. In a strange way, one can admire the carefully worked out design which the child, Kitty, developed and built painstakingly for her voyage in life. Given her experience, it certainly seemed a reasonable and hopeful way of trying to navigate among dangers whose terrors and pains Kitty had already experienced all too woundingly. It just was founded on too little understanding of the intrinsic nature of the voyager herself and thus of what is involved in being fully alive.

For Kate did need others. Not as pleasant options of life, but as essential to self-realization. But to need others is to open ourselves to the possibility of real hurt. The deepest emotional wounds always have their source in caring relationships. Thus, when we try to build defenses by avoiding close relations, terror colors our discovery that the need of others has still survived. This is especially so when we uncover the deep need of a particular other.

Very often, the reactions to such discoveries are great anxiety followed by heedless rage. Finding his safety torn open, the anguished person seems driven to announce by his actions, "I cannot endure the terrible danger of needing you, and the only way I can avoid that danger is to destroy you. If you do not exist, then I can't need you, and most importantly, I won't run the risk of losing you." There is little doubt that some of the ghastly news stories of violence within families ("Father slays sleeping family; turns gun on self," "Estranged wife attacks husband") are products of this very impulse.

Sometimes the rage takes a different route. Recoiling from the impulse to destroy the needed and loved one, the frantic person turns the rage against himself. Repeatedly, patients who feel this panic have spoken of impulses to mutilate themselves, to slash their faces, breasts, or genitals, or to commit suicide in a way that will destroy their appearance. Clearly, since these parts of the body are those most involved in interpersonal closeness, the wish is to destroy the vehicles of relationship and intimacy, the means for seeking fulfillment of the terrible need.

In time, Kate began to reexamine what she had long felt were the essentials for her to exist. She found that she could tolerate pain—indeed, that she had been tolerating a great deal of it for a long time. When she was a child, being abandoned by her mother amounted to being abandoned by a large part of Kate's world. As an adult, she thought she had once again experienced the catastrophe of desertion when I announced my plan to leave. But somehow she persevered through hell and found that she was not destroyed, that she could relate to me and to others, that she could endure change, that she could still be alive and inwardly aware.

Beyond the characteristics that I have already related, Kate's experience highlights some additional aspects of being fully alive and fully human:

I am a being that is continually in process, changing, evolving. *I cannot look for a stable, fixed identity. Whatever I experience, I experience in transit. There are no fixed identities, and when I attempt to freeze my nature, I unwittingly destroy myself.*

To be human is to need and want;[5] *it is to be incomplete, hungering, continually needing; it means for life to be ever open, uncertain. Trying to be totally self-sufficient in order to be safe is a hopeless effort, sure to yield new anxiety, sure to end in desperation. Only as I allow myself full awareness of my needs and wants can I approach real wholeness.*[6]

My needing always includes the need of relationships with others, *and that is frightening because I never can control those others. Since they have their own centers and since they are continually changing as I do, there is always the possibility that I will lose them. It is dangerous to need others, but it would mean killing my own vitality to try to deny that need.*

Thinking of Kate, I feel a special warmth, similar to that comrades who have gone through battle together often feel. To be sure, there are unique feelings of closeness for each of the people with whom I work intimately in the manner I've been describing, but Kate certainly has her special place. Her wit and quick tongue are very present in my thoughts when I recall our work together. Sometimes those talents were used to sting me accurately and acutely; sometimes they were applied fondly.

Kate found she could reinterpret her needfulness and her changingness. Need became a way to relationship, to deeper connectedness with others. Change became a part of her outlook. Of course, Kate has retained a tendency to discover some new solution to life's problems, some new philosophy or diet or exercise program or whatever, and to plunge into it as though she has finally come upon the answer to all questions. The difference is that now Kate can come to the end of her enthusiasm with disappointment, feel a wry amusement at herself, or sometimes endure genuine pain, but she no longer has the feeling of total catastrophe such as once nearly destroyed her.

Recently, I had a visit with Kate and her new husband. Their marriage, now several years old, has gone though some intensely stormy times, but they both have access to their inner sense, and they are—as Kate demonstrated herself to be—tough fighters who really hang in for the long haul. The result is that their marriage is an eminently growing, healthy relationship.

As we filled each other in, Kate was obviously full of excitement. "Jim, you know Hugh and I have this new program we're using to train all kinds of people—industrial managers, engineers, professional people. It's really so important for them, and it's making such a difference in the way they see themselves and their work. . . . "

"Sounds good. What's the basic idea of your program?"

"Well, it's hard to put in a few words, but basically it's to help them recognize that life is constantly changing, that nothing important in themselves or their work is ever really the same."

And so Kate has embraced change, and Kate is changing, but Kate is changeless too.

8

DUALITY
AND OPENNESS
A Personal Epilogue

I am sixty years old.[1] What a strange, incredible statement that is. Men who are sixty are leaving middle age and becoming "older" men (not quite "old men"). I'm barely middle-aged. I know it. I can feel it. I am still trying to find out how to be a person, a professional man, a husband, a father. The actuarial tables say I have thirteen more years to live. What crap! Thirteen years ago I was forty-seven; when I see a man forty-seven today, I think of him as young. (That feels like an older man's thought; I wish I hadn't had it.) I was forty-seven, and my children were twenty and sixteen. Not babies by any means. I was in the full tide of life, but I didn't know it. What happened?

Sixty years old. In thirteen years I'll be seventy-three! That can't be. It seems so terrible, so deathly. It's all happening too fast. I have been hurrying along, trying to do things right, trying to enjoy the good things I have, trying to learn, always trying to learn, trying to be more the way I want to be. What is that?

For sixty years I've been trying to get myself ready to live the *real* life. For sixty years I've been getting prepared to live . . .

278

as soon as I found out how . . . as soon as I made enough money . . . as soon as I had enough time . . . as soon as I became more like the person I could trust. Lately I feel as though I know a little more about how to live, how to be a friend, how to be real with people, how to face things within myself. Lately I feel more hopeful for me. But then I look at numbers like sixty and thirteen and seventy-three. Am I too late?

I have always wanted to be one of the "right" people, always since my earliest recollections. The trouble is that the definition of *right* keeps changing. About the only thing that is constant about it is that the right people are somehow and significantly different than I am.

My mother was a great admirer of "cultured people." Very early I somehow got the idea that such people had a different skin texture than most people—maybe it was because another favorite word of hers described cultured people as *finer.* Beyond that none of the words—*right, cultured,* or *finer*—is much help to me in my search.

In time, though, I began to form an image of how such people live. Their home, clearly is a house on a hill, and a more costly house than our depression-wounded family ever rented. They doubtlessly lived in that house for several generations at least, and they had college educations—something neither my parents nor their brothers or sisters had—and "professions" instead of jobs.

Trying to track down how to be one of the really "right" people is very much like trying to catch the abominable snowman. There are many tracks and a myriad of supposed eye-witness accounts, but each lead plays out in a way that leaves the searcher more lost than before. And looking back, I see so many landmarks behind me that I am hard put to know which were really significant.

There is an abandoned construction shack in the big vacant lot, and we explore it with trepidation and excitement. There is little in it but a plank seat and a broken knocked-together writing surface and dust and us—two little boys and one little girl. But it is strangely exciting because only we are in it and because it is somehow shut off from the world—even though the world is just outside and all around. To celebrate that curious feeling we dare each other into undressing and looking wonderingly at what is disclosed and trying to understand the coded message our senses send but ending up unsatisfied with vague touchings.

Somehow mother knows. She always knows. She asks questions; she challenges evasions I scarcely knew I'd offered. She seeks information in a way that gives mysterious, intriguing suggestions. Finally, I sob the story out, and she is terribly shocked, she says. She's coldly aloof, and I am filled with shame and the sense of having lost the sole stable foundation of my world. Only after a long, long period of crying with my face in her lap do I finally promise enough—is there ever enough?—to win back her crucial acceptance. I will, I must be good, be right.

Being "right" is so important and so easily lost. Obviously, being right means pleasing the teachers, and that means being a "sissy." Clearly, being right means not being like Dad, who is loving but undependable, and who gets drunk whenever we really need him.

Somehow by junior high school I decide to trade in being right at school for being one of the guys, and I like the bargain. But soon I'm into being right as a Boy Scout, and that proves a way to be right and be part of the gang too. Merit badges and special awards and finally being a camp counselor attest to my rightness. And I like to dance and hold girls in my arms but I am careful not to "try anything" because obviously that isn't right. And oh, how I yearn to try something. Only by myself—in terrible shame and continually renewed and continually broken resolutions—do I let the hidden, the wrong part of me have brief life. I know how bad this is—"self-abuse, the solitary vice, it will weaken your mind, it will make you unable to have children," I've been well taught.

And so the explorations go. In some ways, I get confirmation of being right—recognitions, offices, approval. But always the secret self must be hidden, that I know is not right. It is shameful because it is sexual, because it is emotional and unpractical, because it really wants to play many times when I force it to work, because it likes to daydream instead of being realistic. Two selves: gradually one becomes more public, the other more hidden.

The depression dies in the wartime boom. I marry my student sweetheart just before Hitler marches into Poland. A graduate degree, a new-found confidence in my own powers, and war-created needs for psychologists help me move into more exciting positions. I must be doing it right. And still the shadow, the wrong self is always there.

I take a doctorate in clinical psychology in the great wave of postwar educational enthusiasm. I teach in a university and begin to publish professional papers. With two colleagues, I start a private practice group, and we devote many hours over nearly fifteen years to developing our knowledge, skills, and self-awareness. And, unwittingly, I have planted a time bomb in my life.

To practice psychotherapy, I find, is to be drawn gradually into deeper and deeper engagement with the people who consult me, with many different personalities. Where once a week was enough at first, our work begins to call for twice, then three and four times a week. This reflects our increasing recognition that the goals we seek are those of major life change, that the forces we must combat are deeply entrenched, and that the work of disentangling life-long patterns and of winning through to new perspectives is the most engrossing that I and those with whom I work have ever known. And that involvement is of many kinds: I am caught up in ways that carry me beyond my depth in relating, in attempting to be open and genuine, in trying to bring about changes in others, in seeking to be more of a healer than one person can be for another, and—hidden in the background—in trying to mend the split within myself by mending those I find in my patients.

Thus the realizations about our human experience accumulate, and slowly the cost of living my dual life becomes clear. My efforts to share these growing recognitions at home seem only to flaunt my greater engagement outside the home, and so they are not valued. I go into psychoanalysis and spend many hours on the couch trying to expose and rid myself of my duality, trying to cover and justify it. The analysis ends inconclusively, with that duality more painful than ever and more than ever in my awareness.

The burden of being dual weighs most heavily on me in my home and marriage. Daily there is the contrast of my increasing genuineness with others, and I am guilty and torn. In my marriage, I feel—rightly or wrongly—that there is acceptance only for my "right" self. Thus the end is inexorable. We really have love for each other—to the extent that we have really known each other—

and so the tearing apart wounds us both. She has been a good wife as best she knew how to be, and I a good husband and father within my own now-obviously-distorted image. But it will not hold together any longer, or else I cannot help it to do so. As kindly as I can, but inevitably cruelly, I leave the house on the hill and the companion and stranger with whom I've shared so much and with whom I've never been able to be whole. I leave the two grown children whom I know so incompletely and who know me so little. I tried to be everything for them that my father was not for me—financially dependable and known and respected in the community—but I did not know how to be *me* with them.

And now the time of change, the time of healing, of hope for a new life. The secret self is secret no more. I swim in shame and find I do not drown. With new relationships, I gradually risk letting more and more of me be known, and I find I am welcomed. In a new marriage, I discover how pervasive was my need to hide my inner life, how much I took being separate for granted. But this woman shares my work and my valuing of completeness and challenges and supports me in trying to be whole. We adopt a daughter with whom I am determined to be a "Dad" and not simply a distant good provider. We join a community of six families and move to a new area to explore a more interdependent and intersupportive way of living. And the old split diminishes.

So is it over, is it healed? Am I "right" at last? No; no to each of these. It is not over; the split is still there—although so small in comparison to before. I heal and I tear open and I heal a bit more. And I am giving up being right in favor of trying to be who I am.

Throughout this book I have tried to phrase one fundamental message. It is, it seems to me, by far the most important message I have learned from all the years of my life and of my work. Yet it is the most difficult one to impart of any teaching life has given me. Again and again, I find that those to whom I speak or write take other—and to me, lesser—points as more fresh or meaningful. This fundamental learning about life is so embedded in what is familiar that it is difficult to point to or to see.

In this last chapter, and by way of summary of what I deem

most important in all I have tried to say, I want to enlarge on the significance of our lost sense, the inner awareness that has the potential to let each of use live in wholeness and with true realization of his or her unique nature. I want to talk about how important that awareness is to having our own lives truly, and then I want to talk about my conviction that this lost sense is our avenue toward the most profound meaning of life and the universe. These are grand assertions, to be sure, but I believe them literally.[2]

Trying to be who I am turns out to be almost as hard as trying to be who I should be. But with time that gets better. Patiently, Kate and Hal and Jennifer and the others who come to me for help—all of them teach me. Again and again, I have seen a person turn his life around when he began to open up to his inner awareness, began to attend to his own wantings, hopes, fears, intentions, fantasies. So many of these people did as I did—they tried to dictate what should be going on within themselves rather than to discover the true flow of their experiencing. To dictate in that way is a way of death; it kills the actuality of our being. Only the inner awareness makes genuine living possible, and it only is the sole guide to my being truly in my own life.

I was never taught to listen within myself. Instead I was taught to listen to the outside—to parents, teachers, Boy Scout leaders, professors, bosses, the church, the government, psychologists, science—almost any outer source of instruction in how to live my life. What promptings came from within, I early learned to regard as suspect, as probably selfish and irresponsible, as likely to be sexual (a terrible possibility) or unloving toward mother (even worse). Inner promptings—as it seemed all authorities agreed —were random, undependable, and in need of immediate and thorough control. At first, others would exert those controls, but if I were the right kind of person (there it was again), in time I would enforce these same controls on myself, just as though parent or teacher or policeman were right there (as they were, in my head).

So now when I came to try to listen to myself, there were so many stations jamming the signal that it turned out to be very hard to discern my own voice. I would not even know that I had such a voice were it not that thousands of hours of listening to the people who come to me demonstrated beyond question that it exists in each of us and that our task is to reclaim this, our birthright, which has been partly or wholly covered over. Thus I have come to believe that even I have such an inner sense, a guiding inward knowing.

All very well, a reader may say, but aren't these people who have been your teachers neurotics and fundamentally unstable? Only someone who is not quite right would have to have such intensive therapy or would go into such an extreme reaction to what happened there, true? After all, we—most of us that is—don't get so hooked on a doctor that we think we've got to have him or the whole world will fall apart, don't go around smashing furniture or screaming or doing the other bizarre things these people did. How can you apply what you learned from them to normal people?

The truth is that these people are not basically different, or abnormal. Doubtlessly, friends or family members sometimes knew of periods of unhappiness or distress, but both before and after therapy most of these people were not strange in any extreme way. To be sure, Kate was lonely and rather dogmatic; Frank was certainly argumentative, ever verging on hostility; Jennifer was hyperconscientious; and so on. But they were not much different from you or me. None of us are totally free from our own stresses and oddities.

The seemingly unusual behavior described in these pages is a relatively open expression of the tensions and emotions all of us carry—but often suppress—within ourselves. It would be a safer and saner world if more of us could find outlets as ultimately filled with growth (and as harmless to ourselves and others) as Larry breaking the chair, Hal screaming, or Kate endlessly walking.

Each person works out a way of being in the world that is a reasonable compromise between the way he sees himself and his own needs and the way he sees the world with its opportunities and its dangers. Unfortunately, both sets of perceptions are usually based on the outlook of a child, and in our culture we are given little help in revising our outlooks as we grow into adults. Thus, we develop ways of being that are shrunken and life-constricting. *What we call intensive psychotherapy is really a crash educative process that seeks in two or three years to catch up on the maturation stunted by twenty, thirty, or more years of trying to live out a child's view of life.*

An adult approach to life has been gradually taking form for me as I have listened to people talk about their lives over the past thirty years. One big surprise that has emerged is how hard it is for any of us to consider his own life fully and candidly. Nearly everyone who consults me does so because he is not satisfied with how his life is going; each has tried various other courses to make his life different, but these efforts have not worked out satisfactorily. One would expect, then, that each of these people has already spent a lot of time thinking and rethinking how his life is going and what he can do to make it more the way he wants it to be. Not so. Not one person who came to see me really knew how to basically reconsider his own life, even though he would certainly have undertaken such a reconsideration without hesitation in his work or in some other area of his external life if it wasn't going as he wanted. To the contrary, these people uniformly—just as in my own case—had habits of mistrusting, devaluing, and avoiding their inner experiencing.

Again, I want to emphasize that this curious lack of ability to take stock of one's own being is not just something that characterizes people who are "patients" in intensive psychotherapy. I've recognized it in various groups I've led—people who are successful business, technical, and professional workers, people who by no stretch of the imagination can be labeled and dismissed as neurotics or hippies or immature. I've found it equally true of my colleagues and friends, when we've let down the social barriers and talked deeply with each other. And I found it, most certainly, in myself.

To be sure, every one with whom I've worked has spent a tremendous amount of time and emotion thinking *about* himself. Looking in a troubled way at the person I think myself to be can take the form of futile worry, of angry self-blaming, of sad self-pity, of elaborate planning and scheduling for myself, of resolutions and checklists, of self-punishment, or of any of numerous other efforts to change the actions or feelings of that elusive and troublesome *self*.

The people whose growth experiences were traced earlier in this book had each engaged in endless ruminations about their lives. Larry tried to analyze his panics as dispassionately as any business proposition. Jennifer continually followed herself around criticizing nearly everything she said and did, trying to remake herself. Frank groused and blamed everything and everybody around him, while within himself he worried and ached to be different without quite knowing what he wanted or what he could risk trying to become. Louise and Kate, each in her own way, tried to make themselves into the kind of people who would be safe from the hurts others can inflict.

Hal, probably more than anyone else, demonstrates the fallacy of such efforts to repair the self as an object. Intelligent, trained, and earnest, Hal worked at himself endlessly and in a great variety of ways, but he never—before his therapy—really took stock of his life *in and for himself*. He always made himself an object, and he had little or no sense of his subjective center in the context of his own living.

What is involved for the person who wants to take charge of his life? Basically, it is to open one's consciousness as fully as possible to one's own concern for one's life, to the fact of one's being alive here in this particular room at this particular time on this particular day. Most of us, unthinkingly, seem to assume that we really have such awareness and only momentarily allow it to be intruded upon from various sources—social pressures, trying to enhance our images, persistent guilts, and the like. Actually, such free and open awareness is extremely rare, and only those people highly skilled in meditation or certain other contemplative arts seem to possess it to any significant degree.

For myself, I find that being truly aware, authentically aware in my life is a job that I still can do only partially. If I start to think about how I can deal with some choice in my life, I'm apt to take a quick look and say, "Oh, hell, I just don't know what to do." And right at the moment, that's so. It is as though I went to the filing cabinet in my head and found I only had three old bent and bedraggled cards under the topic I was concerned with, and so I slammed the file shut. Then, I usually want to get busy with something else; or when it's really serious, I give over to being miserable. I may say I spent an hour thinking about the matter when I actually did no such thing.

When I really am *aware* about something important in my life, the process is a very different one. First, I kind of "soak in" the issues for quite awhile. I let all angles of it hit me, and I experience the anxiety, anger, tension, or whatever emotions go with it. But I don't, if I can help it, try to solve it right away. Then, when the process is working best, I talk to someone (or if that's impossible I write to myself; but lately I have someone I can really talk with). And all I do when I talk is say whatever comes to me about the matter I'm concerned with—what it feels like and how blocked I feel and whatever else comes to mind about it. And the person I'm talking with just helps me say it all out and avoids advising, criticizing, or getting in my way.

At this point, an interesting thing begins to happen. As I open myself inside so that I say whatever comes to mind, all sorts of new perspectives open up also. What seemed a hopeless situation gradually comes to have other possibilities.[3] Some of these "solutions" are impossible; some are very real but not available to me right now; and some—suddenly I realize—really are on target. Yet, something strange has been happening to that target, to the matter that seemed so big and firm and unyielding; it is undergoing a change. It's as though I can't quite remember what it was. Or maybe it's that I can't remember why it seemed so important, or it may even be that I can't see why it gave me so much trouble or seemed so unsolvable in the first place. Not always, to be sure, but many times, the issue begins to get misty or to change form.

There's still another transformation going on in this process. All along, a part of what's been happening is me—or at least an implicit awareness of myself in relation to the choices I face. When this process goes well, that awareness changes somehow. I think of myself differently, or feel my presence and possibilities differently, or know something new, or remember something I'd forgotten about myself.

Although this description may sound very vague and pretty mystical, I can't reduce it to terms that would be acceptable to most of the psychology that I learned in graduate school. One thing I know, though, is that what eventually comes out of me is more than was put in.

That last sentence is the key one. Something more has emerged from the explorations of my awareness than can be explained as a simple retrieval of past learnings. Nor is it solely the sort of recombination of past learnings that a trial-and-error matching of mental file cards might produce. No, there is only one way to say it that truly feels right to me: Something has been created. New meanings, new perceptions, new relationships, new possibilities now exist where they were not to be found before. In short, my inward vision is a creative process that does more than observe what is already at hand; it brings into being fresh possibilities. This is the astonishing and creative possibility latent in our being.

Unfortunately, this sort of inward perception, this use of our awareness of our own lives, is strangely limited or largely missing in so many of us. I, for one, am only beginning to have really dependable access to it, and I am more fortunate than many.

This realization of how rarely we are authentically aware within ourselves seems to me enormously important. If I have trouble really thinking thoroughly about my life, then it is not surprising that I have difficulty in having the kind of life I want. If this condition is generally shared (and I believe it is), then much personal and social distress may be traced, at least in part, to our inability to use our potentialities knowingly, meaningfully, and purposefully.

After all, if I were about to repair the engine of my car, the first thing I'd want to do is see what state the engine is in right now. Only with a candid and complete assessment of the existing situation and a reasonable appraisal of what needs to be done and what I have to work with to do it—only in this way can I have much hope that my efforts will result in a beneficial change in the engine. It seems as though it should be the same within my own life.

But, of course, it is not the same. I am the very process I want to understand. What I seek to survey includes the surveying itself. The engine doesn't change because I look it over. But when I try to look at my life, I am also trying to look at my looking and that is a very different sort of undertaking.

There is a crucial and very powerful significance to the difference between studying an engine and becoming more aware of my own being. After I've completed my examination of the engine, the real work is just beginning. On the other hand, *when I become fully aware of my own being—including my feelings about my way of being and the way I really want to be—the real work has been done!*

Wait a minute. Think about that difference; it has a tremendous implication. In the difference between the procedure for repairing an engine and the process of growing or changing in our own lives—in that difference lies the whole story of the uniqueness of being human. And that story can be summarized in two very potent recognitions.

First, the *process of being aware is itself the creative, growth-evoking process.* Just that: The process of being aware is, in itself, a creative, a healing, a growth-actualizing force. We have become overly accustomed to think of our awareness as modeled on a movie camera that passively examines but in no way affects what lies before it. Well, it just isn't so. Particularly when we turn that powerful force that is human awareness on our own being, then we are bringing to bear the most potent process we have at our command. If that seems an extreme statement, recall that it is human awareness that harnessed steam, explosives, electricity, and the atom itself. I'm not playing with words. At the most fundamental level where the forces affecting our planet contend, human awareness has repeatedly demonstrated its supremacy. The incredible irony has been how much that power has been devalued for the past two hundred years.

Very simply, what all of this means is that *we don't have to do something to ourselves to become more like we truly want to be; rather, we merely need to be most truly ourselves as we are and most broadly aware of our own being.* It is simple only in conception, however; it is tremendously challenging to make it a reality. The point is that when I'm becoming more fully aware of how I want to be within my own being and of all the influences that have kept me from choosing to actually be that way, then I am already in the process of change. Full awareness is itself the way of becoming the person I truly desire to be.

This idea seems so incredible to us that we often look for some trick of language or imputation of mysticism rather than directly confronting the tremendously powerful nature of our own being. Thus Hal kept trying to learn "how to" be aware of his own inner life, unquestioningly treating himself as though he were a strange machine that he had to learn to operate, separating his consciousness and intent from his inner experience, a disabling self-mutilation. Making oneself into an object in this way is akin to pushing the family car wherever you want to go rather than getting in and driving it.

The second crucially important recognition makes it clear how the process of being aware can have so much power: *The fundamental nature of human life is awareness.* Chew that one slowly; it's got life-changing powers. If you distinguish simple physical existence (such as was typified by the patient-thing in *Catch 22* or the boxer in a coma, both of whom I described in the first chapter) from truly being alive as you and I know it, then it is true that our nature is ultimately epitomized in our awareness. Thus, the more fully aware I am, the more alive I am. The more I distort my awareness, the more I cripple my being alive. The more I increase the range and flexibility of my awareness, the more potent and fulfilling is my experience.

In the above sentences, there has been an "I" who distorted or increased my awareness. Does that deny the sameness of "I" and the awareness? No, it does not. The split between "I" and my awareness is but an artifact of our language. As we saw when Larry was looking for his self, he overlooked his true identity—in other words, his looking. So it is in my case. My true identity is the "awaring"; or, to say it differently, I am the distorting or the increasing. I am not the *product* of these processes; I am the *process.* Thus when I become aware that I have distorted my awareness, I am already un-distorting it; when I become aware that I can increase my awareness, I am already doing just that.

The significance of this identity of our lives and our awaring is easy to overlook. We in our Western culture have been so instilled with an overly objective outlook that we repeatedly try to make objects of our own beings. And there is an object available for such efforts. This is the *self.* The *self* is made up of all the truly objective aspects of our being—or perhaps I should say, of our *having been.* It includes our images of our bodies, our ideas about what sorts of persons we are, our generalizations about how others see us, and our personal histories. The *self,* so conceived, is an abstraction, a perceptual and conceptual object. It is not *who I am;* it is more *what I have been and have done.* The *self* is the secretion of the *I.* It is the discarded skin, the tangible and point-at-able aspect of what has already moved on and is more truly purely process and purely subjective.

When we try to approach our lives objectively, in the same way we approach repairing the car's engine, then we can only deal with the *self*. We have divested ourselves of the living power of awareness, and we engage in a task of trying to remake our lives by rearranging the pictures in the family album. We are working on an inanimate object, so it is not surprising that there is little vital profit in the effort. Some classical psychoanalyses and other overintellectualized therapies seem to be of this kind. They yield immense amounts of information about early childhood experiences and sophisticated theories about personality dynamics, but the patients find their actual lives little changed. The analysis of the *self* is as futile a helping effort as any postmortem. Who I *was* is dead; my awareness (the aware I) is alive now and moving on, ever changing.

Psychotherapists are continually trying to identify the agency that brings about change. If only we could better understand why some people profit so immensely from their therapeutic experiences, while others, apparently very similar, show little or no change. Every therapist, every theory, every technique can claim some successes, and every one must also admit that it has failures. How important are insight, the understanding of the patient's history, the relationship with the therapist, discharge of formerly repressed emotions, and other postulated curative influences?

Sometimes the patient achieves a fresh perspective on his life and his problems—he gets insight, we say—and the results are pervasive and a whole life is changed. At other times, the most carefully worked out understanding of the patient's life and symptoms is as futile as last week's stock quotations. Freud arrived at the recognition that insight alone is not enough. Yet clearly it is crucially important for some people, as every therapist and much imaginative literature attest.

I believe that the key to significant life change is to be found in recovering one's centering of life in one's subjective awareness. Genuine insight is to my mind *inner*-sight, subjective vision. So-called "insight" that is chiefly derived from the therapist's perceptions and interpretations is not inward-seeing; it is objective information about the person the patient has been, but is not evocative of his present being.

Popular literature—in movies, novels, TV stories—has created a picture of the curative effect of a person suddenly "getting" insight, a fresh view of his own life. This has led to what I think of as the "detective story" brand of psychotherapy. Many patients approach themselves in this way and eagerly examine their own actions, words, slips of speech, dreams, and all else for clues from which to build their case. The difference between the "insights" arrived at (whether by the therapist or the patient or both) by the detective story brand of psychotherapy and by the awareness of the inner sense is the difference between an artificial light and full sunshine. The former may show us things we would not see otherwise, but only the latter has all of the nurturing qualities we must have to live and grow.

Inward vision is human awareness breaking the sight barrier. It is the direct awareness of our subjective being. It is visible in its carriers and its effects. "I want a piece of pie," is more accurately expressed as, *"I am the wanting of a piece of pie."*

But, of course, as soon as I put it into words, it is no longer the inner sense I am describing but the objectified work of my inner vision. Only in the unreflective moment of sensing the wanting is awareness alive in me. Now I am the writing of these words. No, not even that; now I am the becoming aware of new pre-words that are in the process of becoming words in my inward ear.

I am the crest of a wave that always has moved on by the time the wave can be identified.

In sum, then, my search has brought me to the realization that each of us has an inner sense, a way of perceiving in our subjective world, but that far too often we have not learned to value and use that vital element of our being. As a result, we are lost in a desert of objectification without the guiding star of our own identity to give us a true course to fulfillment.

Having come to realize the tremendous importance of this inward sensing in our daily living, I begin to be aware that it may point to further significances as well, significances beyond the moment.

I am convinced that we do not live in authentic accord with

our deepest nature. Instead, it seems to me, we live in terms of images of ourselves that are diminished and deformed. We conceive ourselves as machines and animals and assume that these are indications of our nature when they are but the simplest vehicles to our purposes.

The people I have been describing in this book, and many others with whom I've worked, teach me that our nature is far deeper and far less known than we usually recognize. For too much of our lives, we live in terms of shrunken images of ourselves. When Larry saw himself totally in terms of his doing, he experienced himself as dying when he could no longer *do*. When Kate saw herself as unable to stand change or real relationship, she felt driven to desperate measures to suppress her emerging awareness of being in process and feeling need of me. Imagine a tribe of primitives who never learn to stand erect but go around on all fours. Their images of men would keep them prisoners in the same way as Larry's and Kate's images constrained them.

So much is apparent. What we so often overlook is that we are, each of us, similarly living out the images we have learned of what we are and what is possible for us. When we are told that we are animals and that such ideas as "freedom and dignity" are illusions, then we may choose to accept that image of ourselves. It is certainly true that we are animals, just as it is true that we can go about on all fours if we see ourselves as four-footed. The great threat to man in the views so urged on us by the behaviorists is not that they are wrong. The reign of a real misconception about man's nature would be relatively short. No, the danger is not that Skinner and his colleagues are wrong but that they are right. They are right, but right in such a determinedly and destructively short-sighted way.[4]

Pigeons can be taught to peck at a ping-pong ball and cause it to go back and forth on a miniature table. Skinner has done so. What Skinner does not understand, and what many of the popular media reporting his work equally miss, is that Skinner did not and cannot teach pigeons to *play* ping-pong. Skinner succeeded only in making little ball-pushing machines out of pigeons. However pigeons may *play*, it certainly is not in this mechanical and unnatural fashion.

Human beings can be reduced to the level of the white rat

or the pigeon. Human beings can be made into machines. A truncated view of man's nature can be used to control him, just as Skinner urges. But will man still be human if he becomes the equivalent of the ball-pushing pigeon?

When I think about the kind of psychotherapy that most engrosses me these days, I find I am using words that were once strange in such contexts: I am most involved in work with those patients who permit me to share their search for the god hidden within them. (For those who still find the word *god* an obstacle, it is possible to get something of the same idea by substituting the term *creativity,* but the significance is not fully the same, at least for me.[5])

It is my belief that each individual human awareness is a unique part of the universe. Each continually processes the stuff of being, and in this way each awareness is similar to a plant or animal or even to a river or mountain. Each receives some portion of the flow of being (sunlight, pull of gravity, chemical composition of the air) and processes it according to its own nature (metabolism, yielding to erosion, decomposition), and then contributes to the total cosmic system (exhaling carbon dioxide, reflecting light). In these cycles, the stuff of the cosmos is changed in form, but it is neither added to nor subtracted from. We call this "the law of the conservation of matter."

But an individual human intelligence is not *only* like an animal or a river or a mountain. Each person also has the potential of bringing into the universe something new, something that has not existed before. In the realm of meaning, the human being not only processes existing conceptions in new patterns, but he may in some cases create genuinely new meanings or interpretations. This is a god-like potential, and it is inherent in our deepest nature. If true creativity is a mark of the divine, then the creation of new meanings, new perceptual experiences, new relations, new solutions bespeak the god that is in our deepest being.

There is more to this enlarged picture of the role of human beings in the universe: For the most part, the world and the cosmos—as far as we know—seem to rock along like a marvelous watch that was wound up long ago and now goes ticking its way through near eternity. Clouds form from condensation and bring water inland to drop it on dry areas that produce green things that facilitate condensation and so on. The whole contraption seems beautifully engineered to maintain itself with factory sealed parts.

Of course, sometimes man comes along and starts tinkering and prying open some of the seals (and eating of the apple), and then the great watch seems to pause or to change its rhythm at least a beat or so. And, of course, man is part of the whole thing anyway. But man is something else as well. Man is a different part of the whole system, for man knows about the system and man knows about man. It's pretty sure that man doesn't know all—or probably not even a major portion—about either the system or himself, but just the fact that he knows makes it a whole new ball game. In the long run (one hundred years, a million?), it may be better or worse (for whom or what?) that man knows, but that's beside the point. The point is that he *does* know.

And that is another very real god-quality that we men have: We participate in the greatest creation job going on. We create not only new meanings and perceptions within our own subjective worlds. We also are—as far as we know—the only parts of the whole cosmic system that knowingly select out of the infinite storehouse of what-might-be some of the elements of what-actually-is. Thus, we men serve as architects of the actual, continually remaking what is real, and for good or ill trying to bend it to our own purposes.[6]

Thus when I speak of a search for the god hidden within the person, I mean quite literally that I believe that within each of us is the divine—the potential to create and the awareness of knowingly contributing to the determination of what will be real.

This creative process of exploring and opening my awareness is a genuine venturing whose outcomes cannot be anticipated; nor can its furthermost possibilities be exhausted. From such trips I may emerge with much more than a solution to a problem or a decision about a difficult choice. Although the extent to which different individuals can and do choose to forge their ways through this process varies widely, many achieve a revitalized sense of their own identities, potencies, and of the possibilities open to them. In those instances in which we are most courageous and able to venture with little distortion into the depths of our being, we return with the sense of having seen god.[7]

Man knows god in his deepest intuitions about his own nature. Deep within me, far beyond the reach of words, I feel at times a sense of possibility for myself, for all men, which is so breathtaking, so transcending of our usual concerns (and yet not belittling of them) that I know I will never see its realization—at least in this life. I think that is a vision of god.

The further I can intuit into my own potentialities the nearer I come to seeing god. I do not think there is an ultimate point. I do not conceive god as a fixed entity or being. It seems to me that god is the dimension of infinite possibility; god is all possibility. Thus god is The All. Within myself, I have a sensing of all possibility, even though I cannot perceive anything even close to that immensity.[8]

As we discover our own sense of possibility, we uncover more and more of our deeper natures, and thus we lay bare more of our own aliveness. To know (in the deepest sense of knowing) what could be is to be enlivened to what is. To know how one might be fully alive is to be discontent with what is plastic and partial in the way one is now alive. To recognize the fullness that awaits one is to be hungry for richer living.

We are all god-seekers, all of us. Atheist and agnostic and devout worshipper alike. We can no more give up that quest than we can stop the flow of our awareness. To be aware is to be concerned with what is and what is not, with being and nonbeing. And the only way we can be aware of nonbeing, of what is not, is by thinking of what might be. It is impossible to think of nonbeing. We try to imagine it but end up imagining a something that we know (we think) is nonexistent. But, of course, it is no longer nonexistent once we have thought of it; it exists, if nowhere else, in our imaginations, and that is indeed the same cradle from which have sprung all of man's creations.

And when we think of what-might-be-but-is-not-yet, we think of what we would wish were true. It is inevitable that our thoughts contrast *what is* with *what we wish for,* and soon we are imagining how we ourselves might be, and so we are launched on the search for God.[9] This is the God above god.[10]

I believe God is identical with man's deepest longings for his own being.

NOTES AND REFERENCES

In this book I have tried to share my experiences in conducting intensive psychotherapy. I am quite aware that these experiences are idiosyncratic to me in important but unknown amounts. Still, I am genuinely happy that a number of my colleagues have told me of resonances they find in their work. These people know how lonely—*mirabile dictu*—such work can be and how reassuring it is when we converge.

In presenting the stories of Laurence, Jennifer, Frank, and the others, I have not tried to detail the clinical and technical concerns that were an important part of my work. It will be apparent to those who are experienced in this field that intensive psychotherapy demands a great deal of the therapist in terms of being continually aware of how a myriad dynamic influences can interplay. I make this point here because I would not want what I write to lend any support to the "do whatever feels good" school of psychotherapy that seems epidemic at times and that betrays many promising young would-be therapists and their clients.

Psychotherapy is an art form. An art form seriously practiced by an artist worthy of that name calls for cultivated sensitivity, trained skills, disciplined emotion, and total personal investment. To bang on a piano or throw paint on a canvas is not to be an artist, although the naive may be unable to distinguish such products from those of matured talents. Psychotherapy demands discipline from its responsible practitioners above all else. Only after one has mastered the fundamentals, steeped himself in the diversity of human experience, and explored more advanced possibilities can he improvise and create meaningfully and responsibly.

In a previous book, I described in a systematic way the principles that have guided me in the development of my way of working with the people who consult me. See *The Search for Authenticity: An Existential-Analytic Approach to Psychotherapy* (New York: Holt, Rinehart & Winston, 1965). In that book, I set forth the conceptions my practice was teaching me about what it means to be a human being. I said that I looked forward to having my perceptions change with further experience, and that is the way it has turned out. Yet the basic ideas about both therapeutic methods and the human situation that made sense to me then are still part of my thinking. Thus, I will frequently cite that earlier book in these notes, and readers who wish to understand further the background of what this book presents may refer to it.

Preface

[1] This incident was also described in J. F. T. Bugental, "Psychotherapy as a Source of the Therapist's Own Authenticity and Inauthenticity," *Voices: The Art and Science of Psychotherapy,* 1968, *4* (2), 13–21.

[2] This book, of course, will only describe one psychotherapeutic approach. There are a great many approaches, and the reader considering entering psychotherapy should go to the library to find other descriptions. Unfortunately, at least to my knowledge, no adequate catalog of the various orientations in this diverse field exists.

Chapter 1: The Lost Sense of Being

[1] The terms *the lost sense, the existential sense,* or other such phrases are not ones I use in talking with my patients about their inner experiences. These phrases are useful to me in my own thinking and teaching. When I work with a patient, I try to find words

that are unique to his or our experiences, such as "your I-voice," "two inches back of your belly button," or "getting in touch with your center." See J. F. T. Bugental, *The Search for Authenticity* (New York: Holt, Rinehart & Winston, 1965), p. 125.

[2] The essence of a person lies in his uniqueness, and this is the aspect of him that is most often suppressed by his training, just as it is the part of his being for which dependable access to the inner sense is truly essential. Cyril Connolly is reported to have written: "Never again make any concession to the 99 percent of you which is like everybody else at the expense of the 1 percent which is unique." Quoted by Charles McCabe, *San Francisco Chronicle*, September 28, 1973.

[3] Leonard and Lillian Pearson provide a systematic and very readable introduction to using inner awareness to guide one's eating habits and thus to establish healthful and comfortable dietary patterns. See *The Psychologist's Eat-Anything Diet* (New York: Wyden, 1973). See also A. H. Maslow, *The Farther Reaches of Human Nature* (New York: Viking, 1971), pp. 210–211.

[4] George Leonard writes: "Then, too, we find it easy to be dumbfounded by the amount of information that can be stored in an advanced computer, until we begin to consider that a single ordinary-sized gene can be arranged in some 10^{600} different ways. (To get an idea of the magnitude of this number, you might bear in mind that the entire universe contains only an estimated 10^{80} atoms.)" "In God's Image," *Saturday Review*, February 22, 1975, p. 13.

[5] Rollo May sees the objectification of human beings as a major disorder of our times. He speaks of "modern man's most pervasive tendency—which has become almost an endemic disease in the middle of the twentieth century—to see himself as passive, the willy-nilly product of the powerful juggernaut of psychological drives." *Love and Will* (New York: Norton, 1969), p. 183.

Paul Tillich wrote: "Man resists objectification, and if his resistance to it is broken, man himself is broken." *Systematic Theology*, Vol. 1 (Chicago: University of Chicago Press, 1951), p. 98.

[6] J. Heller, *Catch-22* (New York: Dell, 1962).

[7] This continuum is adapted from one I presented in "Ex-

istential Non-Being and the Need for 'Inspiriting' in Psychotherapy," in P. Koestenbaum (Ed.), *Proceedings of the First West Coast Conference on Existential Philosophy and Mental Health* (San Jose, Ca.: San Jose State College, 1967), pp. 24–39.

[8] See J. F. T. Bugental, *The Search for Authenticity* (New York: Holt, Rinehart & Winston, 1965), pp. 189–216.

[9] "Self-Actualization and Beyond," in J. F. T. Bugental (Ed.), *Challenges of Humanistic Psychology* (New York: McGraw-Hill, 1967), pp. 179–186.

[10] *The Farther Reaches of Human Nature* (New York: Viking, 1971), p. 33. See also A. H. Maslow, *Toward a Psychology of Being*, 2nd ed. (New York: Van Nostrand Reinhold, 1968), and *Motivation and Personality*, 2nd ed. (New York: Harper & Row, 1970).

[11] *New Pathways in Psychology: Maslow and the Post-Freudian Revolution* (New York: Taplinger, 1972), pp. 25–26.

[12] *Listening with the Third Ear* (New York: Farrar, Strauss & Giroux, 1949).

[13] For example, *The Book: On the Taboo Against Knowing Who You Are* (New York: Pantheon, 1966).

[14] *Escape from Freedom* (New York: Holt, Rinehart & Winston, 1941), pp. 242–243.

[15] In R. May, E. Angel, and H. F. Ellenberger (Eds.), *Existence: A New Dimension in Psychiatry and Psychology* (New York: Basic Books, 1958), p. 44.

[16] *Ibid.,* p. 77.

[17] An earlier draft of this chapter appears as J. F. T. Bugental, "The Listening Eye," *Journal of Humanistic Psychology*, 1976 (in press).

Chapter 2: Laurence

[1] Another account of Laurence's experience in psychotherapy will be found in J. F. T. Bugental, "The Self: Process or Illusion?" in T. C. Greening (Ed.), *Existential Humanistic Psychology* (Belmont, Ca.: Brooks/Cole, 1971), pp. 57–71. That earlier account provides a broader discussion of the problem of identity but gives less of the actual clinical interaction. The book in which it appears

is worthy of comment since the editor, Thomas Greening, has presented a striking range of papers on the theme of existential humanistic psychology in such a way as to call on us to go beyond narrow academic categories and confront the phenomenon of man himself.

[2] For some people, a sense of this exhilaration may be obtained through a simulation of death. An account of a set of exercises used in creating such a simulation will be found in J. F. T. Bugental, "Confronting the Existential Meaning of 'My Death' Through Group Exercises, *Interpersonal Development,* 1973 –1974, *4,* 148–163. In that report, the "Orpheus Experience" is described; this involves relinquishing many of the attributes of thingness. Some participants emerge from this experience with the feeling of being truly liberated.

[3] For some years, I experimented with asking people to give answers to the simple question, "Who are you?" See J. F. T. Bugental, "Investigations into the 'Self-Concept': III. Instructions for the W-A-Y experiment," *Psychological Reports,* 1964, *15,* 643–650. Examination of the answers showed that most were really statements about *what* the person saw himself to be rather than *who* he experienced as his being. Indeed, it is difficult to imagine many answers—with the partial exceptions of the person's name and the pronoun "I" that would be truly *who* responses. Chapters Eleven and Twelve of J. F. T. Bugental, *The Search for Authenticity* (New York: Holt, Rinehart & Winston, 1965) enlarge on this issue of identity. See also M. Hammer, "Quiet Mind Therapy," *Voices: The Art and Science of Psychotherapy,* 1971, 7 (1), 52–56, and "A Therapy for Loneliness," *Voices: The Art and Science of Psychotherapy,* 1972, *8* (1), 24–29.

[4] Paul Stern speaks of the patient's need to "undergo great anguish to come to grips with his buried truth." Laurence needs the assurance of knowing my steady presence if he is to make such a descent into his personal hell. In full, the quotation reads: "We demand of the neurotic that he be ready to undergo great anguish to come to grips with his buried truth. But he can negotiate the infernal journey to self-knowledge only if his willingness to assume anguish is matched by the therapist's readiness to be available when badly needed. A radical therapy—that is, a therapy which goes to

The Search for Existential Identity

the roots of the neurotic's predicament—will expose him to the terror of feeling totally forsaken and alone, but, paradoxically, he can plumb the depths of his aloneness only in the protective presence of a fellow being." *In Praise of Madness: Realness Therapy—The Self Reclaimed* (New York: Norton, 1972), p. 115.

[5] This incident is not an isolated one. Repeatedly with patients with whom I have worked long and very closely, some sort of communication not dependent on explicit speech occurs. Doubtlessly, many kinds of influences are at work—memory of earlier discussions, intuition based on empathy and similar backgrounds, and telepathy. I know that last one is not supposed to be scientifically respectable yet, but I'm convinced that some degree of thought-sharing is a frequent part of many relationships, even though it is invisible because it is so completely taken for granted.

[6] Destructiveness is a frightening potential of human beings. It is the power to transform what is in existence into non-beingness. It is, in Erich Fromm's view, "rooted in the very existence of man, and having the same intensity and power as any passion can have. But—and this is the essential point of my argument—it is the *alternative* to creativeness. Creation and destruction, love and hate, are not two instincts which exist independently. They are both answers to the same need for transcendence [of being solely creature and object]. . . . " "Value, Psychology, and Human Existence," in A. H. Maslow (Ed.), *New Knowledge in Human Values* (New York: Harper & Row, 1959), pp. 151–164. In breaking out of his object-self, Laurence's destructiveness was a means to creativity, to the experiencing of his true subjecthood.

In a different context, Rollo May observes that there can be an "ecstasy in violence. There is a joy in violence that takes the individual out of himself and pushes him toward something deeper and more powerful than he has previously experienced." *Power and Innocence: A Search for the Sources of Violence* (New York: Norton, 1972), p. 177.

[7] Confronting the meaning of nothingness has too long been kept in the realm of the religious and the philosophical. It is a fundamental psychological phenomenon and needs much more attention. See M. Hammer, "A Therapy for Loneliness," *Voices: The Art and Science of Psychotherapy*, 1972, 8 (2), 24–29. Michael

Novak has written a very searching examination, *The Experience of Nothingness* (New York: Harper & Row, 1970); and Maurice Friedman, *To Deny our Nothingness* (New York: Delacourt, 1967)', sets the matter before the reader in direct terms.

Emerson wrote, "For every seeing soul there are two absorbing facts—*I and the Abyss.*" From Emerson's journals, quoted in W. E. Bridges, *Spokesmen for the Self: Emerson, Thoreau, Whitman* (Scranton: Intext, 1971)', p. 43.

[8] A. Watts, *Nature, Man and Woman* (New York: Pantheon, 1958)', p. 154.

[9] Thomas Hora has set forth eloquently and simply the necessity of going "beyond self" if we are to be free: "The self is a conceptual center of being, built up from accumulated assumptions about the nature of reality as mediated by the sensory apparatus and discursive thought. . . . The tragic element of the human condition is rooted in that cognitive deficiency which underlies the desire of man to confirm his self as reality." "Beyond Self," *Psychologia*, 1962, 5, 85. (Both sentences are italicized in the original.)

[10] Valuing of the nonhedonic emotions and the unhappy experiences of life is sometimes suspect of being un-American; it smacks of Greek tragedy or Italian opera. Yet, we impoverish ourselves when we make no place for tragedy. See J. F. T. Bugental, *The Search for Authenticity* (New York: Holt, Rinehart & Winston, 1965)', pp. 151–165. In the same way, when we deny the meaningfulness and even expectedness of such feelings as pain, conflict, grief, anger, and guilt, we condemn our being to surface happiness. See J. F. T. Bugental, "The Humanistic Ethic: The Individual in Psychotherapy as a Societal Change Agent," *Journal of Humanistic Psychology*, 1971, *11*, 11–25.

Maslow, in defining "being psychology" by its subject matter, gives an early and important position to these emotions so often treated as intruders in popular thinking about our lives. He includes: "Unhappy, tragic states of completion and finality, insofar as they yield B-cognition [cognition of being]. States of failure, of hopelessness, of despair, of collapse of defenses, acute failure of value system, acute confrontation with real guilt, can *force* perception of truth and reality (as an end and no longer as a means) in some instances where there is enough strength and courage." *The Farther Reaches of Human Nature* (New York: Viking, 1971), p. 127.

[11] An extended discussion of the process nature of being can be found in my earlier presentation of Laurence's experience in psychotherapy. See J. F. T. Bugental, "The Self: Process or Illusion?" in T. C. Greening (Ed.)', *Existential Humanistic Psychology* (Belmont, Ca.: Brooks/Cole, 1971)', pp. 57–71.

[12] The role of the emotions in the total psychological life of the individual is often misunderstood. Larry and others in the "practical world" often tend to think of emotions only as nuisances, as defects in the human design. Nothing could be further from the genuine, human state of affairs. Emotions are true life processes, sources of motivation, and intrinsic to the fulfillment of our being. Rollo May makes clear the linkage of emotions to will or intention:

"What is omitted in my patient's (and our society's) view is that emotions are not just a push from the rear but a *pointing toward* something, an impetus for forming something, a call to mold the situation. Feelings are not just a chance state of the moment, but a pointing toward the future, a way I *want* something to be. Except in the most severe pathology, feelings always occur in a personal field, an experience of one's self as personal and an imagining of others even if no one else is literally present. Feelings are rightfully a way of communicating with the significant people in our world, a reaching out to mold the relationship with them; they are a language by which we interpersonally construct and build. That is to say, feelings are *intentional*." *Love and Will* (New York: Norton, 1969)', p. 91. Italics in original.

[13] Larry's destruction of the chair represented what I think of as "acting in," which is in contrast to the psychoanalytic concept of "acting out." The latter refers to the patient's tendency to substitute overt actions for releasing repressed material into consciousness—as when a patient is consistently late for appointments but does not allow himself to recognize his fear and resentment of the therapist and the therapeutic process. "Acting in" grows out of the reverse process in which the patient uses overt action to increase and reinforce his consciousness of inner experience.

Chapter 3: Jennifer

[1] This chapter is a much revised version of a paper describing Jennifer's experience in psychotherapy (with a different name used for her in that account); it sums up the generalizations about the nature of responsibility that were suggested to me by working with her. See "Someone Needs to Worry: The Existential Anxiety of Responsibility and Decision," *Journal of Contemporary Psychotherapy*, 1969, 2, 41–53.

[2] Jennifer's protests had the quality of a person appealing to some higher power to right what she regarded as the wrongs done her and to absolve her of any guilt in the matter. As a result, she often seemed to be talking *through* me rather than *to* me. Martin Buber says, "By far the greater part of what is today called conversation among men would be more properly and precisely described as speechifying. In general, people do not really speak to one another, but each, although turned to the other, really speaks to a fictitious court of appeal whose life consists of nothing but listening to him." "The William Alanson White Memorial Lectures," *Psychiatry*, 1957, 20, 108.

[3] Jennifer's protests about the "unfairness" of her husband's action reveal the "secret deal" she feels she has with fate. Karen Horney has well described this in *Neurosis and Human Growth: The Struggle Toward Self-Realization* (New York: Norton, 1950), p. 197: "His claims are based . . . on a 'deal' he had secretly made with life. Because he is fair, just, dutiful, he is entitled to fair treatment by others and by life in general. This conviction of an infallible justice operating in life gives him a feeling of mastery. His own perfection therefore is not only a means to superiority but also one to control life. . . . Any misfortune befalling—such as the loss of a child, an accident, the infidelity of his wife, the loss of a job—may bring this seemingly well-balanced person to the verge of collapse."

[4] Jennifer wrestles with an issue that confronts our whole society—perhaps even our whole world. The conflict of individual rights and group needs poses a dilemma that threatens to overwhelm our most cherished liberties. See, for examples, F. W. Mat-

son, *The Broken Image: Man, Science and Society* (New York: Braziller, 1964)'; M. Mayer, *On Liberty: Man v. the State* (Santa Barbara, Ca.: Center for the Study of Democratic Institutions, 1969)'; A. Wheelis, *The Moralist* (New York: Basic Books, 1973).

We are in the midst of a great turmoil that has many roots and many meanings, and the conflict between subjectivity and objectivity in viewing people can also be thought of as characterizing the period we're living in. This issue is by no means a new one. The values inherent in individuality and the values intrinsic to the social good have often conflicted throughout man's history. Today they seem to be confronting each other with especial intensity.

[5] Alan Button has dramatically shown how the unreachable mother may produce the cruel and vengeful child-adult. *The Authentic Child* (New York: Random House, 1969)', p. 29.

[6] Ugo Betti, an Italian judge and playwright, wrote, "No adult person . . . can be anything but doubtful that those poster labels, good and evil, can be pasted on anything." From *The Gambler,* Act III; quoted in E. K. Bugental (Sister Marie Fleurette, I.H.M.)', *Words of Ugo Betti: Innocence and the Process of Justification in the Late Plays of Ugo Betti* (Los Angeles: Immaculate Heart College Press, 1965).

[7] An extremely valuable treatment of issues relating to responsibility and blame and their connection to feelings of power and powerlessness is contained in R. May, *Power and Innocence: A Search for the Sources of Violence* (New York: Norton, 1972). See also M. J. Barry, "Depression, Shame, Loneliness, and the Psychiatrist's Position," *American Journal of Psychotherapy,* 1962, *16,* 580–590; J. F. T. Bugental, *The Search for Authenticity* (New York: Holt, Rinehart & Winston, 1965), pp. 300–304; and J. F. T. Bugental, "The Flight from Finitude: Sadism, Exhibitionism, and Political Madness," *Voices: The Art and Science of Psychotherapy,* 1974, *10* (1), 40–46.

[8] In "The Humanistic Ethic: The Individual in Psychotherapy as a Societal Change Agent" (*Journal of Humanistic Psychology,* 1971, *11,* 11–25), I have examined further how couples may free themselves of preoccupation with blame. Others have also examined this issue in relation to marriage: N. O'Neill and G.

O'Neill, *Open Marriage: A New Life Style for Couples* (New York: Evans, 1972); C. R. Rogers, *Becoming Partners: Marriage and Its Alternatives* (New York: Delacorte, 1972).

[9] Repeatedly, I find myself seeking an answer to this dilemma of the human condition: our treasured subjecthood and the sheer weight of the necessity to accept objectness for ourselves and others. Yet I know I won't find *the answer*. Indeed, the very idea of an ultimate answer is a contradiction in itself. I know further that the matter is not one in which either subjectivity nor objectivity can, must, or should ultimately triumph. The paradox must be embraced, not resolved away.

[10] Allen Wheelis in *The Moralist* brings his relentless intellect and his deep compassion to bear on the inexorable issues of morality, goodness, justice, and the other values by which we try to guide our lives or to pass judgment on ourselves and others. (New York: Basic Books, 1973.)

[11] "We know in our practice of psychoanalysis that *lack of freedom* is shown in all aspects of the patient's organism. It is shown in his body (muscular inhibitions) and in what is called unconscious experience (repression) and in his social relationships (he is unaware of others to the extent he is unaware of himself). We also know experientially that as this person gains freedom in psychotherapy, he becomes less inhibited in bodily movements, freer in his dreams, and more spontaneous in his unthought-out, involuntary relations with other people." R. May, *Love and Will* (New York: Norton, 1969), p. 199.

Chapter 4: Frank

[1] See J. F. T. Bugental, *The Search for Authenticity* (New York: Holt, Rinehart & Winston, 1965), pp. 39, 309–313.

[2] "The basis of man's life with man," says Martin Buber, "is two-fold, and it is one—the wish of every man to be confirmed as what he is, even as what he can become, by men; and the innate capacity in man to confirm his fellow-men in this way. That this capacity lies so immeasurably fallow constitutes the real weakness and questionableness of the human race: actual humanity exists

only where this capacity unfolds. On the other hand, of course, an empty claim for confirmation, without devotion for being and becoming, again and again mars the truth of the life between man and man." "The William Alanson White Memorial Lectures," *Psychiatry,* 1957, *20,* 102.

³ Rollo May tells of a patient who said, "Rage is the dynamic which makes me autonomous, independent of my parents. If I don't have my rage, I don't have my strength." *Power and Innocence: A Search for the Sources of Violence* (New York: Norton, 1972), p. 137. Frank recognizes, as did May's patient, the survival function of the apparently "negative" emotions.

⁴ M. J. Barry provides a capsule characterization of loneliness such as Frank experiences. "Depression, Shame, Loneliness, and the Psychiatrist's Position," *American Journal of Psychotherapy,* 1962, *16,* 580–590. See also Moustakas' classic studies, for example, in B. Marshall (Ed.), *Experiences in Being* (Belmont, Ca.: Brooks/ Cole, 1971), pp. 53–60.

Frank has many of the characteristics of *The Outsider,* as Colin Wilson (New York: Dell, 1956) has portrayed him.

⁵ The image of the solitary self-reliant man who needs no one, lives by no law but his own, and struggles alone with his demons is a popular one, especially with highly intelligent, young men. It is the *Steppenwolf* figure as portrayed by Hermann Hesse (New York: Holt, Rinehart, 1963), and it also is celebrated by no less a mentor than Emerson, who wrote: "There are two confessionals, in one or the other of which we must be shriven. You may fulfil your round of duties by clearing yourself in the *direct,* or in the *reflex* way. Consider whether you have satisfied your relations to father, mother, cousin, neighbor, town, cat and dog—whether any of these can upbraid you. But I may also neglect this reflex standard and absolve me to myself. I have my own stern claims and perfect circle. It denies the name of duty to many offices that are called duties. But if I can discharge its debts it enables me to dispense with the popular code. If any one imagines that this law is lax, let him keep its commandment one day." From "Self-Reliance," quoted in W. E. Bridges, *Spokesmen for the Self: Emerson, Thoreau, Whitman* (Scranton: Intext, 1971), p. 38. (Italics in the original.)

Extreme self-reliance is an ideal that was popular during the late Victorian period (consider, for example, Bryon, Wagner, Burton) and that has again become somewhat popular among young people today. It is an understandable reaction against the many pressures for conformity and the loss of individual identity, but in its way it makes the same mistake as the position against which it reacts. Man is always *a part of* other men as well as being *apart from* them. The paradox must be embraced if we are to claim our full potential; suppression of either aspect can only lead to a crippled being.

⁶The emasculation of intentionality through unwillingness or inability to make a commitment is a very common pattern. People who experience this syndrome feel miserable, long for the interest that would arouse them from emotional lethargy, and experience themselves as without any inner impulse to action. This is the end product of the denial of the inner sense of being that might bring intentionality to focus and provide a sense of direction to life. Our culture's heavy emphasis on objectivity as the only reality, on treating persons and one's own self as objects, on impersonality in most public realms leads directly to this anaesthetizing of the inward vision and the loss of effective intentionality. Rollo May says, "Detachment and psychopathic acting out are the two opposite ways to escape confronting the impact of one's intentionality." *Love and Will* (New York: Norton, 1969), p. 260. It seems to me that detachment and acting out are also products of the loss of effective awareness of one's own inner aliveness. Such a loss of inward vision, of deep knowing from within, sets up a pattern that cycles on itself—in which the person, lacking real access to his inner vision, finds himself unable to make effective commitment and thus experiences a lack of effective intentionality. Such a person seeks stimulation from the outside through acting out or gives up on life, taking refuge in detachment. But neither route leads lastingly to real satisfactions, and so he may let go of whatever marginal commitments he does have, and his alienation intensifies.

In this view, the key element is the inner life awareness, the existential sense. This is always implicit in May's account, though not brought out into explicit detail. For this reason the full power of May's exquisitely worked out exposition may be missed.

Chapter 5: Louise

[1] A. Wheelis, *The Moralist* (New York: Basic Books, 1973), p. 6.

[2] J. F. T. Bugental, "The Flight from Finitude: Sadism, Exhibitionism, and Political Madness, *Voices: The Art and Science of Psychotherapy,* 1974, *10* (1), 40–46.

[3] The inner sense is attuned to our own unique being. To be authentically in our own lives, we must express that uniqueness as well as our common bond with all men. Emerson expressed this recognition in terms that now seem quaint and that emphasized his orientation—in other words, the *apart from* aspect of the human paradox: "It seems as if the Deity dressed each soul which he sends into nature in certain virtues and powers not communicable to other men, and sending it to perform one more turn through the circle of beings, wrote *'Not transferable'* and *'Good for this trip only,'* on these garments of the soul. There is something deceptive about the intercourse of minds. The boundaries are invisible, but they are never crossed." From "Uses of Great Men," quoted in W. E. Bridges, *Spokesmen for the Self: Emerson, Thoreau, Whitman* (Scranton: Intext, 1971), p. 33. (Quotation marks and italics in the original.)

[4] Throughout the history of psychotherapy, the issue of what degree of involvement between therapist and patient is appropriate has been strongly disputed. Similarly, the extent to which usual social taboos could be allowed to dictate the actions of therapist and patient (as opposed to what they might say) has repeatedly produced intense and self-righteous pronouncements—on both sides of the matter. "Talk about it, but don't do it," has been the maxim that has guided much psychotherapy, at least in public accounts. Freud's early collaborator, Breuer, first astonished Freud by attributing some neurotic symptoms to "the marriage bed." E. Jones, *The Life and Work of Sigmund Freud,* Vol. 1 (New York: Basic Books, 1953), p. 248. Then Breuer withdrew from further work with Freud because of the younger man's involvement with the messy sexual concerns of his patients. *Ibid,* p. 253. Freud, in turn, disciplined and disowned several of his own disciples for their in-

volvements, which he found unacceptable. Thus the story continues, inevitably.

On the one hand, there is the social code born of Victorian morality and mechanomorphic views of man's nature. It insists on a detached, antiseptic, and manipulative view of the psychotherapeutic process. On the other hand, there is the existential reality of living human feelings, impulses, needs, and relationships. This body of vital experience shines through the shabby garment of what is proper and makes evident what a betrayal of trust may be concealed by giving first priority to traditional folkways. Life often shows a complete disregard for such niceties and instead is involving, messy, and ruthless. See A. J. Horner, "To Touch—or Not to Touch," *Voices: The Art and Science of Psychotherapy*, 1968, *4* (2), 26–28.

[5] Hellmuth Kaiser, a creative and courageous psychotherapist with whom I was privileged to study, wrote, "I cannot tell what the experience of the patient is but I know what one experiences, as therapist, when one feels a bit freer to leave the rules behind and venture in—well, what could I call it?—that no-man's land of undiluted humanity!" In L. B. Fierman (Ed.), *Effective Psychotherapy: The Contribution of Hellmuth Kaiser* (New York: Free Press, 1965), p. 168.

[6] My account of this incident may strike some readers as incredibly naive or timid. Nudity and varying degrees of open sexuality in all sorts of settings have become so much more familiar than they were a mere ten years ago. Many younger readers will probably find it hard to understand either Louise's shyness or my internal conflict or why the whole thing has any importance to an existentially oriented psychotherapy. Other readers will be shocked by my disclosure and will see in the description further evidence of the decay of moral and professional standards that they regard as important.

The extent to which the body is a feared and powerful totem in our culture is worth sober consideration. The courage and directness of such a production as *Dionysus in 69* with its complete nudity and explicit sexuality throws into sharp relief the hypocrisy and evasions of our more usual experience. See R. Schechner, *Dionysus in 69: The Performance Group* (New York: Farrar, Straus & Giroux, 1970). Similarly, the professional responsibility and courage of the Masters and Johnson sexual therapy program in providing "partner surrogates" warrants a salute to these pioneers—although they have now discontinued this procedure. See W. H. Masters and V. E. Johnson, *Human Sexual Inadequacy* (Boston: Little, Brown, 1970), pp. 146–156.

[7] E. A. Levenson, *The Fallacy of Understanding: An Inquiry into the Changing Structure of Psychoanalysis* (New York: Basic Books, 1972). This book is a challenging and fresh perspective that may open new dimensions in psychotherapy.

[8] "There is required a self-assertion, a capacity to stand on one's own feet, an affirmation of one's self in order to have the power to put one's self into the relationship. . . . For if one is unable to assert one's self, one is unable to participate in a genuine relationship." R. May, *Love and Will* (New York: Norton, 1969), p. 146.

"Genuine conversation, and therefore every actual fulfillment of relation between men, means acceptance of otherness." M. Buber, "The William Alanson White Memorial Lectures," *Psychiatry*, 1957, *20,* 102.

"Closeness as it is accessible for an adult illuminates more than anything else could the unbridgeable gap between two individuals and underlines the fact that nobody can get rid of the full responsibility for his own words and actions." Hellmuth Kaiser, in L. B. Fierman (Ed.), *Effective Psychotherapy: The Contribution of Helmuth Kaiser* (New York: Free Press, 1965), p. xix.

I find it significant that this basic fact of human existence—that relationship is only possible when there is separateness—can be so completely unfamiliar in the popular folk psychology. Instead, the myth of "two souls blending into one" is still dominant, and many a person feels secretive and ashamed because he does not really want to give up his separateness to the one he loves. And many others so readily put all of their own individuality on the altar mislabeled "love" and then feel betrayed because they do not achieve blissful union ever after.

Perhaps the false ideal of "two who are one" is nurtured by our only half-aware recognition of how much true intimacy is bound up with the imminence of relinquishment. Union denies separateness, denies an end, suggests an eternity of common experience. The intrinsic separateness of authentic relationship always carries within it the evidence and source of ultimate parting. For me at least, my own companion in separate-but-relatedness has said it best:

"This is the paradox about which I write: only at the moment in which I allow myself fully to realize my joy and my communion with another do I touch that intensity of pain which bids me let the moment go. I can only experience the joy when I do not clutch and freeze it; and yet when I do not imprison it, I must let it separate from me and die. And when I experience this moment as it moves through me, I see that I grow older, that the very vitality of the love between my husband and myself, the lovely easy sharing of the moment, must also move on. We must move where we must, and someday, finally, we too must separate and die." E. K. Bugental, "November, 1969: On Intimacy and Death," in B. Marshall (Ed.), *Experiences in Being* (Belmont, Ca.: Brooks/Cole, 1971), 50.

⁹ The effectiveness of a person who does not have access to his own inner vision is often much diminished. It certainly was true of Louise: one of the most evident gains from her therapy was her better use of her capacities. When a person is too concerned about the opinions of others, he is constricted in his employment of his talents. Karen Horney says, "Observation and critical intelligence are no substitute for that inner certainty with reference to others which is possessed by a person who is realistically aware of himself as himself and others as themselves, and who is not swayed in his estimate of them by all kinds of compulsive needs." *Neurosis and Human Growth: The Struggle Toward Self-Realization* (New York: Norton, 1950), p. 295. (This entire quotation was in italics in the original.)

¹⁰ Changes in our folkways about nudity and sexuality are occurring rapidly, yet I am convinced that only time can help us sort out the genuinely liberating from the compulsively reactive. The need to defy the repressions of the past lingers in the subterranean recesses of many of us. See J. F. T. Bugental, "Changes in Inner Human Experience and the Future," in C. S. Wallia (Ed.), *Toward Century 21: Technology, Society, and Human Values* (New York: Basic Books, 1970), pp. 283–295.

Psychotherapists have begun, cautiously, to question the validity of limits set by cultural fashions and mores but seldom tested against the intrinsic needs of our work. Most psychotherapists know of experiments in enactments involving aggression, anger, nudity, intimacy, sexuality, and other formerly taboo areas, but there has been an understandable reluctance to air these matters publicly—especially since there is a marked cultural lag in what is accepted and since malpractice suits are an ever-present threat to innovations. See J. Asher, "Sex Bias Found in Therapy," *APA Monitor*, April 1975, *1*, 4; J. Bensman, "The Sexual Revolution and Cultural Styles: A Reactionary Point of View," *Psychoanalytic Review*, 1970, *57*, 405–431; J. F. T. Bugental, "Psychotherapy as a Source of the Therapist's Own Authenticity and Inauthenticity," *Voices: The Art and Science of Psychotherapy*, 1968, *4* (2), 13–21; C. C. Dahlberg, "Sexual Contact Between Patient and Therapist," *Contemporary Psychoanalysis*, 1970, *6*, 107–124; and M. Shepard, *The Love Treatment: Sexual Intimacy Between Patients and Psychotherapists* (New York: Wyden, 1971). The whole matter has been brought more into the open by the growth center movement with its frequent acceptance or even endorsement of nudity, whole body massage, sensual pleasure, and limited sexuality. See, for example, J. Howard, *Please Touch: A Guided Tour of the Human Potential Movement* (New York: McGraw-Hill, 1970).

[11] "The body needs to be accepted, aye exulted in, lusted in, loved, and respected. Conflicts will emerge as the 'bodily armor,' in Wilhelm Reich's phrase; they will always be there as part of bodily expression. But conflicts can be met constructively, while nothing at all will occur positively if the body remains walled off." R. May, *Love and Will* (New York: Norton, 1969), p. 266.

Chapter 6: Hal

[1] J. F. T. Bugental (Ed.), *Challenges in Humanistic Psychology* (New York: McGraw-Hill, 1967).

[2] So many people who come to see me find this point difficult to grasp. We are all conditioned by our culture—and especially by education and popular psychology—to treat ourselves as objects; thus, we cannot readily understand what it means to think from

within ourselves. This difficulty becomes critical when we are trying to take stock of our lives, when we are trying to help them be as we deeply want them to be—as in the work of intensive psychotherapy.

An analogy may make the contrast between human beings and machines clearer. When a machine that has been working properly starts malfunctioning, we want to have someone who is expert on such machines examine it, determine the source of the difficulty, and take whatever steps are needed to clear the trouble and return the machine to smooth operation. How the operator of the machine feels about the trouble is as unimportant as how any other person at hand feels. Even the feelings of the trouble-shooting expert are of minimal importance as long as he is adequately motivated to do a prompt and thorough job. And certainly no one will be as silly as to think the machine has any feelings in the matter.

This model of repair works very well for many situations. It is even used, with some degree of success, when the machine involved is the human body. But when we come to deal with human feelings, we are entering a totally different realm.

In the truly human sphere, subjective experience is the central source of how we live and what we do. This means that the thoughts, images, feelings, attitudes, and emotions that we experience within ourselves are crucial to our choices and commitments in life. Thus each of us, consciously or not, willingly or not, is the subject of his or her own life. When we come to meet any given situation in our lives, all that we are, all that we have created out of our responses to life is brought to bear. It is not possible to treat one part of our internal experience—for example, some emotional problem such as Hal's rage at his son—in isolation, just as it is not possible to take any one color out of a painting without destroying that painting. This truth about the nature of our being—that we are basically subjective wholes—distinguishes us from objects (such as machines) and makes the model of repair inapplicable to our emotional lives.

³ Some form and period of "waiting" is often necessary as a patient comes to the point of giving up his old way of being in the world, confronts the no-thingness of his being, and readies himself for what he may choose next in his life. This is a time of relinquish-

ment, of death, of endings. It is a time of discovering the role playing that has been taking the place of authentic being in the patient's
life. See A. Watts, *Nature, Man and Woman* (New York: Pantheon, 1958), p. 153. It is well characterized in a fitting metaphor
of Emerson's:

"Let a man empty himself of all display even if thereto he
need to stop all action. Inaction will not last long. Action is as
natural and inevitable as rest and presently he will be impelled to
do somewhat which he can do in as great a mind as his repose. He
that waits for this rising of the general tide in his particular creek
or bay, he that does nothing until he can act wholly and earnestly
has the immense advantage of not being a part but of merging his
private nature in the world and he makes on you the same refresh-
ing impression that stars and waters do. His action, his word gives
to vulgar actions and words an impertinent and mean appearance
whilst the air gladly bears his accents and the sun and moon shine
friendly on his form." From "Being and Seeming," quoted in W.
E. Bridges, *Spokesmen for the Self: Emerson, Thoreau, Whitman*
(Scranton: Intext, 1971), pp. 62–63.

[4] See the discussion of the existential crisis in J. F. T. Bugental, *The Search for Authenticity* (New York: Holt, Rinehart &
Winston, 1965), Chapter 10.

[5] "Within his methods the psychotherapist has to do only with
guilt feelings, conscious and unconscious. . . . But within a comprehensive service to knowledge and help, he must himself encounter
guilt as something of an ontic character whose place is not the soul
but being. He will do this, to be sure, with the danger that through
his new knowledge the help which he is obliged to give might also
be modified so that something uncustomary will be demanded of
his method; indeed, he must. be ready even to step out of the established rules of his school. But a 'doctor of souls' who is really one—
that is, who does not merely carry on the work of healing but enters
into it at times as a partner—is precisely one who dares." M.
Buber, "The William Alanson White Memorial Lectures." *Psychiatry*, 1957, *20*, 115.

[6] "Man has no nature," writes Ortega y Gasset, "only history. Now this vision, too, is fading. Our time of arrogance is coming
to an end. We cannot go back, cannot believe again in a fixed

human nature, good or bad, but are learning to accept a fundamental ignorance. Not an ignorance to be conquered by more knowing, but one which will recede forever before our ever longer cognitive reach, recede and grow larger, never even in principle to be eliminated. It is true we are what we do, and true we can do as we choose, but always we do and choose more than we know." Quoted in A. Wheelis, *The Moralist* (New York: Basic Books, 1973)', pp. 112–113.

[7] In retrospect, I can see that Hal's period of "waiting" was a period of readying himself for decision. Relinquishing his old, constricted way of being in the world, he needed to make anew the choice to live (both to choose to be alive rather than to commit suicide and to choose to take the responsibility for his life rather than try to give it over to knowledge and science). Only when he was ready to decide for life could he really get perspective on his being. Rollo May writes of a truth that he feels is generally overlooked: "The patient cannot permit himself to get insight or knowledge until he is ready to decide, takes a decisive orientation to life, and has made the preliminary decisions along the way." R. May, E. Angel, and H. F. Ellenberger (Eds.), *Existence: A New Dimension in Psychiatry and Psychology* (New York: Basic Books, 1958), p. 87.

[8] The fundamental therapeutic gain is the gain of the inner sense of being, the immediate intuition that May calls the *"I-am* experience" and that is the underpinning of all other gains. "We may well be suspicious that solutions to a person's problems in psychotherapy which do not presuppose this 'I-am' experience in greater or lesser degree will have a pseudo quality." R. May, E. Angel, and H. F. Ellenberger (Eds.), *Existence: A New Dimension in Psychiatry and Psychology* (New York: Basic Books, 1958), p. 44.

Chapter 7: Kate

[1] A. H. Maslow talks of a new type of man, Heraclitian, to whom continual change is the expected, the normal state of affairs, and he predicts that "the society which can turn out such people will survive; the societies that *cannot* turn out such people will die."

The Farther Reaches of Human Nature (New York: Viking, 1971)', p. 59. (Italics in original.) As Maslow's naming of the new man reminds us, the recognition of continual change as a fact of life goes back at least to the Greeks. *Vide* R. May, *Love and Will* (New York: Norton, 1969)', p. 78. Still, we do not live in terms of such realistic expectations. We create our social institutions as though we had discovered immortal and immutable truths, and we live our individual lives as though we are momentarily on the verge of arriving at a finished state of being which will thereafter require only minor adjustments and polishing. See A. Toffler, *Future Shock* (New York: Random House, 1970)'; notice the title he has given the first part of his book, "The Death of Permanence."

[2] See J. F. T. Bugental, *The Search for Authenticity* (New York: Holt, Rinehart & Winston, 1965), pp. 43–45.

[3] "Nature ever flows," Emerson says, "stands never still. Motion or change is her mode of existence. The poetic eye sees in Man the Brother of the River & in Woman the Sister of the River. Their life is always transition." From Emerson's journal, quoted in W. E. Bridges, *Spokesmen for the Self: Emerson, Thoreau, Whitman* (Scranton: Intext, 1971)', p. 53.

[4] These were very apprehensive days for me. I cared for Kate very much, feared what her rage and desperation might impel her to do, hung on to faith in her will to choose life. She was never really out of my thoughts, and I had to make and remake my own resolution to trust her life-will, just as Kate herself had to choose repeatedly. As May puts the issue quite bluntly: "The patient can indeed destroy himself if he so chooses. . . . The symbol of suicide as a possibility has a far-reaching value; Nietzsche once remarked that the thought of suicide has saved many lives. I am doubtful whether anyone takes his life with full seriousness until he realizes that it is entirely within his power to commit suicide." R. May, E. Angel, and H. F. Ellenberger (Eds.), *Existence: A New Dimension in Psychiatry and Psychology* (New York: Basic Books, 1958), pp. 89–90.

[5] The denial of wanting is, it seems to me, an increasingly frequent pattern in the affluent, middle-class, American culture. Indeed, I believe that we really are crippled in our capacity to want. Rollo May speaks of patients who "have developed the goal of 'not

wanting,' a kind of cynical or despairing aim of not wishing for anything." Of such people, he says, "The person lives by the formula 'It is better not to want,' 'To want exposes me,' 'To wish makes me vulnerable,' 'If I never wish, I'll never be weak.' " *Love and Will* (New York: Norton, 1969), p. 264. May also reports the views of Father William Lynch who believes that "it is not wishing which causes illness but *lack of wishing.* He holds that the problem is to deepen people's capacity to wish, and that one side of our task in therapy is to create the ability to wish." *Ibid.*, p. 215. (Italics in original.) I would only dispute the idea of "creating" the ability to wish. That potentiality is, to my mind, built in, but in far too many of us it has been layered over with destructive learnings. The therapeutic task is to uncover or release the capacity for healthy wanting.

[6] The healthily functioning person who is truly actualizing his own potential for life is one who is centered in his subjective awareness of being, his sense of his own existential being. Such a person experiences his wanting in a direct way as an outward reaching from that inner center toward objects or activities that will be completing or fulfilling. Such awareness of wanting is in contrast to what most of us experience as we are played upon by a variety of outer inducements and instructions—advertisements, suggestions of other people, ethical systems—while we try to thread our way through conflicting inner responses to discover what it is that we truly want. We fear our naked wanting, suspect it will reveal us to be greedily selfish, will bring about conflicts in which we will lose out, will only be futile, and yield but the pain of frustration. My observations over many years, by the way, convince me that the pain of frustrated wanting is nothing compared to the anaesthetized living of blinded wanting. See the discussion of wanting in J. F. T. Bugental, "Existential Non-Being and the Need for 'Inspiriting' in Psychotherapy," in P. Koestenbaum (Ed.), *Proceedings of the First West Coast Conference on Existential Philosophy and Mental Health* (San Jose, Ca.: San Jose State College, 1967), pp. 24–39.

One of the most useful questions I can ask a patient is, "What do you really want right in this moment; what can you discover within your own center right now that you want for yourself?" Most people find that an extremely difficult and conflict-disclosing query. Ruth Cohn has described a "game" that she plays with herself and encourages friends and patients to play. It is very simply to make a contract with herself that "I must do what I want to (for ten minutes)." As she says, "People report very different experiences. Frequently, there is a great sense of relief resulting in a lovely feeling of serenity and being at one with self and the world. Some people experience anxiety and panic which usually disappears within a few sessions of playing the game. To them, the permission to do 'what I want to' and not 'what I should do' appears to hold an awesome threat." "I Must Do What I Want to (for ten minutes): A Therapeutic Game for Therapists, Patients and Other People," *Voices: The Art and Science of Psychotherapy*, 1968, *4* (2), 30.

Chapter 8: Duality and Openness

[1] An earlier version of the latter portion of this chapter appeared in J. F. T. Bugental, "The Search for the Hidden God," *Voices: The Art and Science of Psychotherapy*, 1971, 7 (1), 33–37.

[2] George A. Kelly, whom I proudly claim as one of my teachers, once said rather casually, "The key to man's destiny is his ability to reinterpret what he cannot deny." This simple observation is one of the most profoundly optimistic statements about human nature I know. Kelly built a careful and fertile conception of the psychology of personality and of a psychotherapy that releases the person's capacity to make just such creative reinterpretations. This book, to my mind, is in the tradition of Kelly's teachings, although it does not employ his particular vocabulary or techniques. See *The Psychology of Personal Constructs* (New York: Norton, 1955).

[3] Thomas Hora saw this dis-covery of new possibilities in a somewhat different, but compatible, way. "Transcendence and Healing," *Journal of Existential Psychiatry*, 1961, *1*, 501–511.

Hora envisioned man's role as being the manifesting of transcendent truth. "The therapist's and patient's concern is with truth as it reveals itself *through man*. For man *does not produce truth, he manifests it and is defined by it*. The capacity for cognitive transcendence is realized through a process of *freeing the mind of*

its epistemic prison. Which means that the liberation of consciousness from ingrained categories of thought becomes an important
aspect of the existential therapeutic process." "Existential Psychotherapy," *Current Psychiatric Therapies,* 1962, 2, 31.

[4] Skinner has won publicity largely as a result, it would
appear, of brash dogmatism, an utter disregard of the tenets of logic,
and an unfailing sense for showmanship. His best known book is
composed chiefly of verbal sleight-of-hand and logical absurdities.
See B. F. Skinner, *Beyond Freedom and Dignity* (New York:
Knopf, 1971). Typically, he will select some aspect of human experience (such as the concept of "freedom") and then equate it
with one of many superficial and objective phenomena with which
it may have some association (such as the words used in writing
about freedom!). Then he dashes into windmill battle against his
self-selected "opponent," after which he proudly announces the
demise of the original human experience! In all, it is a performance
similar to shooting a picture of a lion with a popgun and proclaim-
ing that one has slain the king of beasts.

In fairness, it is gladly recognized that Skinner's experimental
work is by no means as jejune; were he only more responsible in his
generalizations from his evidence, the results would be most welcome.

As a phenomenon, Skinner is interesting and even a bit
frightening. His statements have won him magazine cover photographs and TV talk show prominence to the extent that many
people in the general populace feel he is a representative of the
science of psychology. One can only speculate on the epidemic
proportions of the existential anxiety associated with confronting
our limitedness and our inability to direct our lives as we wish.
Panacean claims are eagerly responded to when such fears are so
prevalent.

[5] "A man is a god in ruins," Emerson's "Orphic poet" sang.
And he continued: "Man is the dwarf of himself." Our intuitions
that we know not our true nature are as old as man himself. The
balance of Emerson's paragraph offers one vision:

"Man is the dwarf of himself. Once he was permeated and
dissolved by spirit. He filled nature with his overflowing currents.
Out from him sprang the sun and moon; from man the sun, from

woman the moon. The laws of his mind, the periods of his actions externalized themselves into day and night, into the year and the seasons. But, having made for himself this huge shell, his waters retired; he no longer fills the veins and veinlets; he is shrunk to a drop. He sees that the structure still fits him, but fits him colossally. Say, rather, once it fitted him, now it corresponds to him from far and on high. He adores timidly his own work. Now is man the follower of the sun, and woman the follower of the moon. Yet sometimes he starts in his slumber, and wonders at himself and his house, and muses strangely at the resemblance betwixt him and it. He perceives that if his law is still paramount, if still he have elemental power, if his word is sterling yet in nature, it is not conscious power, it is not inferior but superior to his will. It is instinct." From "Nature" quoted in W. E. Bridges, *Spokesmen for the Self: Emerson, Thoreau, Whitman* (Scranton: Intext, 1971), p. 47.

[6] In these days of pollution, exhaustion of natural resources, energy crises, and an immense technology of murder, it is all too evident what great issues for the world—our only world—and for ourselves are involved. Loren Eiseley, sensitive observer and rich interpreter, says it succinctly: "Men, unknowingly, and whether for good or ill, appear to be making their last decisions about human destiny." *The Unexpected Universe* (New York: Harcourt Brace Jovanovich, 1969), p. 39.

[7] The discovery of the deeper, subjective reality of our being is an intensely moving experience. Often it is described in words that suggest religious (but not necessarily dogmatic or denominational) meanings. James V. Clark has recorded this event of seeing the transcendent possibility in oneself and others in a provocative paper. "Toward a Theory and Practice of Religious Experience," in J. F. T. Bugental (Ed.), *Challenges of Humanistic Psychology* (New York: McGraw-Hill, 1967), pp. 253–258.

[8] "The fundamental impulse in both science and religion is the singular impulse of man to appreciate the nature of his existence in time, in space, in history, and in his peculiarly self-conscious corporeality." D. Bakan, *The Duality of Human Existence: An Essay on Psychology and Religion* (Chicago: Rand McNally, 1966), p. 5.

Bakan continues: "All that falls under the heading of either science or religion issues from this singular impulse. The self-definitional activity of man, in substance and in concept, is his most abiding characteristic beyond any specific definition of him; and both the scientific and the religious enterprises are expression of this self-definitional activity. *This impulse presupposes that the manifest is but the barest hint of reality, that beyond the manifest there exist the major portions of reality, and that the function of the impulse is to reach out toward the unmanifest.*" (Italics in the original.)

[9] Thomas Hora lists as the ultimate transcendence the "transcendence of the separation between man and Ultimate Reality (God)." "Transcendence and Healing," *Journal of Existential Psychiatry*, 1961, *1*, 502.

[10] Paul Tillich writes, "The soul of the wise man is similar to God. The God who is indicated here is the divine Logos in unity with whom the courage of wisdom conquers fate and transcends the gods. It is the 'God above god.' " *The Courage to Be* (New Haven, Conn.: Yale University Press, 1952), p. 15.

INDEX

N

Neurosis, Maslow on, 11
Neurosis and Human Growth (Horney), 305
NIETZSCHE, F., 318
Nihilism, seeking safety in, 139, 309
Nudity, 311-312, 313-314; in patient's photos of self, 172-175, 176, 184, 189; and swimming, 168-169

O

Objectivity, 6-7, 193; case history of Hal, 190-236; and identity, 14-15, 54, 301; loss of, 292. *See also* Subjectivity
O'NEILL, G., 306, 307
O'NEILL, N., 306

P

Panic experiences, 16-25, 28-33, 43, 46, 52, 53, 55, 123, 285
Parents, 142, 238-240, 282, 315; alcoholic drinking by, 240, 255, 265; attitude of, toward childhood sex, 280; death of, 143, 144, 147, 186; father's anxiety over children, 192-205, 208-211, 213, 220, 234; influence of, over patients, 67, 68, 71, 118-119. *See also* Childhood
Patients, characteristics and behavior of: anger (*see* Anger); anxiety about relating, 119; attitude toward length of therapy, 19-21; attitude toward work, 34, 40-42, 49-50; behavior under medical care, 26-28; concealment of emotion, 118; control of conversation by patient, 16, 18, 19; degree of involvement with therapist, 114, 115, 281, 310-311; denial of wanting, 318-319; detachment, 35, 44, 49-50, 309; eagerness and impatience, 31; emotional involvement with others, 132; failure to keep appointments, 263-266, 269-270; fear, 16-17, 19, 39-40, 124-125, 243; first interview, 15-21, 58-65, 241; happiness in misery, 110; intensity, 22, 59, 62, 123, 129; introspection, 35; lan-

guage as indication of mood, 35, 220-221; lists of topics to discuss, 59, 65, 66, 68, 69; mood changes, 42-43; new subjective state, 253; nudity, 172-175, 176, 184, 189, 311-312, 313-314; "orderly thinking," 29; panic experiences, 16-25, 28-33, 43, 46, 52, 53, 55, 123, 285; payment for treatment, 106, 119, 122, 139, 235, 262; personal appearance, 15-16, 54-55, 129, 135, 143, 176, 192, 241, 256-257, 266-267, 270; petty larceny, 103-104; "playing God," 219-220, 222-226, 231, 233, 234, 236; punctuality, 15-16; reaction to children, 250-253; reading habits, 105-106, 110-112, 113, 119, 136; remininiscences of childhood events, 244, 246; reversal of therapist's role, 235-236; risking ridicule, 112, 129; sarcasm, 82, 117; screaming during therapy, 229-230, 234; self-consciousness, 129; self-hatred, 268-269, 275-276; self-improvement, 119; self-reliance, 308-309; sex (*see* Sexual behavior); sleep during therapy, 198-199, 203-204; substitution of therapists, reaction to, 257-263, 267-271; suicidal tendencies, 58, 60, 63, 64, 65; talking to self, 202-203; termination of therapy, 50-51, 98-100, 185, 230-231; transference, 244-245; unconscious communication, 46, 61, 302; unconscious sense of humor, 106; urgency and impatience, 22; violence in therapist's office, 46-49, 54, 229, 304. *See also* Interpretations of therapist
PEARSON, L., 5, 299
Phenomenon of Man, The (Teilhard de Chardin), 110
Process living, 34, 39, 40, 52-55, 235, 237, 273, 276, 287-290, 293-295, 304
Protesting, significance of, 57, 305
Psychedelic experience and identity concept, 14-15, 300-301
Psychotherapy, 249, 292; defined,